Nero Caesar Augustus

Emperor of Rome

David Shotter

PEARSON

Longman

Harlow, England • London • New York • Boston • San Francisco • Toronto
Sydney • Tokyo • Singapore • Hong Kong • Seoul • Taipei • New Delhi
Cape Town • Madrid • Mexico City • Amsterdam • Munich • Paris • Milan

PEARSON EDUCATION LIMITED

Edinburgh Gate
Harlow CM20 2JE
United Kingdom
Tel: +44 (0)1279 623623
Fax: +44 (0)1279 431059
Website: www.pearsoned.co.uk

First edition published in Great Britain in 2008

ISBN: 978-1-4058-2457-6

British Library Cataloguing in Publication Data
A CIP catalogue record for this book can be obtained from the British Library

Library of Congress Cataloging in Publication Data
Nero Caesar Augustus : emperor of Rome / David Shotter. – 1st ed.
   p. cm.
   Includes bibliographical references and index.
   ISBN 978-1-4058-2457-6
   1. Nero, Emperor of Rome, 37–68. 2. Emperors–Rome–Biography.
3. Rome–History–Nero, 54–68. I. Title.
DG285.S536 2008
937'.07092—dc22
[B]

                                 2008017472

10 9 8 7 6 5 4 3 2 1
11 10 09 08

Set by 35 in 10/14pt Galliard
Printed and bound in China (GCC)

The Publisher's policy is to use paper manufactured from sustainable forests.

CONIVGI KARISSIMAE MEAE

Contents

ॐৡৰৡৰৡ

CONTENTS

List of Photographic Plates

List of Coins

❧❧❧❧❧

(These images of coins are reproduced by Courtesy of the Trustees of the British Museum)

1   *Denarius* of Claudius, showing Agrippina (obverse) and Nero (reverse)
2   *Cistophorus* of Claudius' reign from Ephesus, showing Claudius and Agrippina together
3   *Aureus* of Nero, showing (obverse) Nero and Agrippina facing each other
4   *Denarius* of Nero, showing (obverse) jugate busts of Nero and Agrippina
5   *Aureus* of Nero, showing (reverse) oak-leaf crown
6   *Denarius* of Nero, showing (reverse) Nero and Poppaea
7   *Denarius* of Nero, showing (reverse) Nero radiate
8   *Denarius* of Nero, showing (reverse) Jupiter the Guardian
9   *Denarius* of Nero, showing (reverse) the Temple of Vesta
10 *Sestertius* of Nero, showing (reverse) Ceres
11 *Sestertius* of Nero, showing (reverse) Triumphal Arch
12 *Sestertius* of Nero, showing (reverse) Harbour at Ostia
13 *Dupondius* of Nero, showing (reverse) Nero's Market-Building
14 *Dupondius* of Nero, showing (reverse) the Temple of Janus
15 *As* of Nero, showing (reverse) Apollo Citharoedus
16 *Tetradrachm* from Alexandria, showing Nero (obverse) and Poppaea (reverse)
17 *Denarius* of the Civil War, showing (obverse) the 'Health of the Human Race'
18 *Denarius* of the Civil War, showing (obverse) the Deified Augustus
19 *Denarius* of Galba, showing (reverse) the Rebirth of Rome

List of Figures

Preface

If there is one Roman Emperor about whom some knowledge has passed into general circulation, it must surely be Nero Claudius Caesar Augustus, who succeeded his adoptive father, Claudius, as Emperor on 13 October AD 54 at the age of nearly seventeen. Fourteen years later, on 9 June AD 68, Nero committed suicide, deserted by many of Rome's nobility, declared a public enemy by the Senate, and facing a military coup d'état that aimed to replace him with Servius Sulpicius Galba, the Governor of one of the Spanish provinces (*Tarraconensis*).

That fourteen-year reign was marked by dramatic events, such as Nero's murder of his mother, the Younger Agrippina, in AD 59, the murder of his wife, Octavia, three years later, the Fire of Rome in AD 64, and the merciless attack on the Christian community in Rome in the aftermath of the Fire. These events are the ones likely to be most familiar to a modern lay audience. However, a principal purpose of this book is to put these events into the broader context of Nero's fourteen-year reign.

As we shall see,[1] surviving Classical writers are mostly critical of Nero, even abrasively hostile towards him; they reflect the disappointment, even disgust, felt by many after his reign was over. A few contemporary writers, however, carry a more favourable, even hopeful, view of Nero's Principate: most of these were writing early in the reign, when it seemed to many, for a while at least, that a new 'golden age' had been born with the accession of an Emperor with youth and physical attractiveness on his side. For them, Nero appeared to be the antithesis of the dour Tiberius, the excessive Caligula, and the uncharmingly eccentric Claudius.

Despite some dire deeds on Nero's part, mostly concerned with the insecurity he felt about his position, for some this initial sense of optimism was never completely lost. For these amongst his subjects, the 'People's Emperor' never completely disappointed. Hence, the appearance after his death of false Nero-figures, as some perhaps cherished the hope that Nero was indeed still alive, awaiting the right moment to reclaim his kingdom.

One act, however, ensured that posterity would not be kind to Nero's memory: his savage attack on the Christian community in Rome, following the Great Fire, that was yet another sign of his insecurity, made it inevitable that the developing Christian Church would entertain no mercy for the last of the Julio-Claudians. This may even have helped to determine that the works of certain writers of antiquity would not survive through the late-Roman and early-medieval periods; there will have been no room in Christian libraries for those writers who failed adequately to condemn Nero's behaviour towards the Christians. Released in the early-fourth century from the shackles of persecution, the early Church rounded – sometimes almost hysterically – upon Nero. Some even branded him the Antichrist, who would return to wreak havoc and destruction upon the earth.

Modern writers, however, are generally more balanced: whilst few, if any, would try to construct a blameless Nero, most, whilst acknowledging the gravity of his crimes, have tried to find something positive in his behaviour. Whether or not Nero was personally responsible for the better acts of his reign, it is clear that not all was doom and gloom.

Nero was young at the time of his accession, hardly ready to accept in full the responsibilities that went with supreme power, and perhaps placed by some on a pedestal which no act of his could possibly justify. The result of this was inevitable disappointment and frustration for his subjects – and, therefore, given his craving for popularity, for Nero too.[2] Nero was weak, too easily undermined by his own insecurity and too readily influenced by the agendas of others – good and bad. Further, Nero was culpably self-indulgent as, in a sense, he had been encouraged to be by the sycophancy of many of those around him.

Thus, although the ultimate verdict on Nero is bound to be harsh, there are logical – and not always discreditable – explanations for some of what he did. As Cornelius Tacitus, the historian of the early-second century AD, wrote of the Julio-Claudian Emperors in general, the severe criticism of posterity might sometimes mislead. At the end of the day, however, Nero's character was not that of which sound Emperors were made; nothing makes this clearer than the important oration placed by Tacitus into the mouth of

Nero's successor, Servius Galba.[3] This oration, which has been viewed by some as a 'manual of statecraft' and which was delivered by Galba to his intended successor, Piso Licinianus, forms a kind of posthumous critique of the Julio-Claudian Emperors in general, and of Nero in particular.

Many of the events of Nero's life and reign have, over the years, also caught the imagination of the popular media: historical novels such as Robert Graves' masterly *I, Claudius*, films, such as *Quo Vadis?*, with the then youthful Peter Ustinov taking the part of Nero, television dramatisations on *The Caesars* and *Rome*, educational programmes, such as *I, Caesar* and *Nero's Golden House* and many others have provided a bill of fare for the growing number of people outside the narrow academic community who are captivated by Imperial Rome, or by this or that Emperor, the most popular of whom is likely to be Nero.

People inevitably wish to learn the answers to questions, such as 'Was he mad?'; 'Was he really as bad as he has been made out to have been?'; 'Was he typical of his times?'; 'Did he have any redeeming features?'; 'Was there any shape or coherence to his reign?'. These are amongst the questions which this book sets out to discuss; hopefully, as a result of that process, whilst Nero may not appear any more lovable, he will, at least, become a more coherent and intelligible character.

Acknowledgements

I should like to express my gratitude to Peter Lee for the originals of the maps upon which Figures 2.3, 6.1 and 9.1 are based; also to Dr Roger Bland, Head of the Department of Portable Antiquities at the British Museum, for his help in the preparation of illustrations of the Neronian coins; my thanks are due, too, to Professor Anthony Birley for his many helpful suggestions for improvements in the text; also to Professor Herbert Benario, Professor Michael Fulford and Dr David Woods for allowing me access to papers of theirs in advance of publication. I am grateful, too, to Jean Creed, the wife of my late colleague, John Creed, for permission to cite passages from his privately – published translation of Lactantius' *On the Deaths of the Persecutors*. Finally, I owe a great debt of gratitude to my wife, Anne, both for her help in the preparation of the manuscript, and for living with Nero for a very long time 'without any complaint'.

The publishers are grateful to the following for permission to reproduce copyright material:

Figure 7.1 redrawn from *Swan Hellenic Cruise Guide Book*, reprinted by permission of Swan Hellenic (Swan Hellenic 2002); Figure 7.2 *Etruscan and Roman Architecture*, reprinted by permission of Penguin Books Ltd. (Boëthius, A. and Ward-Perkins, J. B. 1970).

Plate 1 and Plate 13 The Bridgeman Art Library; Plate 2 akg-images, London/Erich Lessing; Plate 14 Anderson/Alinari Archives, Florence; Plate 25 © The Art Archive/Corbis; Plate 26 Professor Paavo Castrén.

In some instances we have been unable to trace the owners of copyright material, and we would appreciate any information that would enable us to do so.

Introduction: The Quest for Nero: The Principal Sources

The life of no Roman Emperor is independently verifiable: the modern historian of the Classical world has to work with a variety of ancient sources of information, if he or she is to make progress in separating truth from fiction. These ancient sources come in many different forms – for example, writers whose works survive wholly or in part to the present day, official and semi-official documents (usually inscribed on stone or bronze), that may offer a brief snapshot of a person, an event or an incident. These can sometimes be usefully and meaningfully compared with the texts of Classical writers; an example of this is an oration given by the Emperor, Claudius, to the Senate in AD 48 on the occasion of the introduction of some Gallic notables into senatorial membership, and the version of it provided by Tacitus.[1] In addition, we may consult coin-legends, extant buildings which may offer an insight into contemporary life-styles and, in Nero's case, even a piece of popular art in the form of the work of a graffito-artist.[2] The present chapter will consist of a discussion of the most significant of these sources, and of factors affecting their use; this synopsis will be supplemented by an Appendix[3] providing brief details of other relevant sources and how they may be accessed.

It may come as a surprise to a contemporary audience to learn that the task of the modern historian who is concerned with the ancient world is not limited to the analysis of writers who were themselves classed in antiquity as historians; to the surviving ancient historians of Nero's reign we have to add biographers, satirists, philosophers, a playwright and poets of various types. Some of these were contemporaries or near-contemporaries of Nero, but most – and certainly the most significant – wrote after the events, and so were themselves dependent on earlier sources, most of whose works no longer survive to allow us to assess the use that was made of them. Further, it has not infrequently been asserted in the past that contemporary documentary evidence, such as inscriptions and coin-legends, is independent and thus provides a corrective to the written sources. It must be kept in mind that such material is not independent, but is simply different, in that it reflects the government's own view of itself.

The principal literary sources for Nero's life and reign are the *Histories* and *Annals* of Publius Cornelius Tacitus (*c.* AD 57–120),[4] the *Lives of the Caesars* of Gaius Suetonius Tranquillus (*c.* AD 70–140),[5] and *The History of Rome* of Dio Cassius (*c.* AD 160–230).[6] These authors not only composed works which differed considerably in character, but also enjoyed rather different backgrounds. Tacitus and Dio Cassius were both historians, but followed rather different traditions of historiography; Suetonius was not a historian at all in a formal sense; his list of writings comprises various types, including biographies.

Tacitus was a first-generation senator, whose family probably came from northern Italy; he enjoyed a successful senatorial career, which spanned five decades – from the late-70s to the second decade of the second century AD – rising to the consulship in AD 97 and to the prestigious proconsulship (governorship) of the province of Asia in *c.* AD 112.[7] He must have shown clear political promise from an early age, as he was chosen as a suitable husband for the daughter of the senator, Gnaeus Julius Agricola, who became governor of Britain (AD 77–83) and whose biography was one of Tacitus' earliest literary compositions.[8]

Suetonius, Tacitus' near-contemporary, was not a senator, but a member of the equestrian order, the second rank in Roman society; like Tacitus, he too appears to have been of Italian origin.[9] As an equestrian, he filled a number of secretarial posts in the Imperial civil service, rising to senior rank under the Emperors, Trajan (AD 98–117) and Hadrian (AD 117–38). He was, however, dismissed by Hadrian in *c.* AD 122, apparently as the result of an indiscretion rather than a serious crime, along with his friend, the Prefect of the Praetorian Guard, Gaius Septicius Clarus.[10]

The family of Dio Cassius, on the other hand, came from Nicaea (in the province of Bithynia, in Asia Minor); he was, however, a Roman citizen and, like his father, Cassius Apronianus, was a member of the Roman Senate.[11]

Dio himself enjoyed a successful, if unspectacular, political career, rising to two consulships – in AD 205 and 229; although, evidently, not a particularly active participant in day-to-day senatorial business, he will, however, as a senator, have been well aware of the harsh and disdainful treatment meted out to senators by his own contemporaries, the Severan Emperors,[12] particularly Septimius Severus and his elder son, Caracalla.

These authors, then, chose different types of writing; even the two historians, Tacitus and Dio Cassius, followed different historiographical paths. Ever since the fifth century BC, writers of history in antiquity had fallen into two observable groups: one of these chose to write up lengthy periods, usually commencing with the mythological past, for which plainly the chief source was tradition, rather than other writers whose statements could be checked. The greatest Greek exponent of such writing was Herodotus of Halicarnassus (Bodrum, in modern Turkey), but his work was evidently looked down upon by some as 'unscientific'.[13] The alternative was to choose a relatively short and up-to-date period for study, for that, earlier writers could be checked and eye-witnesses consulted. The most famous Greek practitioner of this type of historiography was the Athenian, Thucydides, in his account of the Peloponnesian War between Athens and Sparta in the late-fifth century BC.[14]

Rome, too, had exponents of both approaches to the writing of history: the 'Herodotean' style was followed by the Augustan historian, Livy, and later by Dio Cassius, who elected to cover the history of Rome up to his own times in eighty books – truly a colossal undertaking. Tacitus, on the other hand, followed the 'Thucydidean' example, and chose shorter periods of recent history: his earlier work, the *Histories*, covered the period AD 69–96, that embraced the latter part of the civil war that followed Nero's death and the reigns of the three Flavian Emperors, Vespasian (AD 69–79) and his two sons, Titus (79–81) and Domitian (81–96). Much of this work is lost, the manuscript breaking off during the account of the events of AD 70. The *Histories* was followed by the *Annals*,[15] that covered the Julio-Claudian Emperors, Tiberius (AD 14–37), Gaius (37–41), Claudius (41–54) and Nero (54–68). From this work, the books dealing with the reign of Gaius and the early years of Claudius, as well as the final two years of Nero's reign are missing. Tacitus also indicated[16] that he intended, in old age, to write up the reigns of Nerva (96–98) and Trajan (98–117), although there is no evidence that he ever fulfilled this promise.

In using Classical sources, such as Tacitus, it is important that we keep in mind aspects of the writing of history in antiquity, that make the finished product different from what we should expect of a historian writing today. In the first place, although such works were committed to writing early on, 'publication' took the form of literary launches that will have consisted of a recital of a work (or part-work) before an invited audience. We know from Tacitus' contemporary, the satiric poet, Juvenal, that such audiences could be extremely critical and were evidently easily bored.[17] Thus, communication between author and audience had to be vital and immediate:[18] there was no place for modern luxuries of presentation, such as cross-references, footnotes, appendices, plates and figures. Much more was, therefore, expected of the delivered word, and its ability to retain the audience's attention; it is thus important to remember that such works were thought of as 'works of art', that necessarily placed a premium on stylistic and presentational aspects: in such circumstances, we can begin to understand why Classical historians did not provide detailed discussions of their sources of information or extended descriptions of military campaign-routes. The liveliness of the narrative had to be maintained by, for example, such practices as the inclusion of speeches composed for historical figures (whether there was any legitimate source for these or not), by the inclusion of descriptions of omens and prodigies, and by speculation on the motivations of historical characters. Such features were not viewed as optional extras, but as vital elements of the process of communicating with the audience.

This should not, however, be taken to mean that the writing of history in the Classical period was all style and no substance: it is clear, for example, that Tacitus was extremely anxious not just because he feared that he might not be able to hold his audience's attention[19] – important though this was – but also that he might not be able to uncover the truth in his researches.[20] In particular, he cites the facts that one-man rule had had the effect of making government more secretive about its activities, and that there was a real problem with the sources of information upon which he had to rely. Those writing during an Emperor's reign might falsify their accounts through ignorance of the truth or for fear of speaking out,[21] whilst those who published after an Emperor was dead might write with a venom that could easily be mistaken for independence of judgement. A very similar point is made by the Jewish historian, Flavius Josephus,[22] who had been taken prisoner during the war with Rome (AD 66–70), brought to Rome and subsequently patronised by Vespasian and his family.[23]

Unsurprisingly, Tacitus' opinion of Nero was not favourable, although the historian did show more restraint than some other writers in the matter of certain allegations commonly made against the Emperor. On the other hand, Tacitus provides us with an oration, that may be regarded as a clear view of the failings of Nero and his Julio-Claudian predecessors; historically, this oration[24] was put into the mouth of Nero's successor, Servius Galba, as he addressed his own intended successor, Piso Licinianus, in January of AD 69. It is not known whether any form of a genuine version of this oration had survived to be consulted by Tacitus, or whether the historian was simply following the stated practice of the Athenian, Thucydides, of putting into the mouths of his characters 'sentiments proper to the occasion'.[25]

Galba's oration has been seen by some as an expression of Tacitus' own views: in it the Emperor is made to argue that a ruler such as Nero served only to highlight the dangers of a dynastic system of succession and that it was Piso's duty to restore confidence in the Principate[26] as an institution after the aberration that Nero represented: 'Nero', says Galba, 'will always be missed by the worst of Rome's citizens; it is our job to ensure that he is not missed by the better ones also'. Under the Julio-Claudians, and Nero in particular, Rome and the Empire had been treated as if they were the private property of the Emperor. However – and it might seem particularly appropriate in Nero's case – others, especially senators, bore a measure of responsibility for inflating the Emperor's *ego* by their meaningless flattery of everything that he said and did.

The main account of Nero's reign is to be found in Tacitus' later work, the *Annals*. It has been argued[27] that this work was composed in three groups of six books (hexads), of which the account of Nero's reign occupied the whole of the final one. As we have noted, of the third hexad only Books 13–15 and a small part of 16 have survived; it remains uncertain whether the final books, although written, have been subsequently lost, or whether Tacitus did not live to complete them;[28] in support of the latter viewpoint, it has been suggested that the unusual citing of sources in the Nero-books may point to the possibility that these books had not received their final edit.

In all, Tacitus mentions five writers whose works he had consulted;[29] three of these were historians – Marcus Cluvius Rufus, Fabius Rusticus and the Elder Pliny (Gaius Plinius Secundus). Cluvius Rufus was a senator and courtier of Nero, who accompanied the Emperor on his visit to Greece in AD 67; despite this, he won the praise of the Stoic, Helvidius Priscus, for having caused no-one any harm.[30] It is thought likely that Tacitus' less critical observations about some events of Nero's reign may have originated with Cluvius Rufus. We shall also see later that Cluvius apologised in advance to Lucius Verginius Rufus, Nero's commander in Germania Superior in AD 68, for taking a critical line towards Verginius' conduct during the rebellion of Julius Vindex.[31] Fabius Rusticus and The Elder Pliny are regarded as having been more hostile towards Nero than was Cluvius Rufus.[32] In the case of Fabius Rusticus, who was a protégé of Nero's tutor and adviser, Seneca, this may have been due to Fabius' high (perhaps over-high) regard for his patron and to Nero's growing antipathy towards Stoics (UC). The hostility of references to Nero in Pliny's surviving *Natural History* suggest the likelihood of a similar tone having been taken in his general history which Tacitus consulted. Pliny will have conformed to the anti-Neronian stance that became usual during the reign of Vespasian.

It was common practice for members of Rome's noble families to write up their memoirs; Tacitus cites two such works – those of Nero's mother, the Younger Agrippina, and of his eastern commander, Gnaeus Domitius Corbulo.[33] Whilst Tacitus makes no specific comment about Agrippina's memoirs, he clearly found Corbulo's rather self-important in tone. It is also known that Suetonius Paullinus, governor of Britain at the time of Boudica's rebellion,[34] composed his memoirs, although it is not known which parts of his career they covered, nor whether Tacitus made any use of them. Tacitus further informs us that he consulted the official publication of the proceedings of the Senate (*Acta Senatus*);[35] as well as this, he will have had the testimony of eye-witnesses available.[36]

Although Tacitus does not *explicitly* subscribe to the view, supposedly advanced by the later Emperor, Trajan, that Nero's first five years in power were generally characterised by a better standard of government than what followed, he does appear in practice to have had some sympathy with the notion. Tacitus does not, however, allow his reader to overlook the fact that this five-year period was also marked by Nero's planning of his mother's murder, the likely murder of his step-brother, Britannicus,[37] together with the exiling of two senators, Rubellius Plautus and Faustus Cornelius Sulla, who appear to have committed no crime beyond that of having familial ties with the ruling house. From AD 59, however, the historian paints a deteriorating picture; under the influence of less scrupulous advisers, Nero murdered his wife, Octavia, as well as the two senators (mentioned above) whom he had already exiled. As time went on, an accelerating number of senators and others fell victim to Nero's sense of insecurity and his growing obsession with his personal popularity. Yet, in these later years, on two matters over which the majority of sources evidently took a harsh line, Tacitus was more cautious: he did not lay at Nero's door the blame for setting the Fire of Rome in AD 64, and, when discussing the Emperor's building-projects, he allows that Nero may have been swept along by the extravagant ideas of his architects.[38]

Tacitus does, therefore, produce an account of Nero that is seriously critical of the Emperor, although he was sufficiently independent in his thinking to remain open to the possibility that some writers and commentators may have been too ready to denigrate everything that Nero did.

Dio Cassius differs from Tacitus – and not just in the type of history that he chose to write: as we have seen, his account of Nero's reign (Books 61–63) is a small part of a much larger undertaking. Much of what Dio originally wrote, however, has come down to us not precisely as he wrote it, but in the form of quotations and summaries put together by a number of Byzantine monks. For example, most of the material dealing with the early Emperors, including Nero, has come down to us through Xiphilinus, a monk of the eleventh century.[39] It can be disturbing to discover, in Book 63 for example, that deals with the fall of Nero and the rebellion of Vindex, differing details of what Dio is reported by different summarisers (epitomators) to have written.[40]

For the substantial task that he had undertaken, Dio claims to have read widely,[41] although he leaves no indication of which particular sources he relied upon most heavily. It is thought, however, that, whilst he may not have made much direct use of Tacitus and Suetonius, there is enough common ground between them to suggest that Dio probably did use sources that they used. For example, his hostility to Nero makes it very likely that he did consult the works of Fabius Rusticus and the Elder Pliny.[42] He may thus have woven together material from a number of sources with observations of his own. Essentially, Dio's is a narrative history, and his interpretative power is rarely displayed as anything other than a noticing of the obvious. Qualitative judgements in Dio are rare, although in Nero's reign he does mark the contrast between his subject's performance as Emperor and his performances on the stage.[43] He also observes, in his account of Nero's tour of Greece in 67, that most of the masks for female theatrical parts were fashioned to resemble Nero's dead wife, Poppaea Sabina. Although his narrative embraces a number of important changes in the manner of government, Dio was sufficiently removed in time from the 'good old days' not to be sentimental about them; he recognised that one-man rule was a necessity. Thus, Augustus takes on a principal importance for him, together with material which facilitates comparison between Augustus and what came later.[44]

Dio makes considerable use of speeches, although these are not generally, as are a number of those in Tacitus, vehicles for his own thinking. They appear to explore such contemporary issues as, for example, in the lengthy 'bedtime-dialogue' between Augustus and Livia, the matter of the conduct of Gnaeus Cornelius Cinna Magnus, and how to deal with it.[45] As such, it exhibits similarities with the treatise, *On Clemency*, which Seneca composed for Nero. The very length of Dio's piece on this and other occasions suggests that it may have derived from the set-compositions which emanated from the rhetorical schools; such pieces also serve, as with Tacitus, to introduce variety and a sense of drama into narrative passages. Like Tacitus, too, and probably for the same reason, Dio shows a liking for reports of omens and portents.[46] We also find occasional trite aphorisms:[47] one example is a comment upon the household of Augustus, that is clearly intended to refer forward to the Severan Emperors, under whom Dio lived and worked.

Dio, then, leaves us in no doubt that his history is what it purports to be – the *story* of Rome: it has little analysis, and no ulterior motive beyond moralising. For Dio, one feels, the eighty books were the achievement in themselves.

Suetonius has often been criticised as a *historian* of inferior quality; it is of obvious importance, therefore, that we recognise at the outset that, in his *Lives of the Caesars*, he was writing biography, not history, and thus worked with different criteria in the selection and arrangement of his material. Suetonius' early career was spent in teaching and writing; since teaching involved the collection of relevant and striking examples from literature for his students to use, it may be that it was this part of his life that gave him his obvious liking for compilation, which is very evident in *Lives of the Caesars*. By nature, he appears to have been fussy and superstitious,[48] but was admired by Pliny for his sense of honour and integrity.[49] Pliny enjoyed him as a literary companion and, particularly, for the care that he took over his composition.[50]

As we have seen, Suetonius' career in the Imperial secretariat was cut short in AD 122, when he was dismissed by Hadrian. This certainly seems to have left him with a sense of bitterness, and critical references to Hadrian and the Principate have been detected in some of the *Lives*.[51] More significantly, however, his dismissal denied him access to the imperial records that were so vital to him as a unique source for *Lives of the Caesars*. It is clear, for example, that the *Lives* that were evidently researched and written up after his dismissal, including that of Nero, are on the whole shorter and less well illustrated from his sources. By contrast, the earlier *Lives* contain relevant material quoted from such sources as Augustus' correspondence, to which it seems that our other sources did not have access. It does not appear that Suetonius can have survived much beyond *c*. AD 140.

In the *Lives of the Caesars*,[52] the research-characteristics that emerge most clearly are attention to detail, that may be used to correct other writers, and diligence in compilation – as can be seen in such subjects as the discussion of Caligula's birthplace,[53] his quoting from Augustus' correspondence, that is done *verbatim* rather than integrated into his narrative,[54] and in his favourable comments upon Nero's poetry, that may have been intended as a contradiction of Tacitus.[55] As a biographer, Suetonius does not respect chronological development,[56] as would have been natural for a historian, but treats his subjects by dividing their lives and characteristics into topics, and then compiling as much material as possible to inform those topics.[57]

The *Lives of the Caesars* follow a similar general pattern: they begin with a survey of family-history, the early life of the subject (with appropriate omens and anecdotes), and his career to the point of accession to power. The subjects' lives are then treated under headings, that are not necessarily clearly indicated in the text, such as wars, legislation, buildings, virtues, vices and so on, and concluding with physical characteristics and death (again, with appropriate omens). All of these sections are illustrated with collections of facts and anecdotes, although the amount of information given varies from subject to subject. The topics do not necessarily appear in the same order in each *Life*, and are sometimes overridden by more general divisions – as in the *Life of Gaius Caligula*, where a division is announced between the acts of 'the Emperor' and those of 'the Monster'.[58] As one would have expected, Suetonius concentrates almost exclusively on the character in question, whilst other names and contexts are kept to a minimum. In the *Life of Nero*, for example, no mention whatever is made of events in Britain and Parthia/Armenia. Occasionally, too, he writes of what appears to have been a general characteristic of his subject when, in fact, the only evidence may have consisted of a single incident.[59] This can obviously be misleading for those attempting to use *Lives of the Caesars* as a normal historical source.

Suetonius' predilection for scandalous material has often been noted, although this is much more likely to have been due to an interest in the curious than to a liking for the scurrilous and salacious. For example, the fulsome details of Tiberius' alleged perversions whilst in retirement on the island of Capri[60] bear more the signs of diligent research and composition – something that can be recognised in the titles of some of Suetonius' lost writings.[61] We need not, therefore, see in Suetonius the signs of a malicious man, but one whose temperament suited him to listing, compiling and categorising. At the same time, we may also perhaps glimpse the same indecisiveness that Pliny observed in Suetonius' personal life;[62] indecisiveness may indeed, on occasion, have led to serious inconsistency, as when, in two separate *Lives*,[63] Suetonius gives very different impressions of the nature of activities in Germany during the reign of Gaius Caligula.

In conclusion, it may be that, for Suetonius, the amassing of information was one thing, but coming to critical decisions about it quite another.

Chapter One

The Political Background to the Reign of Nero

In 31 BC, Gaius Julius Caesar Octavianus,[1] better known to history as Augustus Caesar, defeated his arch-rival, Marcus Antonius (Marc Antony), at the Battle of Actium, off the west coast of Greece. From what had started twelve years earlier as the Triumvirate of Antonius, Lepidus and Octavian, charged with the task of putting right the problems of the Roman Republic, Octavian was now left as the undisputed master of the Roman world; he put in place the system of government that is usually called the Principate, after the status-title (*princeps*/'first citizen'), by which Octavian – or Augustus Caesar, as he was named after 27 BC – preferred to be known.

In so doing, Augustus effectively brought to an end the governmental system that we call the Republic, formed from the Latin words, *Res Publica* ('the common concern').[2] During the period of the Republic,[3] that according to tradition was founded in 509 BC, Rome had grown from a small and embattled city-state to become the mistress of a prospering Empire which encompassed the Mediterranean lands, Asia Minor, as well as much of central and western Europe.

A cornerstone of the Old Republic, as people came to refer to it, was the avoidance in government of dominance (*dominatio*) by any single individual or group. Three elements were perceived as making up the Republic's government: the annually-elected executive officers (or 'magistrates', as the

Romans referred to them), of whom the chief were the two consuls. They were kept in check both by the fact that each year there were two of them, and by the tradition, regarded by many as a requirement, that, in carrying out their duties, they should consult the Senate (a body composed largely of former magistrates) during their year of office and, at the end of it, should give an account of their conduct to the People who had elected them.

The Greek historian, Polybius (*c.* 208–126 BC), who lived in and admired Rome, regarded this interconnection in government between magistrates, Senate and people as the crucial factor in providing the Old Republic with stable government and in preventing the advent of a king-like figure who might attempt to usurp the reins of government.[4] Indeed, the word, *rex* ('king'), was one of the harshest terms of political abuse in Rome during the period of the Old Republic, as can be seen in Julius Caesar's famous declaration that, despite all the power that he came to hold, he was 'not king, but Caesar'. The only circumstance in which the Republic's constitution was effectively set aside was in the event of a grave emergency, when the annual magistrates could be replaced by a *Dictator* – but then only for six, or *in extremis* twelve, months. For Polybius, writing in the tradition of Greek political thought, that embraced Plato and Aristotle, this form of government seemed ideal and stable, because it held in balance the three principal constitution-types of Classical antiquity – monarchy, aristocracy (oligarchy) and democracy. In Rome, the magistrates provided the monarchic element, the Senate the aristocratic, and the people the democratic.

Nowadays, however, it is generally thought that this stability, that was so highly prized, was due less to magistrates, Senate and people representing three equal partners in government than to the fact that the Republic's aristocracy (the *nobiles*[5]) monopolised the magistracies, formed the Senate and, through a voting-system that favoured the rich and powerful,[6] dominated the popular assemblies. In reality, then, provided that the voice of the ordinary people was not ignored, the Old Republic was an oligarchy that itself was dominated by a small number of exceedingly powerful families who regarded the Republic as in effect their own property. This was made clear when, in 50–49 BC, Julius Caesar and his rival, Pompey (Gnaeus Pompeius Magnus),[7] were propelled into a civil war that neither of them really wanted, and against which the Senate had voted by a margin of 370 votes to twenty-two, only to be railroaded into war by the intransigence of spokesmen for the twenty-two; such, through the agency of the veto of tribunes of the plebeians, was possible in the Roman Republic.

So, what undermined the so-called 'Polybian balance' and the stability that it appeared to guarantee? Although many different factors can be isolated, the overarching cause was the growth, from the mid-third century BC, of Rome's overseas Empire. Territories, first in Italy and then overseas, were acquired, more often than not as an accident of successful warfare; overseas, acquired lands were formed into provinces or occasionally left, temporarily at least, under the control of a pro-Roman local ruler. In its early years, Rome was essentially a city-state with interests largely confined to Italy; the new Empire, however, forced upon her an obligation to the overseas provinces to provide good government, as well as maximising the opportunities to exploit the human and material resources provided by the provinces.

The growth of the Empire brought money and slaves into the Roman system at a level previously not contemplated; through these means, individual Romans were able to finance ambitions more extensive than before, whilst the advent of large numbers of slaves generated more leisure-time for aristocratic households, greater profits on the land, and a source of 'cheap blood' that could be used to entertain the people in the arenas. Society, thus, moved away from what many Romans, in retrospect at least, saw as the good-old-days, when individual and family values were simple and wholesome and when the family prided itself on its self-sufficiency and respect for Rome's traditions.[8] In his 'Roman Odes',[9] the Augustan poet, Horace (Quintus Horatius Flaccus) stressed the obligation that rested upon Augustus to revitalise such old values.

However, in the event, the most damaging change that came about as a result of the Empire's growth was the need for a larger, more permanent and better-organised army, that had previously been raised from property-owners on a campaign-basis. The Republic's solution to this, put in place in the late-second century BC, was far from satisfactory: troops continued to be recruited largely for campaigns, but from the whole citizen-body, and thus required settlement-packages on their return to Italy. No automatic provision was made for this other than by army-commanders, who were also Rome's leading politicians, using their weight and influence to secure the best settlement-packages possible. Soldiers were thus thrown inextricably into the arms of their commanders who, in their turn, soon appreciated that they had acquired a new and irresistable weapon in the fulfilment of their political ambitions. Stability, therefore, in the final century of the Old Republic gave way to the near-constant threat of civil war. As the Roman politician and orator, Marcus Tullius Cicero, succinctly put it, 'faced with armed force, the laws fall silent'.[10]

Some, such as Cicero, began to see that the ultimate solution to this – although an unpalatable one, given Roman prejudices against one-man rule – was to entrust the oversight of government to an individual who had sufficient wealth, power and influence to guarantee its continuing integrity and stability. In other words, a king-like figure who was not a king and who could be trusted not to submerge the state in the dangers flowing from his own personal ambitions and from the envy of others. What is more, this had to be done against a background of an army that respected and identified with its general (*imperator*/'commander')[11], of a people who required the provision of food and entertainment ('bread and circuses'), and of a Senate that, whilst not totally opposed to change, was sensitively mindful of its traditional rôle and privileges, and thus fit to play a leading and responsible part in the Republic.

Cicero frequently[12] looked for a state of affairs in which all 'good men' (the *boni*, as he called them) would come together as a 'Union' (*consensus bonorum*). On occasions, he appears to have thought of this within the historical context of the second century BC, with Publius Cornelius Scipio Aemilianus as the leading figure (*moderator*); on other occasions, he appeared to be thinking more specifically of his own times, when Pompey would save the Republic as the *moderator*, with Cicero himself as his chief supporter and adviser.[13]

The achievement of such a *consensus* represented an extremely difficult challenge, particularly in a Republic in which politicians were traditionally obsessed with the acquisition of personal glory and success that were 'worthy of their ancestors'. Cicero's *moderator* would need to be extraordinarily modest and self-effacing to be able to carry through the rôle that Cicero seems to have had in mind. So who might undertake such an overarching rôle? The list of failed attempts to create harmony and stability had grown during the turbulent years of the first century BC, prominent amongst them Sulla,[14] Pompey and Caesar. Could Caesar's great-nephew and adopted son, the future Augustus, succeed? Although an early career, marred by bloodshed, thuggery and dissimulation, hardly appeared promising, Augustus Caesar emerged as one of those people who, through a combination of realism and spin, managed to reinvent himself – to outward appearances, at least.

It was fortunate for him that his chief rival, Antony, decided – albeit for reasons that were, for him, perfectly logical[15] – to leave Rome and base himself in the East, lured there by the charm, but also by the wealth, of Cleopatra, queen of Egypt. Such orientalising never went down well with Rome's traditionalist aristocracy; Nero, too, was to discover the reality and the danger of this. Augustus was, therefore, able conveniently to present himself as the defender and upholder of the time-honoured traditions of the Roman West. By so doing, he gathered around himself men from a variety of backgrounds, most of whom combined loyalty to him with effective conduct. Such a man was Marcus Agrippa, Nero's great-grandfather; it was Agrippa who effectively won the battle of Actium for the young Caesar.

Again, the deaths of both Antony and Cleopatra in 30 BC and the deaths or disgrace of many of their supporters left the future Augustus without obvious rivals for power; as Tacitus put it, 'the Julians had no leader but Caesar'.[16] Many of the great aristocratic families were lulled by Augustus' own blood-connection with the Julian family, and the fact that his wife, Livia Drusilla,[17] came from the heart of that aristocracy made him appear convincing as one of them in head and heart. In fact, they had little option: Actium left Augustus as *de facto* head of the whole army and, in popular eyes, the only man who could prevent a return to the uncertainties and dangers of civil bloodshed. Beyond this, Augustus knew that, whilst public relief after Actium might provide him with a 'honeymoon period', he had to deliver on stability and prosperity and he had to show that, in essence, he was restoring, not destroying, the Republic. Politics and personal inclination demanded reform, but reform that was firmly embedded in Rome's traditions.[18]

There is no doubt that, during the half-century that separated the victory at Actium from Augustus' death in AD 14, the *princeps* had his hands firmly on the levers of control. His reform of the army, making it permanent, well-paid, loyal to him as its commander and reliant on him as the provider of its retirement-gratuities, was the key to this. However, by placing the army in groups in the frontier-provinces and delegating day-to-day control of it to men whom he trusted, he avoided the appearance of overbearing control on his part, although the *esprit de corps* that was engendered in these groups, with their local loyalties, was to have dire consequences by the end of Nero's reign.[19] Augustus, then, guaranteed the army's rewards and ensured that its commanders were men loyal to him. The fact that each year was inaugurated with oaths of allegiance to Rome, Jupiter and the army's *imperator* not only guaranteed Augustus' continuing supremacy, but also placed him into a totally traditional context. Even the nine thousand troops who made up the Praetorian Guard (imperial bodyguard) were barracked in small units outside, rather than in, Rome, and thus did not obtrude upon the popular consciousness. In terms of appearance, however, it was a mistake, although perhaps an inevitable one, on the part of Tiberius to yield to the arguments of Lucius Aelius Sejanus, his Prefect of the Guard, that he should barrack the Praetorians together in Rome itself.[20]

The actual powers that Augustus held were rooted in the traditions of the past; writing of his power-base in this renewed Republic, Augustus said: 'I excelled all in *auctoritas*, but of powers I possessed no more than my colleagues in the several magistracies'.[21] *Auctoritas* (prestige), however, was all-important, and Augustus possessed it by virtue both of his achievement of ridding Rome of civil war and of his descent from the aristocratic Julian family (*gens Iulia*). All of the Julio-Claudian Emperors who followed him enjoyed *auctoritas* by virtue of their descent from Augustus and the Julian and Claudian families. The significance of this is emphasised by the experience of Vespasian, who came to power in AD 69 and who obviously enjoyed respect for his achievements. However, he lacked *auctoritas* because of the fact that he was not descended from a senatorial family – a point that was not lost on some of those in the Senate.[22] Thus, at the beginning of his reign, Vespasian needed to set about acquiring his own *auctoritas* and in this way to compensate for family-origins that were regarded as inadequate.[23]

Whilst cynics might carp at the plurality of Augustus' powers,[24] he could point out that his tenures of office all respected the traditional principle of accountability that had been a corner-stone of *libertas* in the Old Republic.[25] *Libertas* (freedom), indeed, was a concept indissolubly associated with the Old Republic; in practice, its application during the period of the Republic had been chiefly directed to the interests of the governing (senatorial) class and their ability to pursue their political careers without hindrance from others.

Augustus was wise enough to leave in place the old offices of state, such as the consulship, and to keep them subject to annual election, although the exercise of authority in these posts was, in practical terms, reined in by the

Emperor's own powers. However, he recognised the importance of leaving open to men the ability to rise through the tiers of office (*cursus honorum*), an aspect of *libertas* for which, in the Old Republic, men had been prepared to go to war and even to lay down their lives. Nonetheless, Augustus and his successors ensured that they retained a measure of control over the outcome of elections.[26] At the same time, however, the fact that the security of public and personal life in Rome so clearly depended upon the *auctoritas* and continued presence of Augustus allowed these offices of state to be used by him to manage Rome and the Empire along the lines that he desired.

Similarly important in the Augustan Republic was that potent symbol of Republican tradition, the Senate. Augustus himself attended its meetings on a regular basis, put a great deal of business before it and respected its decisions; the Senate even acquired an enhancement of its judicial functions. The *princeps* used the Senate in important ways: it was the vehicle for much of the legislation that he wished to see passed, and it provided a point in the system through which Augustus could introduce into the administration men of wealth and talent from outside Rome and even Italy. This gave meaning, as the later Emperor, Claudius, was also to observe, to the practice of granting the rights of Roman citizenship widely, and ensuring that citizenship was seen as conferring obligations[27] on the recipients as well as providing privileges and opportunities.

In the Augustan state, the only bodies which visibly lost powers were the assemblies of the people, although they remained of ceremonial relevance. Already, it was regarded as more important to keep the people fed and entertained rather than informed and involved. It is little wonder that the historian, Tacitus, describing the street-battles that took place in Rome in AD 69 in the civil war between the supporters of Vitellius and those of Vespasian that followed Nero's death, observed that the people watched these as if they were just another arena-spectacle.[28]

However, Augustus' position as a holder of 'tribunician power' made him the heir to the patronage and protection of the plebeian people that had been an original rôle of the tribunes of the plebeians in the Old Republic. Thus, his substantial programme of public works ensured not only that Rome became a capital city that was visibly worthy of its imperial rôle, but also that there was work by means of which men could earn money – a point which the later Emperor, Vespasian, is said to have emphasised in his building of the Flavian Amphitheatre (or *Colosseum*) in Rome in the 70s.[29]

As we have seen, the Augustan poet, Quintus Horatius Flaccus (Horace), was one of a number of writers who were patronised by Augustus; whilst the Emperor did not force words upon them, it is clear that they all 'sang from the same hymn-sheet'. All of them – the epic poet, Virgil, the historian, Livy, as well as Horace himself – wrote in a way that heralded the Augustan age as representing the climax of respect for Rome's traditional values and aspirations, as enshrined in the Old Republic. Augustus' own respect for the gods, for family and for tradition was his *pietas* (piety/sense of duty); in the context of Virgil's poem, the *Aeneid*, it was this virtue that drove the hero, Aeneas, forward to complete his divinely-appointed task of founding the city of Rome, however hard that proved to be. As we have seen, Horace, in his six 'Roman Odes', describes the ways in which the latter years of the Old Republic had represented a decline in Rome's traditional standards. In nothing is Horace more insistent than in the field of religion, the rock upon which the Roman state was founded.

It is clear that respect for the old cults had declined in the later years of the Old Republic, with educated men turning with increasing frequency to philosophy; the turmoil of the period of civil wars that preceded Augustus' victory at Actium was seen as caused by the gods' anger at the neglect and disrespect that they had suffered. It was, in other words, a prime duty incumbent upon Augustus to set traditional religious practices back into order. Not only did Augustus do this, building or rebuilding a large number of holy places,[30] taking on the rôle of *pontifex maximus* (chief priest), but it is clear that he relished it, giving it prominence in his account of his reign in the *Res Gestae Divi Augusti*. Whilst there was a place in Rome for certain new cults from the growing Empire, such as Mithraism from the Middle East, these could be associated with traditional deities, but never allowed to displace them. After all, the religious ceremonies and priestly pronouncements of the Old Republic had been vital to its success and, on a more cynical level, provided a powerful means of political manipulation on the part of the political establishment.[31] The gods were much more the levers of political control than the dispensers of religious comfort. 'Jupiter', wrote Cicero, 'is called Best and Greatest not because he makes us just or sober or wise, but rather healthy, rich and prosperous.'[32] In Roman religion, material aspirations far outweighed the spiritual.

The historian, Cornelius Tacitus, shows[33] that, in the wake of Augustus' death, some people were critical in their assessments of him, looking beyond the apparent stability and prosperity to murkier dealings. However, for most, the success of Augustus lay in his restoration of peace and of significant aspects of a traditional life that was seen once more to be important, and yet surmounting the turmoil of the recent past by exercising a firm control over the Republic's business. In a sense, the Principates of Augustus and of his successor, Tiberius, might be said to have represented an intermediate stage in the development of Rome's government. A stage that was transitional between the Old Republic and its traditions of aristocratic government[34] and the open autocracy which characterised the reigns of so many of Augustus' successors – including his great-great-grandson, Nero Claudius Caesar Augustus.

In retrospect – and, indeed, during his lifetime also – Augustus was criticised for one serious manifestation of autocratic rule – his insistence upon a dynastic succession-policy. Indeed, as we have seen, Tacitus[35] put into the mouth of Nero's successor, Servius Sulpicius Galba, an oration that is, in effect, a critique of dynasticism. In it Galba observed, as he reflected on the period between Augustus and Nero, that Rome had become 'the heirloom of a single family'. Galba – and he was right in principle – saw this pursuit of a dynastic succession-policy as a damaging break with a past which Augustus had seemed so keen to respect and embrace. Further, the operation of Augustus' policy of retaining power in the hands of his family, the Julio-Claudian dynasty (31 BC–AD 68), has been seen by many in more recent times as one of the more murderous episodes in Roman imperial history. Tacitus himself implies that Augustus got away with his autocracy because so many who might have challenged him had been killed in the civil wars of 44–31 BC, or were subsequently bought off.[36]

It is clear, however, that, for many, the Augustan era was one of exceptional achievement and satisfaction; some, it is implied,[37] hoped – or even believed – that Augustus might prove to be immortal. What might happen in the event of his death posed a worrying prospect. The *princeps* had, after all, crafted his Republic over a period of time; it was suited to its times and to its creator and his contemporaries. Any successor would have to 'pick it up and run with it', whatever the circumstances of his accession, whatever people's views of him and whatever his own temperament. Hopefully, his advantage would lie in his *auctoritas* (prestige) which derived from who he was and what he had achieved.[38]

Over time, Augustus had, within his family, an abundance of potential successors. However, one by one 'a cruel fate', often regarded as a euphemism for dynastic blood-feuding, disposed of them.[39] In the end, only his stepson, Tiberius Claudius Nero (or Tiberius Julius Caesar, as he was known after his adoption as Augustus' son and heir in AD 4) remained. Tacitus[40] shows how acutely aware Tiberius was of the pitfalls of dynastic succession; he wished fervently to be 'seen to have been the Republic's choice, not the lame product of an ambitious wife imposing her will on her ageing husband'. Further, he was at pains to show that he had no wish to be anybody's master (*dominus*).[41] Once, when addressed as such, he retorted sharply that he was 'master' to his slaves, 'general' to his armies and '*princeps*' to his fellow-citizens.[42] Although Tiberius notably lacked the Augustan charisma that would have convinced his contemporaries of it, it is clear from his actions that Tiberius wished to develop his tutelage of the Principate along studiedly Augustan lines[43] – that is, maintaining it as a 'Republican Principate'.

Tiberius, however, despite many obvious admirable qualities, was no Augustus: he could not easily adapt his own rather dour personality and caustic tongue to suit the required diplomatic charade.[44] Whilst he endeavoured to uphold Augustan precedent and act as he believed Augustus would have done, his lack of the easy and confident manner that had characterised his predecessor precluded the achievement of the kind of genuine relationship with his contemporaries – particularly senators – that he so anxiously desired. Galba was later to acknowledge ruefully what a difficult, yet vital, task this was.[45] In short, Tiberius was not trusted, and his reaction to this failure (as he saw it) and his consequent frustration was to withdraw into himself and to rely on those whom he thought that he could trust, such as the infamous Lucius Aelius Sejanus[46] and Naevius Sutorius Macro, his successive Prefects of the Praetorian Guard. Further, the concentration of the Praetorian Guard in Rome itself, that Sejanus requested and achieved, inevitably heightened the appearance of a military dictatorship. The influence of men such as Sejanus and Macro blighted Tiberius' Principate and he spent his last ten years in self-imposed seclusion on the island of Capri. His reputation in that period as a cruel, perverted and sadistic tyrant could not be ameliorated by anything that he had accomplished in his earlier years; for most, it simply confirmed their worst fears.

That Tiberius wished to govern after the Augustan pattern seems clear; his actions towards and words of respect for the magistrates and the Senate mirrored a genuine attitude of mind on his part. Indeed, Tiberius' frustration at not being able to match Augustus' ease of deportment in government is dramatically borne out by the opening sentence of a letter which he sent to the Senate from Capri, and which is quoted (with minor differences) by both Tacitus and the biographer, Suetonius: 'If I know what to write to you, senators, or what not to write, or how to write it, may heaven consign me to a worse death than I feel myself dying day by day.'[47] Tiberius understood well enough that he had failed, although understanding of his most significant failing eluded him: 'why had all this happened to him despite his good intentions?' Ultimately, imperial (and often imperious) letters to the Senate from the Emperor on his island-retreat could not adequately replace Augustan engagement with the Senate in its debates. Tiberius had known (and warned) at the outset that only Augustus could carry the burden of Empire;[48] he had hoped to be able to do his best to maintain the Augustan Republic: he died, however, an autocrat, hated and feared by the majority of his subjects.

For the last seven years of his sojourn on Capri, Tiberius had the company of his great-nephew, Gaius Caesar, popularly known as Caligula;[49] whatever the truth regarding the quality of life on the island, it can hardly have been an uplifting and improving experience for a young man in his early twenties. Tiberius died (or, according to some, was murdered) in March, AD 37; it remains unclear whether he named Caligula as his successor, or – characteristically, perhaps – left the matter for the Senate to resolve. In any case, Caligula himself, encouraged by Macro, the Prefect of the Praetorian Guard, rendered any discussion superfluous by assuming power, as if the outcome of any discussion was beyond question. This prelude to the reign proved to be an ominous sign of the shape of things to come.

Caligula was twenty-five years of age when he succeeded Tiberius; his accession was generally welcomed with a popular outpouring of satisfaction that the grim and joyless years of Tiberius were at an end, and his place taken by a young man of whom a very great deal was expected. A few, however, rightly, as events turned out, had their doubts about Caligula's stability and suitability for the job.[50] Even the reviled Tiberius was now credited with prescient observations about the woes that Caligula would inflict upon Rome.[51] Indeed, the new Emperor's widespread popularity at the time of his accession was based upon little more than people's longing for a change and their somewhat ill-judged expectations of the son of the 'dream-couple', Germanicus Caesar and the Elder Agrippina.[52]

In reality, Germanicus, Livia's grandson, although undoubtedly well-meaning, had been largely ineffectual and extremely theatrical in his behaviour. This was shown in his attempts to deal with a mutiny in AD 14 amongst the legions on the Rhine, and in the emotional speech which he made five years later on arriving in Alexandria.[53] Agrippina, the grand-daughter of Augustus, was a lady with personal ambitions, who would have relished the chance to exercise power in her own right, but, failing that, was determined that one of her sons should inherit Augustus' position. A probably ill-conceived conspiracy-theory regarded both Germanicus and his wife as martyrs to persecution by Tiberius and his friends;[54] the accession of any offspring of theirs would be seen as the dawn of a new 'golden age'.

It was, indeed, a new age, but not in the sense that most people hoped and expected: Caligula was a young man who had, throughout his boyhood and youth, basked in a seemingly endless glow of public adoration. By the time that he was growing towards manhood, his father was dead and his mother intent on avenging what she regarded as her husband's murder at the instigation of Tiberius and his mother, Livia. The Elder Agrippina, indeed, was by contemporary standards an extraordinary woman, who was warned by her dying husband not to provoke those in power,[55] rebuked by Tiberius for envious anger because she was not 'queen of Rome',[56] and caricatured by the menacing Sejanus as the leader of a revolutionary party.[57] It is not difficult to see in Caligula's parents two strands of temperament that were prominent in him – his father's theatricality and his mother's obsession with power and her own superiority.

Tiberius' government, which never attained the easy co-operation of the Senate along Augustan lines, had deteriorated fast, with Tiberius issuing peremptory instructions from his island of retirement. This provided no example for the young Caligula to follow. Tiberius had found his relations with the Senate trying and ultimately frustrating, a frustration captured in a private outburst of the Emperor recorded by Tacitus.[58] Caligula's temperament was plainly ill-matched to making further efforts where Tiberius had failed.

More than this, Caligula's descent from Augustus, together with his own popularity and that of his parents before him, bred in him a strong sense of his own superiority, even infallibility. Further, some of his mother's obsession with power had rubbed off on him. The Alexandrian Jewish philosopher, Philo, who was a member of a delegation that came to Rome to discuss with Caligula a catastrophic deterioration in relations between

Greeks and Jews in Alexandria, records an exchange between Caligula and his mentor, the Praetorian Prefect, Sutorius Macro, which sheds a telling light on the way in which Caligula viewed himself:

> *And then does anyone dare to teach me, who even while in the womb, that workshop of nature, was modelled as an Emperor? Does ignorance dare to instruct knowledge? How can they who were but now common citizens have a right to peer into the counsels of an imperial soul? Yet, in their shameless effrontery they who would hardly be admitted to rank as learners dare to act as masters who initiate others into the mysteries of government.*[59]

It was a sentiment with which Nero was later to concur, describing himself as the 'survivor of a family born to rule'.[60]

Despite some seemingly conciliatory gestures in the first weeks of his reign, it is clear that Caligula was his own man, and was determined to rule in a manner that suited him, whatever the precedents. The days for trying to make the Principate look as if it were a reconstituted Republic were over. Indeed, Caligula probably regarded such a political fiction as no longer necessary or relevant; after all, nearly a century had now elapsed since the passing of the Old Republic and, although some descendants of the Republican aristocracy remained in the Senate, they were fast becoming a minority as 'new men' gained senatorial status. Caligula knew best, and some of his ideas, particularly in the field of foreign policy, were not uninteresting, although he appears to have preferred to operate by dramatic gestures (as in Germany and Britain) rather than to engage in the more tedious business of day-to-day administration.[61] In manner, particularly with senators whom he did not trust, he was hectoring, caustic, cruel – even sadistic – and utterly unpredictable. Co-operation with other individuals or bodies was available on his terms – or not at all. In short, Caligula did indeed conduct himself as if born to rule, and completely beyond reproach or the reach of the law.

The dynastic succession-policy created a royal family (*domus Augusta*[62]) and made a king of Caligula, and he could act as he wished. Whether he was also minded to insist upon worship of himself as a god is a moot point;[63] allegations to this effect are made in our sources, although there is no unimpeachable archaeological or documentary evidence from Rome itself to support them. The Augustan system had produced an autocrat; whilst Caligula probably retained his popularity with the masses by playing to their interests, his peers came to see no solution to his autocracy but to assassinate him. Thus, in January AD 41, Caligula was succeeded by a totally unexpected candidate for power, his uncle, Claudius.[64]

Claudius, regarded as a weak-minded imbecile by many of his contemporaries, was not strictly a part of Augustus' direct family; as the son of Nero Claudius Drusus (and the brother of Germanicus), he was Livia's descendant rather than Augustus'. Strictly, therefore, the use of the name, Caesar, in his case marked its transition from a name to a title, as it was to remain for future Emperors. Claudius had had little formal connection with the power-structure under his predecessors, but had spent his time in the study of Rome's past.

If, in their jubilation at the removal of Caligula, senators expected Claudius to revert to an Augustan style of co-operation with the Senate, they were to be disappointed. Claudius' historical studies had probably convinced him that, against the background of an expanding and increasingly multi-national Empire, the Old Republic had less now to offer, and that there was no alternative to the centralised authority of one man. So the new Emperor had no inclination to reverse the trend towards centralisation that had taken place under Caligula. Rather, he wished to rid the system of its total dependence on the unpredictable whims of a man such as Caligula, and to improve its efficiency by developing an administrative bureaucracy. In practice, this failed under Claudius because the Emperor appointed to 'headships of departments' former slaves (*liberti*) from his own household, whom he proved unable to control.

Claudius was attempting to construct an administrative pyramid with himself at its apex; such an innovation would, under any Emperor, have been a difficult and sensitive reform to carry through; senators, as Tacitus observed,[65] were bound to fear a loss of their traditional privileges. Claudius, however, was singularly lacking in the personal charisma that might have inspired confidence in others, and, in the event, the ruthless exploitation by the freedmen of their positions, and their employer, to advance their own wealth and personal ambitions proved totally unacceptable to senators in particular. Not surprisingly, they and others resented the realisation of their own dependence on the goodwill and favours of former slaves and of what they could not help but interpret as the downgrading of their own careers.

Predictably, they blamed Claudius for this; after all, these men were accountable to the Emperor alone. Worse was to follow, as trials that were formerly held in public were now dealt with inside the imperial household itself, with Claudius firmly subject to the influences of these same men. This did not, to senators at any rate, represent any improvement on what had happened under Caligula. Claudius, despite a sounder judgement over state-affairs and a desire to *work* with the Senate, was in practice as much a centralist as Caligula had been. No doubt – and it was not generally seen as an amelioration – Claudius' motive in undertaking his reforms was his desire to secure greater efficiency in government.

A further problem was caused by Claudius' relationships with the womenfolk within the imperial court. As Tacitus remarked,[66] 'Claudius did not like the bachelor-life', and the women he married were as damaging to his reputation as were his former slaves. The Emperor's third wife, Valeria Messalina, bore him two children, Britannicus and Octavia, both of whom were to become important in Nero's life. When Messalina was disgraced and executed for having committed bigamy – an event with a highly political look to it – Claudius was persuaded by pressure within the court to marry his niece, the Younger Agrippina, (daughter of Germanicus and the Elder Agrippina, and the mother of Nero), despite the fact that such a union was regarded in Rome as incestuous.

The Younger Agrippina had two ambitions – to rule in Rome as the Emperor's consort, thus in a sense fulfilling her mother's ambition,[67] and to persuade Claudius to disregard the claims of Britannicus to succeed his father as Emperor in favour of Nero. In this, she was assisted by two extremely able men – Seneca the philosopher, who was Nero's tutor, and Afranius Burrus, the Prefect of the Praetorian Guard. With their help, Agrippina persuaded her husband to break the existing engagement of his daughter, Octavia, to Lucius Junius Silanus[68] in favour of marriage with Nero. This marriage was seen as a vital factor in the legitimising of Nero's position, whilst Britannicus was pushed relentlessly into the background. It has been suggested that this may have been Claudius' way of avoiding conflict between his son and his stepson, although Levick has convincingly argued that Claudius in determined fashion stuck with his original plan for the succession.[69]

An element of imperial administration that had not received a great deal of attention under Claudius' predecessors concerned the status of the Empire's subject-population, especially those who were wealthy. By making grants of Roman citizenship to provincials, Claudius felt that he was recapturing the dynamism of Rome's founding-fathers, that in his view had suffered neglect under his predecessors, and that such a move would enable him to offer them opportunities in the Empire's administration. In this way, the Emperor felt that all would be drawn together in a shared enterprise. It was the reawakening and development of a practice that Rome had long employed in its dealings with defeated enemies in the hope that it would bring the Empire and its subjects closer together. In its turn, it was expected – not without some justification – that this would make internal rebellion less likely and thus obviate the need for an overlarge army that would be expensive to maintain and perhaps politically volatile, and that would also send out signals suggestive of a military despotism on the Emperor's part.

Claudius' reign provided one further sign of things to come that was ultimately to prove ominous for Nero: the plot to assassinate Caligula in AD 41 certainly embraced senators and members of the Equestrian Order, and possibly even Claudius himself. However it was carried to success by officers and soldiers of the Praetorian Guard, who had been persuaded by events and promises to desert their allegiance to Caligula. It was the Guard, too, that physically conferred power upon Claudius, although the Senate was allowed to ratify their choice. This highlighted the sensitivity of the relationship between the Emperor and his Praetorians specifically, and between him and the army in general. Claudius commemorated on his coinage the rôle that the Guard had played in his accession,[70] a decision which clearly indicates his awareness of this new situation. Similarly, there can be little doubt that some of the Senate's distrust of the new Emperor must have sprung from its disquiet at this very public acknowledgement on Claudius' part of the new realities of power. Further, such king-making activities by the army must have revived uncomfortable memories of the chaotic and dangerous latter days of the Old Republic.

Claudius knew that the army had to be kept loyal: in the case of the Praetorians, this could be achieved by means of imperial donatives and a careful choice exercised over the position of its commander. However, his evident favouring of the Praetorians probably caused disquiet in other sections of the army, that were traditionally envious of the extremely favourable conditions of service enjoyed by the Praetorians. Indeed, we may speculate that Claudius' renewed interest in military conquest – in particular, the high-profile invasion of Britain very early in his reign – may not simply have been a symbolic way of signalling his admiration of Julius Caesar, but perhaps also a way of reassuring legions and auxiliaries that they were as vital to him as were the Praetorians. This meant that the Emperor's relationship with the army, that had to a considerable extent been kept from public scrutiny by Augustus and Tiberius, had now come to the forefront of the political agenda. An Emperor who failed to offer suitable recognition of the importance to him of his army would be placing the stability of his position and, indeed, of the Republic itself in considerable jeopardy. The events that were to precipitate and follow the fall of Nero in AD 68 demonstrated that only too clearly; as Tacitus succinctly and famously put it,[71] 'the secret of empire was out, that an Emperor could be made elsewhere than at Rome.'

Thus, the political landscape which greeted Nero when he succeeded Claudius in AD 54, and in which he had to work, had moved a great deal since Augustus' victory at Actium. Although it is true that, by AD 54, the Emperor no longer had to deal with men whose careers had been fashioned during the Old Republic, many of their descendants, who still constituted a sizeable portion of the senatorial aristocracy, remained acutely sensitive to the traditions that they and their families had inherited. So, too, did many of those who had 'inherited' those traditions by winning senatorial status since Actium. The Senate, therefore, still required careful handling, and Emperors who afforded the senators scant regard still did so at their peril.

For Emperors themselves new pressures were added to old: just as care and tact were still required in appearing to avoid disturbing the balances inherited from the Old Republic, it was inevitable that the attention which Emperors needed to devote to new groups – the permanent, salaried army, ambitious and powerful courtiers, provincials, ex-slaves[72] – would severely test the stability of an Emperor's relationship with the Senate. Further, since senators continued to provide the bulk of Rome's provincial and army commanders, the maintenance of this stability had to be regarded as a crucial priority in a political world that was moving relentlessly towards centralisation.

Such dilemmas would have tried the ever-sharp political acumen of a man such as Augustus Caesar: Nero, inexperienced in power and devoted to alternative and self-indulgent pursuits, was to find that test far tougher – and, ultimately beyond his inclinations and capabilities.

Nero's Family

Nero was the last member of the Julio-Claudian dynasty to rule in Rome. Whilst it is clear that he was firmly attached to this dynasty through his mother, the Younger Agrippina, his father, Gnaeus Domitius Ahenobarbus, was a member of another ancient and distinguished Republican family, and one that had its own links with the Julio-Claudians.

In the previous chapter, we saw the importance that was attached by Augustus to the rôle of his and Livia's families[1] in the establishment of the Julio-Claudian dynasty. The Julian and Claudian families were both of ancient origin, and both were from the highest level of the nobility, the patriciate. Legend had it that the ultimate ancestor of the Julii was Iulus, the son of the Trojan hero, Aeneas, who, after the sack of Troy, sailed westwards, eventually founding the city of Rome.[2] In common with many aristocratic families, the Julii also looked back to a divine ancestor – in their case, the goddess, Venus, the mythological mother of Aeneas. Significantly, the new *Forum* begun in Rome by Julius Caesar and completed by his adopted son, Augustus, had as its crowning glory a temple to *Venus Genetrix* (Venus the Founder).

The Claudii were, by comparison, late arrivals in Rome: the Sabine leader, Attus Clausus, is said by Livy[3] to have brought his family to Rome in 507 BC; he was granted patrician status, and changed his name to Appius Claudius. Most generations of the Roman Republic saw members of the Claudian family, of either the Claudii Pulchri or the Claudii Nerones branches, playing an active – and sometimes risky – rôle in political and military affairs.[4] The last generation of the Old Republic had witnessed one of the most wayward members of the family – the individualist and populist, Publius Clodius Pulcher, who had changed the form of his family name from Claudius to the plebeian version, Clodius.[5]

Although of ancient ancestry, the Julii had played a less significant part in Roman politics,[6] perhaps because of their relative impoverishment. However, the last century of the Republic saw a determined (and successful) attempt by Gaius Julius Caesar to improve the family's political and military profile. Caesar had no son, but chose to adopt as his son his great-nephew, Gaius Octavius,[7] who thereby perpetuated the name of Caesar as Gaius Julius Caesar Octavianus. Although the Octavii were a less distinguished family,[8] their nobility was ancient. Octavius' father[9] had sought to improve his family's standing by marrying Julius Caesar's niece, Atia.

Although the concept of family had been central for the governing class of the Old Republic, the fact that a considerable number of families competed for power on approximately equal terms prevented the government from appearing monarchic. After Actium, however, that situation no longer obtained: Rome had become 'the heirloom of a single family'[10] and, because of the strength of its influence, that family was the dominant house. For some, this represented the most obvious contradiction of the traditions and principles of the Old Republic. As Tacitus put it,[11] 'Principate and liberty' were not reconcilable within a dynastic framework, as an essential meaning of *libertas* had been the freedom of men to compete for office on equal terms. It was the break with the dynastic principle, following the death of the last Flavian Emperor, Domitian, in AD 96, that encouraged Tacitus to think in terms of a reconciliation of Principate and liberty under Nerva and Trajan.[12] In effect, therefore, with the abandonment – if only temporarily – of the insistence on a dynastic succession, the Emperor's position had, in theory at least, become the summit of the senatorial *cursus honorum*, open in principle to all senators.

During the Julio-Claudian period, however, the first two *principes*, Augustus and Tiberius, as we saw, were mindful of Republican tradition and endeavoured to avoid obviously disregarding it – except, of course, in the matter of succession. Their successors, however, appreciated that, in practice, they were answerable to nobody: the Emperor was effectively above the law, unless he chose to be bound by it. Nero was born in AD 37 into a family that fully comprehended and lived by this truth.

Nero's family linked the Julii and the Claudii (Figure 2.1): his mother, the Younger Agrippina[13], was a daughter of Germanicus Caesar and the Elder Agrippina.[14] Germanicus was the elder brother of the Emperor, Claudius, and a son of Nero Claudius Drusus and Antonia.[15] Nero Drusus was the younger brother of the Emperor, Tiberius, and the son of Augustus' second wife, Livia Drusilla, by her marriage to the Republican senator, Tiberius Claudius Nero, a man of strong traditional sentiment who, although a one-time associate of Caesar, was bitterly hostile to his memory. Antonia was a daughter of Augustus' sister, Octavia, and Marcus Antonius, Augustus' one-time triumviral colleague. Germanicus, therefore, Nero's maternal grandfather, drew threads of both families together.

The Elder Agrippina was herself a daughter of Julia, Augustus' daughter by his first marriage to Scribonia. Julia played an important and continuing part in her father's dynastic plans, although little good fortune attended these. Her first husband, Gaius Claudius Marcellus and perhaps Augustus' first hope for a possible successor, died young (in 22 BC). Augustus then arranged a marriage between Julia and his old friend, Marcus Agrippa. However, although there was never any question that the plebeian Agrippa might succeed him, the marriage brought together two strands in Augustus' political following – the family of the Julii (Julia) and the 'party rank-and-file' (Agrippa). The linking of these two elements might then produce, in time, a suitable successor to Augustus.

Two sons were produced early in the marriage and were promptly adopted by Augustus as his own sons, with the names, Gaius Julius Caesar and Lucius Julius Caesar.[16] Three more children followed – two daughters (the Elder Agrippina and Julia) and a third son, known as Agrippa Postumus because he was not born until after his father's death in 12 BC. The death of Marcus Agrippa precipitated a crisis in the family; Julia needed a husband, and her children a guardian. The choice fell upon Livia's elder son, Tiberius. Whilst Livia no doubt viewed this as a god-given opportunity to advance her family, Tiberius saw it as a personal disaster; he had little time for Julia, and he was being forced to divorce his wife, Vipsania (Agrippa's daughter), and effectively lose his son, Drusus. In addition, Vipsania went on to marry a senator, Gaius Asinius Gallus, whom Tiberius greatly disliked and who tried to adopt Drusus as his own son.[17] It is little wonder that Tiberius emerged from this episode a damaged individual; nor is it surprising that, in 6 BC, he decided to turn his back on it all, and retreat to the island of Rhodes – a

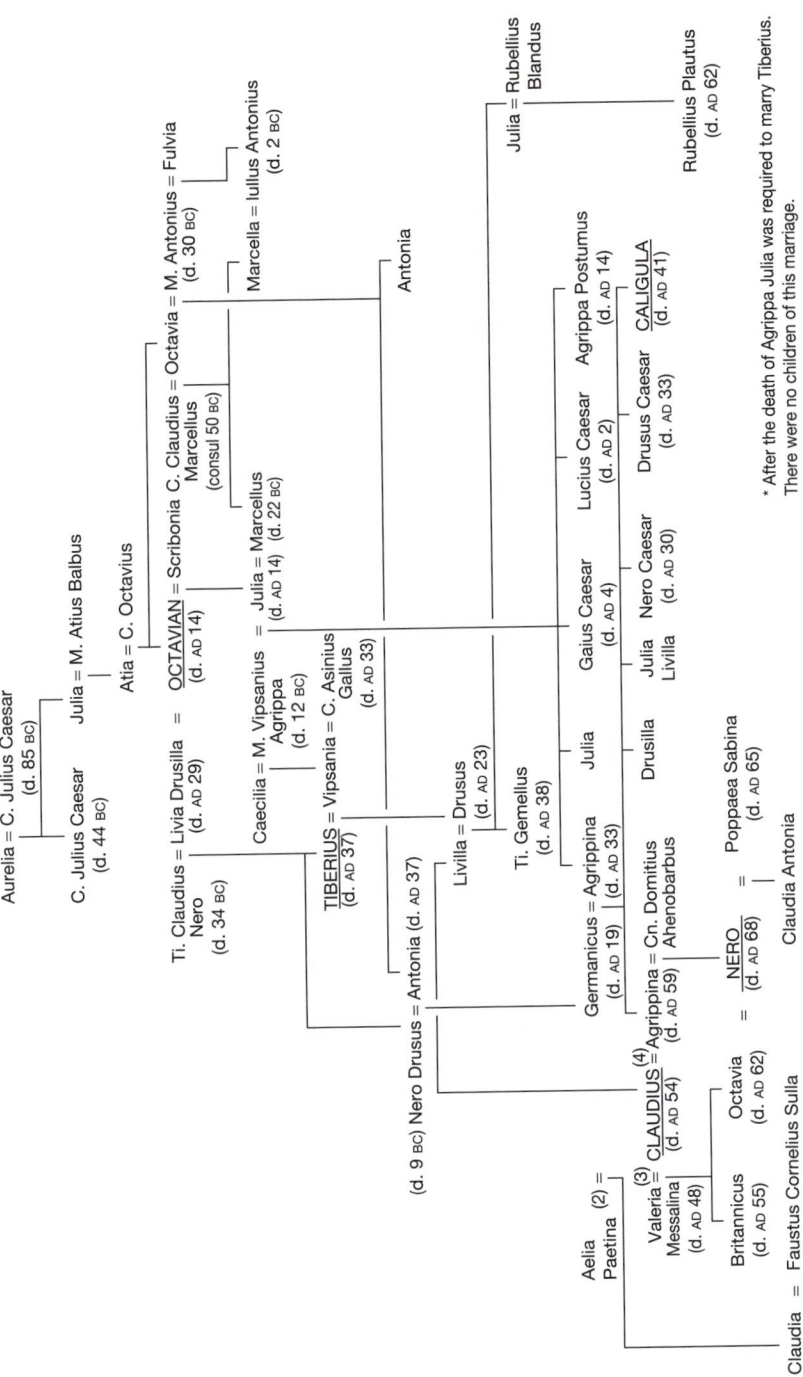

Figure 2.1 Stemma (simplified) of the Julian and Claudian families. Author's own.

retirement that soon turned into a virtual exile,[18] because of Augustus' anger at being 'let down' by Tiberius in this way.

In the meantime, Augustus continued to advance his two adopted sons; in 2 BC, Gaius and Lucius were made leaders of the young nobility (*principes iuventutis*),[19] and their careers accelerated. However, once again dynastic disaster struck. In 2 BC, a scandal broke around Augustus' daughter, Julia, who had been involved in affairs with a number of men whose names sound politically sensitive.[20] Despite the intercessions of her absent husband, Tiberius, Julia was consigned by her father to exile on the island of Pandateria (modern Vandotena) in the Bay of Naples, where she died in AD 14.[21] Hard on the heels of this came the deaths, in AD 2 and 4 respectively, of Lucius and Gaius Caesar, which hit Augustus hard.[22] These deaths, on top of that of Nero Drusus in 9 BC, were beginning to appear more than mere bad luck. People suspected Livia, herself of Claudian descent, of foul play, the purpose of which was to advance the cause of her elder son, Tiberius,[23] who had been allowed to return from Rhodes in AD 2.

There is, however, some evidence at this time of other pressure-groups with an interest in the succession-question. The chief evidence for such pressure can perhaps be seen in the shadowy conspiracy in AD 4 of Gnaeus Cornelius Cinna Magnus,[24] a descendant of Pompey. The year, of course, was the same as that of the death of Gaius Caesar. Dio Cassius has a lengthy, and obviously embroidered, account of a private conversation, apparently held in bed, between Augustus and Livia as to what should be done about Cinna Magnus.[25] The story, if in any way true, seems to point to the existence of a group of conservative senators, mostly with strong traditionalist – even Republican – sympathies whose support inclined towards the aspirations of Livia and a Claudian succession in the person of Tiberius.

One outcome of this was a consulship for Cinna Magnus in AD 5; more significant, however, are signs that Augustus had had to compromise over the succession that, he now evidently accepted, would have to pass from the Julian family to Tiberius. Thus, in AD 4, Augustus adopted as his sons both Tiberius, now to be named Tiberius Julius Caesar, and Julia's youngest son, Agrippa Postumus. In his turn, Tiberius, despite the fact that he had a son of his own, Drusus, was required to adopt his nephew, Germanicus Caesar, who was already engaged to Augustus' granddaughter, Agrippina.[26] These two were held in great affection in Rome – the people's 'dream-couple'.[27] However, before Augustus died in AD 14, there was to be one further dynastic upset: in AD 7, Agrippa Postumus and his sister, Julia, were both banished for reasons that cannot now be satisfactorily reconstructed,[28] but that, according to Dio's account, had something to do with Livia.

In the event, therefore, Augustus allowed power to pass to his stepson, Tiberius Claudius Nero (Tiberius Julius Caesar).[29] Many, including evidently Tiberius himself, regarded his elevation as having been engineered by his mother, Livia, and senators, mostly with strong traditionalist sympathies, who supported her. For many of them, whatever doubts they may have entertained about Tiberius' personal suitability for his elevation, he was to be preferred to the former political outsiders who were now numbered amongst supporters of the Julii. Although Tiberius was generally regarded as an extremely difficult man to fathom,[30] it was felt that he might prove to be more amenable to those of Republican and traditionalist sentiment. His image was not, however, improved by the suspicion that he and his mother had been responsible for the murder of Agrippa Postumus, that occurred shortly after Augustus' death.[31] Inevitably, the rivalry between the supporters of Tiberius and Germanicus (the Claudians and the Julians) increased as a result of these events, and continued to have an adverse effect upon the relationship between the two men themselves, although both appear to have made every effort to play fair by each other: Tiberius advanced his nephew along the path of which he thought that Augustus would have approved, whilst Germanicus was never anything but loyal to Tiberius.

Yet, the Emperor could never rid himself of the conviction that Germanicus might at some stage 'prefer the reality to the expectation of power',[32] nor was Germanicus' obvious and easy popularity with senators, the public and the army likely to do anything to allay the fears and suspicions of the *princeps*. Further, the relationship was not made smoother by the fact that Tiberius, who had in his younger days been a sound and effective military commander, evidently did not rate highly his nephew's performance in his rôle as supreme commander of Roman troops on the Rhine. For most, Tiberius was a reclusive, joyless, suspicious, and perhaps even perverted, old man, whilst Germanicus was seen as, in every way, the dashing hero, the leader-in-waiting, the victim of the malignant envy of Tiberius and his mother. In reality, Germanicus was a decent man, although utterly theatrical in character, as was shown by a dramatic offer of suicide that he made in an effort to bring rebellious troops back to order;[33] his popularity, therefore, is unsurprising. It is evident, too, that he enjoyed dressing up – for example, in imitation of Scipio Africanus, the conqueror of Hannibal – a lapse of imperial dignity for which Tiberius mildly criticised him.[34] Perhaps we can see here the genesis of Nero's lifelong enthusiasm for the stage.

In popular opinion, Agrippina was in every way the ideal partner for Germanicus. directly descended from Augustus (as she once sharply, if tactlessly, pointed out to Tiberius[35]), fearless, competitive, regal in her bearing, profoundly loyal to her immediate family and deeply distrusted by Tiberius and Livia. By Roman standards, she was an unusual woman, not only ambitious for her husband and family but, as it emerged, for herself, also.[36] Tiberius is on record as having on one occasion found it necessary to remind her that it was not her place or her destiny to be 'queen of Rome'.[37] Indeed, even her husband warned her not to overreach herself by offending those more powerful than herself[38] – that is, Tiberius, his mother and the Prefect of his Praetorian Guard, the sinister and ambitious Lucius Aelius Sejanus.

In AD 19, however, disaster struck the royal house once again: Germanicus, still only in his thirties, fell ill and died, whilst representing Tiberius in the East. His very youth was sufficient to suggest to his adoring public that he could not possibly have died a natural death, but must have been the victim of a plot; nor were culprits far to seek – Gnaeus Calpurnius Piso, the governor of the province of Syria, who had been appointed by Tiberius to act as Germanicus' adviser,[39] but who, many believed, engineered Germanicus' death on the instructions of Tiberius and Livia. Germanicus' widow was convinced by this version of events, and predictably cast herself as the avenging angel.[40]

Tiberius might declare his innocence – but to no avail: even though the evidence of Tiberius' complicity in murder was, at best, circumstantial, general opinion held that he hated and feared Germanicus as a rival and so must have removed him. The result was bitterness and suspicion which destroyed any chance of a rapprochement between Tiberius and Agrippina. This cancerous tension within the imperial family was aggravated by Agrippina herself who, contrary to her husband's death-bed advice, could not control her tongue; her dangerous lack of tact and control were exploited at every opportunity by Sejanus.

Sejanus' aims[41] are not clear in all their detail, although they appear to have depended upon effecting the complete isolation of Tiberius – a task made easier by the advancing age of the *princeps*. Frustrated in his efforts to preside over a revived Republic, largely because he could not elicit from others the genuine co-operation he desired, Tiberius turned increasingly to Sejanus, the 'partner in his labours'.[42] Generally suspicious of the intentions of others, it is surprising that it took Tiberius so long to appreciate how completely he was being deceived by Sejanus.

The Prefect proceeded in his plans initially by persuading the Emperor to sanction the concentrating of the Praetorian Guard into a single fortress in Rome.[43] In AD 23, he arranged the murder by poison of Tiberius' only son, Drusus, with the latter's wife, Livilla (the sister of Germanicus), as his mistress and accomplice.[44] Over the next six years, he worked to drive an irreparable wedge between the *princeps* and Agrippina's family. Oblivious to Sejanus' intentions, Tiberius assumed, apparently without question, that Agrippina posed the greatest threat to his security; he was eventually persuaded (in AD 29) to allow the arrest on charges of treason of Agrippina herself, her two older sons (Nero Caesar and Drusus Caesar)[45] and her friend (and a long-standing thorn in Tiberius' flesh), Gaius Asinius Gallus.[46] Of these, Nero Caesar committed suicide in AD 30 or AD 31, whilst Agrippina died in exile in AD 33 as a result of the brutal treatment she had received.[47] Her second son, Drusus Caesar, died of starvation in the same year as his mother, still incarcerated in Rome.[48] At first sight, it is hard to comprehend the viciousness of the posthumous verbal attack launched by Tiberius against Drusus, although we should remember that Drusus had allowed himself to be used by Sejanus in the entrapment of his mother and his elder brother. Of the once-fêted family of Germanicus, only Gaius (Caligula) and his three sisters survived.

If Sejanus' ambition was the acquisition of supreme power and the succession to Tiberius, the removal of Tiberius' son and the political destruction of Agrippina and two of her sons represented major advances. Significantly, too, Sejanus had in AD 27 persuaded the *princeps* that it was not in his best interests to remain in Rome,[49] but that he should go into retirement to his country residence – the *Villa Iovis* – on the island of Capri.[50] Sejanus would thus, backed by the threat of the Praetorian Guard, hold sway in Rome, act as Tiberius' mouthpiece and control all access to the Emperor. In only one feature of Sejanus' planning did Tiberius frustrate his 'partner' – that is, by refusing to sanction a marriage between Sejanus and Drusus' widow, Livilla,[51] regarding it as unsuitable and likely to have a divisive effect upon the imperial family.

It remains unclear how and why Sejanus' plans went awry, although we are informed by the historian, Dio Cassius, that at some time during AD 30, Tiberius was alerted by his sister-in-law, Antonia,[52] to the true character of Sejanus' intentions. Whatever had been revealed was evidently not sufficient to save Agrippina and her second son, Drusus Caesar, although it is apparent that Tiberius did decide to assume a paternal rôle in the cases of Caligula and his sisters, and thereafter kept Caligula with him on Capri. In the autumn of AD 31, as we are told by the satiric poet, Juvenal, a 'long and wordy letter'[53] was sent to the Senate by Tiberius from Capri, that, after a long and devious preamble, demanded the immediate arrest and execution of Sejanus. According to the biographer, Suetonius,[54] the subsequent official explanation of this turn of events was Tiberius' discovery of Sejanus' plotting against the children of Germanicus. Although dismissed at the time as hypocritical, there is no pressing reason to doubt the plausibility of this: one senator was certainly arrested in the aftermath of Sejanus' fall on a charge of having aided the Prefect's plotting against Caligula.[55]

In AD 37, Tiberius died (or was murdered[56]), frustrated and embittered, still in seclusion on Capri. He was succeeded by Nero's uncle, Gaius Caligula, who, as we have seen, entertained a rather different view of his rôle compared with that of Tiberius. His only conceivable rival, Tiberius' grandson, Tiberius Gemellus, was initially treated by Caligula as his likely successor, but as the unpredictable Emperor became increasingly suspicious of those around him, Gemellus was later despatched.[57] However, one positive act of Tiberius during his retirement had been to arrange marriages for Germanicus' daughters: the husband chosen for the Younger Agrippina was Gnaeus Domitius Ahenobarbus.[58] He was considerably her senior and of distinguished Republican lineage but, it appears, of thoroughly uncongenial character.[59] On 15 December, AD 37, Agrippina gave birth to their only son – Lucius Domitius Ahenobarbus, better known to history, after his adoption into the Claudian family, as Nero Claudius Caesar. The fact that the birth was a breech-presentation was regarded as a sinister omen.[60] Ahenobarbus is said[61] to have observed at the time of Nero's birth that nothing born of himself and Agrippina could be anything other than odious and a public disaster.

Nero's paternal family was, through Augustus' sister, Octavia, part of the 'extended' Julio-Claudian network (Figure 2.2). Like the Julians and Claudians, the Domitii Ahenobarbi were a family of great antiquity. The 'brazen beard', the source of the name, *Ahenobarbus*, was said to have been 'conferred' by

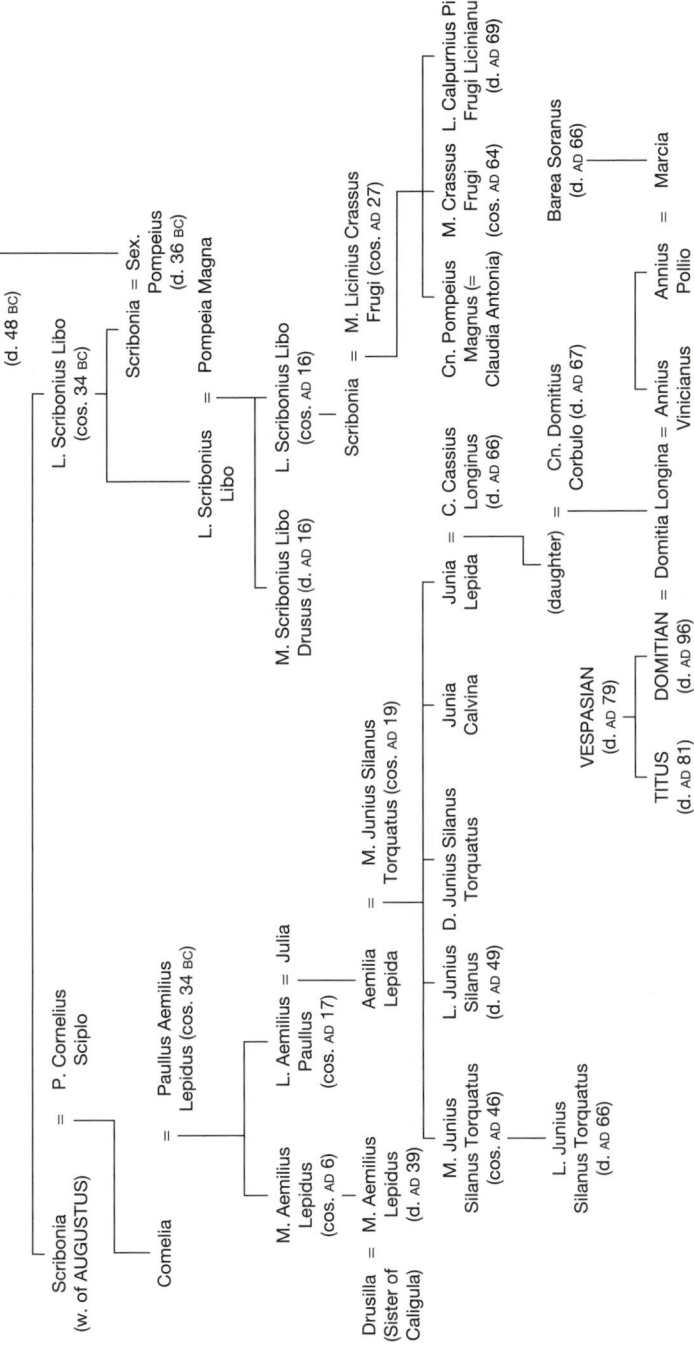

Figure 2.2 Stemma showing some connections of the Julian and Claudian families. Author's own.

'the divine twins', Castor and Pollux, on a Lucius Domitius,[62] when they foretold the outcome of the battle against the Latins at Lake Regillus in 494 BC. The beard was an enduring feature of the image of male members of the family[63] and, although Nero himself is usually shown in his portraits as clean-shaven, there are a few that show him with a beard,[64] including coins of AD 66–7 when the Emperor is known, in fact, to have been clean-shaven.[65]

Suetonius[66] provides a selective synopsis of the family-history and characteristics of the Domitii, and suggests that many of Nero's vices were inherited, and that he made a caricature of the family's virtues. Nero's grandfather, Lucius Domitius Ahenobarbus (consul in 16 BC), was one of Augustus' leading generals, although surviving historians of the period fail to mention his military achievements.[67] He was evidently a man of extreme arrogance and rudeness and, like his grandson, a great enthusiast for chariot-racing, shows in the arena and on the stage.[68] Suetonius mentions that he forced members of the Equestrian Order and married women to act in stage-plays that he put on, and that his conduct in this sphere was on one occasion sufficiently extreme to have merited the censure of Augustus. His son, Gnaeus (Nero's father), is described by Suetonius as sadistically cruel, dishonest, swindling his creditors and embezzling charioteers' prize-money; in fact, a man of 'wholly despicable' character.[69] According to Tacitus,[70] he narrowly avoided being prosecuted for treason and *impietas* towards the Emperor, and was saved only by Tiberius' (for him) timely death. Suetonius adds that he was also accused at that time of incest with his sister, Domitia Lepida.[71]

The legitimacy of Nero's succession was held to depend upon his adoption into the Claudian family and upon his marriage to Claudius' daughter, Octavia. Although it is asserted that he took grave offence at any mention of him as *Domitius* or *Ahenobarbus*,[72] he nonetheless appears to have retained respect (*pietas*) for his father's family, and required the Arval Brethren[73] to observe an annual sacrifice at the family-home on the anniversary of his father's birth.[74] In AD 63, he celebrated games in honour of the Claudian and Domitian families to mark the birth of his daughter.[75] Further, although Vindex's rebels in AD 68[76] tried to aggravate Nero by referring to him as 'Domitius Ahenobarbus', he retorted by saying that it was his intention to resume his paternal name.[77]

Such instances indicate that Nero did retain a traditional respect for his family and for the requirement to live up to the example of one's ancestors (*mos maiorum*). It is also worth noting that the Elder Pliny[78] refers·to the

Emperor as 'Domitius Nero', whilst Nero's contemporary, the poet Lucan,[79] in his account of the civil war between Caesar and Pompey, lavishes praise on Nero's ancestor, the Pompeian, Lucius Domitius Ahenobarbus. Despite this, however, the family's military reputation was one characteristic which Nero did not inherit.[80]

Nero's father evidently had two sisters; the elder of the two is usually named simply Domitia. The younger sister, Domitia Lepida, appears to have been similar in age to Agrippina.[81] It is likely that some confusions between them have occurred in our sources, since both demonstrated their fondness for Nero, and both were enemies of Agrippina. It has been noted[82] that, in ancient texts, although it is never specifically stated that Nero had two paternal aunts, the two sisters appear to be distinguishable by the facts that Domitia is usually characterised as mean, whilst Lepida is associated with sexual impropriety. As we have seen, it was even rumoured that Lepida had committed incest with her brother.[83] In any case, the two had quite different marital histories.[84]

Domitia was embroiled in financial disputes with her brother, although both of them were, in their own rights, extremely wealthy.[85] She had property in Ravenna, where she built gymnasia that were still in use in Dio's time.[86] In addition, she had a villa, with fishponds, at Baiae (on the Bay of Naples), that was evidently coveted by Nero (Figure 2.3). In AD 55, Agrippina referred to her as an 'old woman', and when Domitia was poisoned four years later – at Nero's instigation so that he could inherit the Baiae-villa – Dio observes that she would, in any case, soon have died of old age.[87] Domitia was married to Passienus Crispus who, after their divorce, married Agrippina. In view of Crispus' wealth, this will undoubtedly have been a bone of contention between the two women.

Lepida was married to Messala Barbatus, to whom she bore a daughter, Valeria Messalina, who was to become Claudius' third wife and mother of Britannicus and Octavia. She later married Faustus Sulla (consul in AD 31); their son, also called Faustus Sulla, was put to death by Nero in AD 62 as a potential rival for power. Lepida and Agrippina seem to have competed for Nero's affections, and Agrippina brought about her downfall in AD 54. Like her sister, Lepida was wealthy, and owned property in Calabria and Puteoli (modern Pozzuoli).

Nero's mother, the Younger Agrippina, was in every way her mother's daughter: striking of appearance, forthright – sometimes dangerously so –

Figure 2.3 Map of Italy. Author' own.

and ambitious for power not only for her son but, as we have seen, for herself, too. When she married her uncle, Claudius, in AD 49, Tacitus noted the contrast between her and her predecessor, Messalina, observing that 'this was a rigorous, almost masculine, despotism'.[88] The historian marks one interesting contrast between mother and daughter: whilst the Elder Agrippina is never described as anything other than faithful to her husband and, subsequently, to his memory, her daughter is said to have been 'chaste in her private life, *except in the pursuit of power*.[89] Like her mother, the Younger Agrippina relished a high public profile, and for a while, after the accession to power of their brother (Gaius Caligula), Agrippina and her two sisters, Drusilla and Livia, enjoyed just that, as is demonstrated powerfully by Caligula's *sestertius* of AD 37–8, portraying the sisters as the Three Graces.[90] During the first two years of his reign, members of his family – alive and dead, and including his maternal grandfather, Marcus Agrippa[91] – formed a central feature of Caligula's image-building, that was designed to show him and his family as the true heirs of Augustus Caesar. In this sense, the ambitions of the Elder Agrippina had been realised – and those of her daughter foreshadowed.

As Tacitus had said of Tiberius' Principate, less than halfway into Caligula's reign, fortune seemed to turn sour: in AD 38, his favourite sister, Drusilla,[92] whom the Emperor had already named as his heir, died. In the following year, it is apparent that a conspiracy was detected, evidently centred upon Gnaeus Cornelius Lentulus Gaetulicus, commander of the legions of Upper Germany.[93] The objective of this conspiracy was to assassinate Caligula and to install in his place Marcus Aemilius Lepidus, Drusilla's widower, who was himself related to the Deified Augustus. At any rate, in the aftermath of the conspiracy, Caligula turned upon Lepidus and his two surviving sisters, evidently suspecting them of involvement in Gaetulicus' conspiracy.[94] Lepidus, with whom Agrippina was accused of having had an adulterous relationship, was put to death, whilst Agrippina and her surviving sister, Julia Livilla, were banished and their property confiscated.

The young Lucius Domitius was thus left in the care of his ailing father. In AD 40, however, Gnaeus Domitius died,[95] and the portion of his estate that had been willed to his young son was promptly confiscated by the Emperor. Lucius Domitius was then entrusted to the supervision of his paternal aunt, Domitia Lepida, and was at that time, according to Suetonius,[96] tutored by a dancer and a barber and suffered considerable deprivation. There is, however, no indication that Nero suffered by or resented this; on the contrary, he remained on good terms with his aunt, and his later hostility towards her was born of different causes.[97] It is perhaps worth noting that, in telling this story, Suetonius emphasises[98] the meanness of the aunt in question; that may leave us wondering whether this may have been an instance where the two sisters have been confused by our sources.

Within a few months, however, Caligula had been assassinated (in January, AD 41), and fortune swung again. Claudius, the maternal great-uncle of Lucius Domitius, was proclaimed Emperor and, amongst the new Emperor's early actions, were the recall from exile of Agrippina and her sister and the restoration to the young Domitius of his inheritance. Claudius' accession, however, led to increased tensions within the family, as the daughter of Domitia Lepida, the notorious Valeria Messalina, had become Claudius' third wife and, in February of AD 41, had borne him a son, who was (and is) known as Britannicus,[99] the name given him in celebration of Claudius' invasion of Britain in AD 43. There is, however, no sign that Lepida was on good terms with her daughter, or that she espoused the cause of her grandson, Britannicus, against Nero.

It is hardly surprising, therefore, given Agrippina's great ambitions for herself and her son, that already-existing tensions within the family turned to actual rivalry – initially between Agrippina and Domitius on the one hand and Messalina and Britannicus on the other, and later between Nero and Rubellius Plautus and Faustus Cornelius Sulla. The stage was thus set for yet further murderous episodes of confrontation within the Julio-Claudian family. Immediately, however, in order to fulfil her ambitions, Agrippina had to bring about the destruction of Messalina and Britannicus. Only then, she calculated, would the path to power lie open to herself and her son.

Through generations of politically advantageous marriages, the network of the Julian and Claudian families had become extensive. However, by the time that Nero eventually came to power in AD 54, only Britannicus, the 'last of the Claudians', was regarded as a serious rival. It has generally been assumed that he was murdered in AD 55 at Nero's instigation, although the official explanation, that Britannicus had succumbed to an epileptic seizure, is plausible and might just be true.[100] Yet, there were others who enjoyed a similar place in the Julio-Claudian family-tree to that of Nero himself. Principal amongst these were Rubellius Plautus and Faustus Sulla, although neither of them appears to have entertained ambitions that need have caused Nero alarm.

Rubellius Plautus who, in reality, is probably fairly characterised as a dull and rather boring Stoic, assumed a greater significance than he merited; for he was the son of Rubellius Blandus and Julia, the daughter of Drusus (the son of Tiberius) and Livilla (the sister of Germanicus and Claudius). He was thus the great-grandson of the Emperor, Tiberius and, through his maternal grandmother (Livilla), he was also connected to Octavia, the sister of Augustus Caesar. Faustus Sulla had married Claudia Antonia, the daughter of the Emperor, Claudius; both Faustus Sulla and Nero were thus sons-in-law of Claudius. Faustus Sulla, besides bearing a name that was redolent of the late Republic, could also trace his ancestry back to Octavia through his father's marriage to Domitia Lepida, a daughter of Antonia, who was married to Lucius Domitius Ahenobarbus (Augustus' general, who was consul in 16 BC). This Ahenobarbus played a major military rôle for Augustus on the Rhine, and was also Nero's paternal grandfather.

Thus, as Nero became more sensitive to potential rivals, such men as Rubellius Plautus and Faustus Sulla, although doing nothing positive to arouse the Emperor's suspicions, found themselves assuming a rather larger rôle than either reality or their ambitions and capabilities warranted.

Roman tradition painted the rivalry between members of the Julian and Claudian families in murderous colours. Although some of the accusations may have been founded on little more than rumour, the rivalry had been constant and, at least, divisive. As we have seen from the deteriorating relationship between Tiberius and the Elder Agrippina, this divisiveness provided opportunities for others to make mischief. Although, for Nero, the most obvious dangers may have derived from Britannicus and Octavia, the fact that there were, still living, other descendants of previous Emperors was sufficient to affect political stability through the fear that they induced in Nero and the dangers that in this way they brought upon themselves.

Thus, although many of Nero's problems as Emperor were self-generated, the Julian and Claudian families did not cease to prove disruptive, even in their twilight years, until Nero himself effectively became the last survivor. As Galba showed, the experience of the century from Actium to the death of Nero demonstrated that it was indeed a matter of chance to be descended from a *princeps* and that, consequently, Rome desperately needed a sounder and safer method of emperor-creation that avoided the vagaries and dangers of a hereditary system. This, indeed, is what Tacitus appreciated when he wrote of the 'reconciliation of principate and liberty' that followed the demise of the last of the Flavians in AD 96.[101]

Chapter Three

The Path to Power

᳀᳀᳀᳀᳀

When asked to supply a name for his infant nephew, Lucius Domitius, Caligula is said to have offered *Claudius* as a suggestion – less perhaps of an omen than an attempt to embarrass his sister and their uncle.[1] In the middle years of the first century AD, there was no shortage of men and women who could trace their bloodlines back to the Julii, the Claudii – and even the Antonii. Despite his connections with all three of these families, therefore, Nero would not have stood out as an obvious future candidate for supreme power, although some perhaps might have spared a second thought for the grandson of Germanicus Caesar and the Elder Agrippina.[2]

We are given few details of Nero's childhood, except for some observations by Suetonius.[3] By the time of Caligula's assassination in January of AD 41, Nero had lost his father, whilst his mother was in the exile to which her brother had consigned her, along with her sister, Livilla, believing them both to have been implicated in the adulterous plot centred around their brother-in-law, Marcus Aemilius Lepidus, that had been detected in AD 39.[4]

In addition, although the young Nero had been made heir to one third of his father's estate, Caligula had confiscated Nero's share and placed him in the care of one of his father's sisters, probably Domitia Lepida,[5] the mother of Valeria Messalina, Claudius' third wife, and soon to become the grandmother of Claudius' son, Britannicus. Whether Caligula's motive in confiscating Nero's inheritance was the greed and shortage of money of which he was often accused in antiquity, or whether it was purely political is unclear.[6]

Suetonius tries to suggest that Domitia Lepida's period of guardianship was harsh for Nero, although the only evidence that is adduced in support of this contention is the fact that the tutors who were hired for him were a dancer and a barber.[7] However, those tutors whose names we know[8] include two philosophers (Alexander of Aegae and Chaeremon of Alexandria, who was a noted scholar of his day), together with Beryllus of Caesarea[9] and the freedman, Anicetus, who later became Prefect of the fleet at Misenum[10] and was to gain notoriety for his participation in Nero's murders of his mother in AD 59 and of his wife, Octavia, three years later. Thus, Nero's early education may not have suffered, but may, in fact, have been essentially conventional for young members of the nobility.

However, within a matter of months, Claudius had succeeded Caligula and had recalled Agrippina and her sister from exile; he had also restored to Nero his confiscated paternal inheritance. Indeed, it is not impossible that Nero may have found his aunt's company congenial, and it has been suggested[11] that he may, through her, have made the acquaintance of his later confidant and associate, the uncongenial and unscrupulous Ofonius Tigellinus. Domitia Lepida had been the favourite sister of Nero's father, and it may have been for that reason that she did not relate well to Agrippina. Indeed, Nero may well have found easier company with her than with his domineering and ambitious mother. It is worth noting that Agrippina is on record as having accused her former sister-in-law of 'spoiling' Nero.[12] A further point to note is that Domitia Lepida's relationship with her own daughter was not good; thus it should not necessarily be assumed that she would have favoured her grandson, Britannicus, over Nero.[13]

Agrippina's restoration to Rome will have had a profound influence on Nero's life; like her mother, she was a woman with determined ambitions not only for herself, but also for herself in conjunction with her son. She had also learned a lesson from the dangerous isolation in which her mother had found herself after the death of Germanicus. Soon after her return to Rome, the Younger Agrippina remarried; her new husband was Gaius Sallustius Passienus Crispus, a man of great wealth who was an accomplished orator and a noted wit.[14] This marriage demonstrated Agrippina's single-mindedness, for Passienus Crispus had recently been divorced from Domitia,[15] the other sister of Nero's father; although the circumstances of this divorce are not known to us, it is entirely possible that Passienus Crispus was targeted by Agrippina whilst he was still married to her sister-in-law;[16] Agrippina allowed nothing to stand between her and her ambitions. This marriage will certainly have assisted her in rebuilding her position in aristocratic society; her profile gained from it, as did her wealth, for she accompanied her husband on his proconsulship of the province of Asia in AD 42–3, and was herself celebrated with a statue on the island of Cos.[17]

It appears, however, that the marriage was short-lived[18] and, although there is no evidence of foul play in the matter of Passienus Crispus' death, it undoubtedly left both Agrippina and Nero much wealthier. It also left Agrippina free of marital encumbrance at a time when the political situation in Rome was about to become extremely fluid. In fact, Agrippina's position appears to accord well with Tacitus' observation[19] that her private life was chaste except in the pursuit of power and that she was avaricious for money as the 'stepping-stone to supremacy'.

Of Nero's boyhood little detail survives, although – significantly, perhaps – what does survive offers pointers towards the future Emperor's adult tastes. For example, he is said to have been devoted to chariot-racing[20] to the extent that he would discuss it with his fellow-pupils all through lessons. Music, too, was a popular feature of his curriculum[21] from which he derived great pleasure. His own, later, passion for the games and for personal public performance needs no emphasis; nor were these passing pleasures, for Nero went to great lengths to train his voice[22] and took his art seriously, eventually seeing himself at one with *Apollo Citharoedus* (the Lyre-Player).[23]

Nero's mother exerted an important influence on his education: we are told[24] that she reined in his nascent enthusiasm for philosophy – evidently a sought-after subject for young men of his day. Tacitus informs us[25] that the mother of his future father-in-law, Gnaeus Julius Agricola, had to intervene similarly in her son's curriculum. Obviously grooming her son for his expected station in life, Agrippina gave no reason for the restriction other than that philosophy was not a suitable topic for a boy who would become Emperor. When Nero was ten years old, Agrippina introduced Seneca as his tutor, presumably to train him in rhetoric and, perhaps, to show him a more practical path for his interest in philosophy: a number of Seneca's philosophical treatises that survive were clearly intended to demonstrate the relevance of philosophy to the business of ruling. As we shall see, however, the effect was probably not as intended, for virtues such as clemency (*clementia*) simply encouraged Nero to think of himself as on the fringe of legal constraint and able to indulge his whims – or not – as his mood took him.[26]

Seneca is also said[27] to have tried to prevent Nero from studying the work of the great rhetoricians, anxious, it seems, lest his own offerings should pale before them. According to Suetonius, it was this stifling of Nero's creative outlets that led him to turn towards poetry. Suetonius also explicitly contradicts[28] the assertion, commonly made at the time, that Nero's poetry had little merit, and largely plagiarised the work of others. Nero's artistic interests extended also to painting and sculpture.

However worthwhile many of these pursuits may have been, they exhibit a self-indulgence in Nero that may have been excusable in the boy, but that certainly had no place amongst the characteristics of a future Emperor. Self-indulgence was to remain with Nero as one of his less attractive characteristics in adult life, which is regrettable in view of the fact that he was plainly not lacking in talent, as he is said to have demonstrated at a performance of the 'Troy Game' in the Secular Games of AD 47.[29] By denying her son the challenge of education and exposing him to the superficial, Agrippina (and Seneca) were encouraging in him a sense of necessary dependence upon others from which he was never able to shake himself free. Plainly, in this sense, Nero's future was sacrificed to Agrippina's ambitions – to exercise power with or through Claudius, and to continue such a rôle through her son.

Agrippina's total self-interest was to prove Nero's undoing; 'wife and husband' were, in her mind, to be extended in time to 'mother and son'. It is sometimes suggested that Agrippina, perhaps reflecting on her mother's difficulties after the death of Germanicus, looked to Nero's political future because she realised that, as a woman, she would not easily find a political rôle for herself in Rome. However, this is both to see her in too conventional a light and to underestimate her self-confidence; her ambitions for her son were not a substitute for ambitions on her own behalf; they represented her path to power, a path that was as relevant to Agrippina as it was to her son.

In a well-known passage, Tacitus[30] contrasts Agrippina and Claudius' wife, Messalina, representing the latter as wholly frivolous in her pursuits, whilst Agrippina's thoughts and actions were always firmly focussed on the acquisition of power. Valeria Messalina was of noble birth[31] as well as being Claudius' third wife and the mother of his children, Octavia and Britannicus, the latter of whom was just three years younger than Nero.[32] With such a background, she was probably as determined as Agrippina to fulfil the traditional rôles of a wife and mother of noble birth. Indeed, the notion of rivalry between Nero and Britannicus is marked up early on with the story[33] of the failed plot, organised by Messalina, to secure Nero's assassination. In this, it was said that a snake appeared at the crucial moment from beneath Nero's pillow and scared off the would-be assassins. Suetonius adds that subsequently Agrippina persuaded Nero to wear the snake's skin, set in a gold bracelet, on his wrist, although he evidently discarded it after the murder of Agrippina in AD 59 – an action that he subsequently regretted. It is likely that Agrippina hoped that, by highlighting – even embellishing – the murderous attempt by Messalina, she could play a card that her mother had employed with success – winning public sympathy for the perilous situation, real or imagined, in which the family of Germanicus had been placed by its enemies.

Thus, relations between Agrippina and Messalina were clearly – and understandably – poor, and presumably not helped by the former's feud with Domitia Lepida, that appears to have had some connection with Agrippina's marriage to Passienus Crispus who, as we have seen, had been formerly married to Lepida's sister, Domitia. The situation is reminiscent of the female rivalry about which the Emperor, Tiberius, had been so sensitive after the death of his son, Drusus, in AD 23.[34] Yet, Agrippina is not noted at this stage for any particular act of hostility towards her rival. Indeed, she may have shunned the limelight by remaining on her dead husband's estates during the early- and mid-40s; this may have been a wise move on her part as it was a period in which both Claudius and Messalina were evidently affected by fears of conspiracy. It may, indeed, have been the case that Agrippina, again learning from the painful experiences of her mother, had decided to adopt a low profile and leave room for Messalina to entrap herself. Agrippina was no less sensible than her mother had been of the destiny that befitted a direct descendant of Augustus Caesar.[35]

The trap into which Messalina fell was not long in materialising: driven on by what Tacitus in particular sees as her insatiable lust for men, she had formed a liaison with Gaius Silius, who in AD 47 was consul-designate for the following year.[36] He had, until AD 47, been married to a Junia

Silana,[37] a member of a family of considerable influence during the early Principate, but with little affection for the institution. Further, there was a family-connection between Agrippina and Silius, whose father and mother (Sosia Galla) had been in Germany with Germanicus and the Elder Agrippina and subsequently fell victim to Sejanus' attempts in AD 24 to persuade Tiberius[38] that the Elder Agrippina was the central figure in a plot against him, which was supported by a number of high-ranking family-associates.

As suggested above,[39] whilst it is difficult now to be certain of what was at stake, it is not impossible that the Younger Agrippina was using the younger Silius as an *agent provocateur* in a scheme to destroy Messalina; such might explain what otherwise appears to have been a fatalistic urge on Silius' part to bring the affair with Messalina into the open. In retrospect, it hardly seems to be mere coincidence that it was this episode that restored the Younger Agrippina to a prominent political position. If the affair and subsequent 'marriage' of Messalina and Silius was part of a plot to destroy Messalina, it represented a high-risk strategy if matters went awry, although, as events were to show, the risks were being run by people other than Agrippina. For her, however, it would result in the inevitable destruction of her rival, the probable marginalising of Britannicus and – perhaps most importantly – Claudius' need of a new wife and consort. That there was a conspiracy can hardly be doubted, nor that it went to the heart of the imperial household; but whether Agrippina instigated it or merely took advantage of it will probably never be known. The episode, however, certainly suits her intriguing, as does the involvement of two allies – Claudius' financial adviser, the powerful freedman, Marcus Antonius Pallas, and the Emperor's chief courtier, Lucius Vitellius, who had shared the censorship with Claudius in 47. The Vitellii, too, had a history of attachment to the family of Germanicus.[40]

In Tacitus' account, the affair between Messalina and Silius occupies the closing sections of *Annals* 11; at the opening of the following book, the historian turns to the intense competition to fill the vacancy left in Claudius' household by Messalina's death. It was not simply the case that Claudius disliked being celibate, but also that he needed a strong partner to protect him from real and imagined enemies. Agrippina's advantage over the other candidates, besides her obvious strength of character, was that she carried in her veins the blood of both the Julii and the Claudii. Not only that – and it may have been of significance for the man that Nero became – but the bloodline went back to Marcus Antonius also.

Despite the religious objections to a marriage between uncle and niece, the case presented in Agrippina's favour – principally by Pallas – was so strong as to sweep away the competition. Tacitus observed:[41] 'From this point, the country was transformed. Complete obedience was accorded to a woman. . . . This was a rigorous, almost masculine, despotism.' It will be recalled that Tacitus similarly remarked upon the almost 'mannish' behaviour of Agrippina's mother in her dealings with the troops under the command of her husband, Germanicus.[42]

Agrippina's agenda had two principal aims – for herself to become Claudius' consort and partner in power, a position for which the ground had effectively been laid by an oration made to the Senate by Lucius Vitellius,[43] and the elevation of her son to the position of Claudius' son and heir. This held the promise of her retention of real power in the long term. Her marriage to Claudius took place early in AD 49, on a day that saw the suicide of Lucius Junius Silanus Torquatus. This young man had been engaged to Claudius' daughter, Octavia. It had seemed a totally suitable arrangement, as Silanus was a great-grandson of Augustus, and might reasonably have expected an important rôle as Octavia's husband, if Claudius were to die whilst Britannicus was still in his minority. Certainly, although from a family less distinguished than that of Germanicus, Silanus will have stood out as a potential threat to Nero's prospects.

Thus, even before her marriage to Claudius, Agrippina set in motion the destruction of Silanus through the agency of Lucius Vitellius.[44] Vitellius accused Silanus of having committed incest with his own sister – an accusation that was enough for Claudius to sever the engagement to Octavia, whilst the Senate concurred in his expulsion from that body. In such parlous and humiliating circumstances, suicide was probably Silanus' only realistic option; but by doing it on the very day of the marriage between Claudius and Agrippina, this great-grandson of Augustus made it clear through whose machinations he was ruined. Agrippina's supporters in the Senate lost no time in engineering a decree of that body that Claudius should sanction the marriage of Octavia and Nero; the Emperor duly obliged.[45] It would not appear from subsequent events that Nero ever entertained any affection for Octavia; however, for many, this union represented the strongest feature of Nero's legitimacy as successor to Claudius. Further, the fact that he had Seneca as his tutor set Nero's education on a remarkable footing; no longer for him the more usual type of tutor of Greek origin.

The next stage in Agrippina's plan was to persuade Claudius to adopt Nero as his son. Earlier imperial precedents, mostly of doubtful relevance, were called into play – Augustus' reliance on his stepsons, Tiberius and Nero Drusus, whilst his adopted sons, Gaius and Lucius Caesar, were too young to be considered for succession. It should be noted that Nero Drusus was never adopted by Augustus as his son, and Tiberius not until AD 4, by which time Gaius and Lucius were both dead. The words of Augustus' will made it clear that this decision was made *in extremis.*[46] Tiberius' adoption of Germanicus in AD 4 was also cited, although it is far more likely that this represented Augustus' pursuance of his ambitions for the Julian family.[47]

Nero's adoption by Claudius was confirmed by the end of February, AD 49;[48] the names by which he was thenceforth known were Nero Claudius Caesar Drusus Germanicus.[49] That same year, Agrippina received the title, *Augusta* – the first imperial consort to achieve this whilst her husband was still alive. Nothing could have made it clearer that she was not simply Claudius' wife, but his partner in government. Agrippina had thus achieved the kind of power-base which had for so long eluded her mother.

Nero will, at this stage of his life, have presented an attractive and personable figure, with a future of consequence in front of him.[50] Young, cultured, interested in popular concerns and – perhaps most important – like his grandfather, Germanicus, he was firmly linked by birth, adoption and the promise of marriage to both sides of the imperial family. Indeed, many must have viewed him as the 'new Germanicus' who would in time preside over a liberal, cultivated and popular Principate. For Agrippina, this represented a long-term route to the fulfilment of a family-ambition, whilst, for Claudius, the drawing together of the strands of the royal family offered the prospect of improved security for himself and a continuation of his vision of the Principate. Marriage to Agrippina released him from much of the pressure that he had experienced in the earlier years of his reign. Indeed, from the Emperor's point of view, this provides a rather more positive inter-pretation than the suggestion that he had acceded to all of this simply to protect his son, Britannicus.

Nero's advancement continued in strength from this point.[51] In AD 51, although not yet fourteen years of age, he assumed the *toga virilis* (toga of manhood), that represented his formal entry into public life. Further, a senatorial decree reserved a consulship for him after his nineteenth birthday (that is, in AD 56). He was awarded the title of *princeps iuventutis*, an honorary rôle that gave him titular headship of the young members of noble families, and that had originally been given by Augustus to his adopted sons, Gaius and Lucius.[52] His name was also added to the rolls of the priestly colleges.

Although largely of an honorary nature, these advances singled Nero out for an impressive future, and at a time when his stepbrother, Britannicus, was still only a child. It is, however, worth noting that in the early-50s, despite what was happening in Rome, provincial coinages did give prominence to Britannicus.[53] However, the exceptional brightness of Nero's future was also symbolised (and guaranteed perhaps, in case anyone should entertain lingering doubts) by the donatives made in Nero's name to soldiers and people. The significance of his entry into public life was given expression by his prominent place at the games and by speeches which he made in the Senate between AD 51 and AD 53,[54] some of them in Greek, on behalf of communities seeking imperial assistance. His interest in the eastern part of the Empire at this early stage of his life is demonstrated by the fact that the speeches made on behalf of Ilium (Troy) and Rhodes were more in recognition of their historical status.

In AD 53, Nero's marriage to Octavia was formalised. In order to strengthen Nero's position further, whilst at the same time weakening that of Britannicus, Agrippina secured the dismissal of his tutors and the removal (either by dismissal or promotion) of officers of the Praetorian Guard who were thought to favour Claudius' natural son.[55] These included the two Praetorian Prefects, Lusius Geta and Rufrius Crispinus, and their replacement by a single successor of Agrippina's choosing, the Gallo-Roman, Sextus Afranius Burrus,[56] who was to play such an important part in Nero's advancement over the next decade. In opting for a single Praetorian Prefect, Agrippina invoked arguments similar to those that Sejanus had employed on Tiberius to strengthen discipline and efficiency by military control.[57]

How far Agrippina's influence was beyond attack at this stage is hard to say, although it is worth noting the continuing influence with Claudius, despite the fall of Messalina, of the freedman, Narcissus, the chief supporter of Britannicus within the imperial household. Narcissus' influence, however, was not sufficient to prevent, in AD 54, Agrippina's attack on and destruction of her former sister-in-law, Domitia Lepida.[58] The charges levelled against Lepida were in no way trivial, but designed to deliver a fatal blow. She was accused of plotting against Agrippina, of attempting to steal Nero's affection, and of allowing the slaves on her estates in Campania to run riot and thus endanger the security of Italy. It seems likely, however, that Agrippina's true motive was further to undermine the status of Britannicus by depriving him of possible supporters, in this case his grandmother. However, despite the seemingly obvious signs of Nero's relentless advance, it has to be kept in mind that Britannicus was, in spite of everything that had happened, Claudius' son, and thus represented the first opportunity in the Julio-Claudian period for an Emperor to bequeath imperial power to his own son. Agrippina showed her awareness of this possibility by pushing Nero into the limelight on every occasion.[59] In such circumstances, the possibility would always remain that, at a crucial moment, Claudius' natural son might be preferred to his son by adoption;[60] indeed, Suetonius[61] indicates that Claudius talked of the Roman people at last having 'a true-born Caesar'. Nor should it be forgotten that Britannicus was to assume the *toga virilis* early in AD 55. Agrippina could not, therefore, afford to relax her pressure.

Claudius' death in AD 54 has usually been regarded as an event hastened by Agrippina because of signs that Claudius was showing a renewed affection for his natural son.[62] At the time, it was widely accepted, as the sources show,[63] that Agrippina secured her husband's death by poisoning his food: only Josephus[64] shows caution by representing it as rumour rather than as proven fact. However, given the real chance of a rogue-mushroom being served up alongside harmless varieties, accidental death or, in view of Claudius' frequent over-indulgence, even natural death, must remain as possibilities. Further, the fact that Nero is said to have frequently joked about mushrooms being the food of the gods may point more to the level of his sense of humour than to the integrity of the evidence.[65]

The evidence for poisoning in our sources does indicate the existence of versions that differed in detail, although there is general agreement that the motive on Agrippina's part was to forestall any move by Claudius to reinstate Britannicus as his successor. Tacitus says that the poison was prepared by Locusta, but administered by Halotus, the Emperor's food-taster, who applied it to a dish of mushrooms. In this version, Agrippina had also suborned Claudius' doctor, Xenophon, to apply further poison in the event of the Emperor surviving the initial attempt. Suetonius, on the other hand, has different details, including the fact that Claudius was not dining in the Palace, but on the Capitoline Hill with the priests of Jupiter. He lays the blame on Halotus, or possibly on Agrippina herself. Suetonius, too, carries the story of a further poisoning. Dio says that Locusta prepared the poison, but that Agrippina administered it; in this version, Claudius sank into a coma and had no temporary recovery. It may be significant that Seneca's *Apocolocyntosis*, the source nearest in time to the event, makes no mention of mushrooms, although it does provide evidence of possible illness.[66]

Crucial to Nero's acceptance as Claudius' successor on the death of his adoptive father was the attitude of the Praetorian Guard; continuing apprehension over this explains why Britannicus was not permitted a public appearance, lest it undermine the position of Nero.[67] Thus, with little actual danger threatening from Britannicus, Burrus' own commitment to Nero and the judicious decision to repeat in Nero's name the donative of 15,000 *sestertii* that Claudius had given to each member of the Praetorian Guard on the occasion of his accession in AD 41,[68] ensured that Nero was accepted as Claudius' successor. He duly received all the powers of the Principate, with the exception of the title of *Pater Patriae*, which he argued he had not yet earned.[69]

What Claudius had written in his will on the matter of the succession is not known, because the document was ignored and our sources offer different interpretations of the significance of this.[70] It will never be known whether Claudius named Britannicus as his successor, or whether he named Nero because he genuinely wanted him or because he thought it to be the most effective way of protecting Britannicus' life.

Although it would be foolish, and contrary to the evidence, to believe that Britannicus did not enjoy any support in Rome and the Empire, the majority of people took the line of least resistance, accepting what they were offered and hoping for the best. A papyrus from Egypt, dated 17 November, AD 54, perhaps appropriately captures the mood:

> *The Caesar who has honoured his debt to his ancestors, who is a God manifest, has gone to them; the expectation and hope of the world has been proclaimed Emperor; the good genius of the world and the beginning of all great and good things, Nero, has been proclaimed Caesar. So wearing garlands and making sacrifice of oxen we must all pay our thanks to all the Gods. Issued in the first year of Nero Claudius Caesar Augustus Germanicus, on the twenty-first of the month, Neos Sebastos.[71]*

Chapter Four

The Expectation and
Hope of All the World

※※※※※※※

The best form of State is under a just king[1]

The Egyptian accession-papyrus, dated 17 November, AD 54 – in the first month of Nero's reign – provides an indication of the mood of excitement that greeted the new, young *princeps* and echoes the enthusiasm with which Nero's grandfather, Germanicus, had been greeted on his arrival in Alexandria in AD 19.[2] As if taking up what appeared to be the early policy-message of Nero's government – links with his two deified predecessors, Augustus and Claudius – two of the voting-tribes in Alexandria renamed themselves *Philoklaudios* (indicating Nero's affection for his adoptive father) and *Propapposebasteios* (honouring the new Emperor's great-great-grandfather, Augustus).[3]

In strong contrast to the early coinage of Claudius, that had highlighted the importance of the new Emperor's relationship with the Praetorian Guard,[4] one of Nero's earliest issues[5] (of AD 55) proclaimed a message similar to that emanating from Alexandria. It shows on the obverse side the heads of Nero and his mother, whilst on the reverse, four elephants draw a chariot on which are two male figures seated on chairs, the Deified Claudius and the Deified Augustus. In any case, the choice of dual rôle-models probably represented a sound judgement: Claudius was popular in the provinces, but hated by many in Rome, whilst in Rome Augustus' memory stood head-and-shoulders above those of his three successors, Tiberius, Caligula and Claudius.

With Nero's acceptance in October of AD 54 by the Senate, the people and the Praetorian Guard, Agrippina's triumph seemed complete: she was *Augusta*; she had been her husband's consort in government in a manner unparalleled by the wife of any previous Emperor, even Augustus' wife, Livia.[6] Agrippina's position was open and proclaimed, whereas Livia's had been exercised principally through her influence behind the scenes. Not only this, but Agrippina had personally stage-managed her son's rise and succession; Tacitus pinpoints the significance of this by describing Agrippina's rôle in Nero's succession in language similar[7] to that he had used to describe Livia's in AD 14 in the accession of her son, Tiberius.[8]

The early years of Nero's reign pose a number of questions: why did the strength of Agrippina's position collapse so completely in the early years, even months, of the reign? Where did power and government-initiative really lie in Nero's early years? Were there observable turning-points in the reign and, in particular, to what was the later Emperor, Trajan, referring when he praised Nero's *quinquennium*?[9]

Agrippina's power rested both on the position that she had occupied under Claudius and on what she, not surprisingly, saw as her son's dependence on, and expected gratitude to, her. Nero was, after all, not yet seventeen years of age when he came to power. However, Nero's power did not depend on her to the extent that she imagined: as we have seen, he was the *accepted* choice of the Senate and people. Dio Cassius[10] informs us that Nero was voted the powers of the Principate fully and quickly after Claudius' death; indeed, Dio[11] says that, shortly before Claudius' death, Agrippina had persuaded him to issue a proclamation that Nero was capable of ruling Rome and the Empire. The surviving fragment of the similar law[12] passed sixteen years later for the Emperor, Vespasian, is sufficient to show that those powers were absolute and all-embracing. Previous Emperors had shown that, no matter how respectfully they might talk about freedom and the Senate, the power to act was theirs. Should this be questioned, they had, as Nero stated on this occasion (although with no obvious implied threat),[13] control of the army, which represented the ultimate reality of power in the Roman state. In addition, Nero was the adopted son of Claudius and his chief heir, and he was the husband of Claudius' daughter, Octavia, a point that was, as we shall see, regarded by some as being of considerable significance in the matter of the legitimacy of his position.

Thus, no matter how powerful Agrippina might appear, that power, by definition, rested on a fragile base. Nonetheless, at the very beginning of Nero's reign, it appeared that her expectations were not to be disappointed. Suetonius states[14] that, early on, Nero left policy-decisions to his mother, although the examples of this that he cites were concerned with Claudius' funeral and deification, both of which should be dated to the first weeks of the reign.

Dio, however, says[15] that, at first, Agrippina 'managed for him (Nero) all the business of the Empire. . . . She received embassies and sent letters to various communities, governors and kings.' She also continued upon the murderous path on which she had embarked during Claudius' reign, causing the removal of Marcus Junius Silanus,[16] proconsul of Asia in AD 54. As we have seen, five years earlier she had destroyed his brother, Lucius, to facilitate Nero's marriage to Octavia. More important now, however, was the fact that Marcus Silanus was a descendant of Augustus, and thus a possible rival to Nero. Agrippina may conceivably have feared the vengeance of the Junii Silani now that she was no longer protected by Claudius. Not long after this,[17] Narcissus, Claudius' loyal freedman and perhaps the strongest supporter of Britannicus' claim to power, also died.

It appears that Agrippina had exercised considerable influence over the financial mechanisms of the state from the time of her marriage to Claudius. Of particular importance in this was her close and long-standing relationship with Marcus Antonius Pallas, Claudius' chief financial adviser.[18] It has been suggested that she may even have had her own nominees within the mint, allowing her some influence over coin-types. The earliest gold and silver types from the mint of Rome show clearly the prominence which Agrippina was determined to enjoy.[19] On the obverse of these earliest issues, the busts of Agrippina and Nero faced each other, although the accompanying legend was that of Agrippina; Nero's legend was relegated to the reverse of the coin. A similar emphasis is to be found on the early coinage of local mints in the eastern part of the Empire.[20] It is as if Agrippina was trying to overshadow her son, or perhaps to indicate that his position was totally due to her patronage.

By AD 55, however, a significant change had taken place:[21] the two busts continued to feature on the obverse, but now they overlapped side-by-side, with Nero's occupying the foreground. The obverse legend now consisted of Nero's titles, with his mother's on the reverse. A power-struggle may be discerned, perhaps with Seneca and Burrus, Nero's advisers, achieving some success in their efforts to push Agrippina into the background – to some extent, at least. Coins issued from the Rome-mint after AD 55 did not allude at all to the Emperor's mother; possibly the dismissal of Pallas in that year,[22] which was a decision of Nero's, undermined any remaining influence that Agrippina may have had at the mint.

That the relegation of Agrippina was the aim of Seneca and Burrus[23] may be supported by the fact that Nero's opening speech to the Senate, that was evidently composed for him by Seneca, did include some criticism of Claudius' style of government and the reversal of one of his laws. The comparison with Tiberius and Livia is again instructive.[24] Tiberius may have tried – often churlishly – to put limits on Livia's participation in his government but, far from deprecating the policies of Augustus, he continued throughout his life to show the deepest – even obsessive – respect for them.[25]

We are also told[26] of honours received by Agrippina in the early days of the reign. On his first day in power, Nero gave the watchword to the Guard – *Optima Mater* (the Best of Mothers); the Senate voted her an escort of lictors (official attendants), normally associated with those holding magisterial office, as well as membership of the priestly body associated with the newly-established cult of 'The Deified Claudius'. The Senate decided that its meetings should be held in the imperial palace (on the Palatine Hill), so that Agrippina, albeit concealed by a curtain, could listen in to senatorial business.[27] Further, it is said that Nero walked alongside his mother's litter in public. Obviously, given the significance of her rôle in Claudius' later years, some form of continuity of privilege would have been expected. It should also be remembered that, when Caligula came to power in AD 37 and for some time afterwards, he celebrated most members of his family, dead and alive, on his coinage,[28] evidently conscious of the importance of what thus appeared as a unified imperial family. It was probably also regarded as a good tactic from the point of view of publicity to celebrate the House of Germanicus Caesar, greatly diminished – not to say discredited – though it now was. This may have been considered a wise move to offset any lingering support or sympathy that there may have been for Britannicus, based upon his direct descent from Claudius.

Why, then, should Agrippina appear to have risen to such heights, only to be dashed in a matter of just a few months? Perhaps she was thought to have overstepped the mark represented by her position under Claudius; perhaps Seneca and Burrus always planned to influence Nero in different ways, but felt that this could not be safely attempted in the immediate aftermath of Claudius' death. Indeed, there are signs that the undermining of Agrippina was carefully orchestrated – for example,[29] in the incident when she attempted to greet ambassadors from Armenia in a manner designed to stress her equality with the Emperor. It should be noted here that it was Seneca and Burrus who prompted the action taken by Nero to restrain his mother, albeit in a diplomatic manner. Further, Nero's affair with the freedwoman, Acte,[30] that both offended Agrippina and undermined her influence in the palace,[31] as well as insulting Octavia, was connived at by Seneca and Burrus. This policy, according to Tacitus,[32] was formulated not so much to leave Nero on the margins of government as, on the contrary, to demonstrate to the young Emperor that he had the power and ability to do what he wanted, no matter how much he might annoy his mother by so doing. In other words, Seneca and Burrus were actively engaged in a policy of emancipating Nero from his mother's influence,[33] and the success of their plan may be measured by noting again that the decision to dismiss Pallas, Agrippina's principal confidant, was evidently Nero's alone.

Tacitus,[34] in fact, did not recognise the honours bestowed upon Agrippina at the beginning of the reign as genuinely given. There seem to have been reminiscences of the stratagem employed by Tiberius in AD 31,[35] as he embarked upon the destruction of his Praetorian Prefect, Lucius Aelius Sejanus – initiating some actions that would obviously have been pleasing to Agrippina, but intertwining these with others that carried more worrying implications.

Thus, for example, as we have seen, in his opening speech to the Senate that, Tacitus says, was composed for him by Seneca, Nero spoke critically of aspects of Claudius' government. Agrippina will have derived little pleasure from this, given her own involvement in the latter years of Claudius' government; moreover, she will certainly have disapproved of the reversal of a Claudian law. The most direct criticism of Claudius, however, came towards the end of the year with Seneca's publication of his satire on Claudius' deification, the *Apocolocyntosis* (Pumpkinification). This may have been composed as a piece of court-entertainment for the *Saturnalia*-celebrations in December of AD 54, that festival being one when it was possible to get away with the seemingly outrageous. The criticisms in it of Claudius' government are obvious and unrestrained and, as Griffin has noted,[36] in accord with items in Nero's initial speech to the Senate. They accord, too, with Nero's famous and tasteless joke about mushrooms being the food of the gods.[37] There was little in this that will have given Agrippina much encouragement. Similarly, the *Apocolocyntosis* appears to embrace the notion of a comparison of Nero with Apollo, and the opening of a new 'golden age'.[38] It has, however, been argued by Champlin[39] that the idea of a 'golden age' did not belong to AD 54, but was inaugurated by Nero himself after his mother's murder in AD 59.[40]

In these ways, signs of a weakening of the position that Agrippina had previously enjoyed followed closely upon the heels of Claudius' death; the honeymoon-period between mother and son was, indeed, short-lived. Agrippina will soon have become aware of the fact that her protégés, Seneca and Burrus, were not, as she would presumably have expected, working in her interests; rather, with Claudius gone, they were demonstrating their independence. The situation is reminiscent of that which, two decades earlier, had caused Tiberius, observing the perceived difference between himself and Caligula, to remark cynically on the 'rising and the setting suns'.[41]

As we have seen, Nero's early behaviour – in particular, his cultural pursuits and his affair with Acte – were probably seen by Seneca and Burrus as relatively harmless diversions for the young Emperor, that served to allow them a freer rein. To Agrippina, however, these same activities were manifestations of a much more worrying and, for her, dangerous process – that of her son's evident emancipation of himself from her influence. Thus, the same actions on Nero's part served the agendas of Seneca and Burrus well, but that of Agrippina rather differently. Indeed, Nero's mother, even before the end of AD 54, may have started to experience the same sense of isolation, even persecution, as that felt by her mother at the hands of Tiberius and Sejanus.

If the Elder Agrippina's reaction to her discomfiture had been unwise,[42] her daughter's was no less so: for Nero's mother attempted to regain control of her son by threatening to switch her support to the cause of the young Britannicus. Relations between the two stepbrothers had never been good, and Britannicus' references to Nero's pre-adoption name of Domitius Ahenobarbus[43] will have aggravated tensions – if not worse. Just as pointedly, at the *Saturnalia*-celebrations of AD 54, when Nero was *Rex*

Saturnalicius (king of ceremonies),[44] in order to embarrass Britannicus, he challenged him to sing; the young man rose to the challenge with spirit, singing a poem about the loss of his paternal home and the throne.[45] The sentiments will have annoyed Nero, as will the competence of Britannicus' performance; the Emperor never reacted well to people whom he saw as rivals for public popularity,[46] and decided on the elimination of Britannicus. Indeed, Tacitus,[47] in his account of Britannicus' death in AD 55, poignantly referred to Claudius' natural son as 'the last of the Claudians', but adds that the death – whether in natural or suspicious circumstances – caused little general anxiety.

The official version that was put out was that Britannicus had suffered a fatal epileptic seizure; since this was feasible, it was the more easy for men, such as Seneca and Burrus, to feign ignorance of what had in all probability really happened, although Seneca at least appears to have known.[48] Nor did the funeral offer an occasion for recrimination, as it was held at night and in bad weather, and was consequently attended by few people.[49] It was an ominous sign for Agrippina that neither Seneca nor Burrus ventured any public criticism of this murder, if that is what it was, evidently regarding Britannicus' demise as inevitable in the circumstances. They had clearly decided that it was their own relationship with Nero that was of principal importance; nothing could have served to make the marginalisation of Agrippina clearer or more real.

Indeed, angry recriminations between Agrippina and Nero led to the former's expulsion from the imperial presence. With a typical lack of appreciation of where her own best interests lay, Agrippina proceeded to cultivate further unwise friendships – with her son's estranged wife, Octavia, and, it was alleged, with Rubellius Plautus, a great-grandson of Tiberius. He was connected with the Deified Augustus in a manner similar to that of Nero himself,[50] and whom, it was alleged, Agrippina was trying to incite to revolution. Such people were, in Nero's eyes, rivals to himself for public popularity. Agrippina now found herself in real danger of prosecution, partly because of her own behaviour, but partly, too, through the malevolence of others, principally her former friend, Junia Silana, who now had a grudge against Agrippina over the latter's upsetting of her plans for marriage to a young senator, Sextius Africanus. Agrippina was denounced to Nero by his aunt Domitia's freedman, the actor, Paris, for plotting against the Emperor's life. For the moment, however, Agrippina was saved;

for Nero was dissuaded by Burrus from taking precipitate action against his mother.[51] Silana, however, was sent into exile, although recalled shortly after Agrippina's murder.[52]

In the event, therefore, Agrippina's increasing marginalisation was seen not to be in the best interests of Seneca and Burrus. Not only was she potentially dangerous when forced into a corner, but in reality the Emperor's two advisers still needed Agrippina to be able to exercise some degree of restraining influence on the evermore wayward Nero. Further, they provided a counterbalance to Agrippina's demands of her son. We begin to observe a growing lack of trust on Nero's part in his two mentors, that arose, in part, from their attempts to bring about some degree of reconciliation between Agrippina and Nero. There was also a more discernible departure from the standards of behaviour that they had tried to inculcate into him. It was evidently at around this time that Nero started his practice of touring the streets of Rome at night with friends for the purpose of thieving and instigating violence.[53] As Champlin shows,[54] this behaviour appears to have been restricted to Nero's youth, and probably reflects his indulgence of a fashion amongst young men that had a lengthy history back to the Republic, that seems to have been broadly tolerated as something which boys did; it did not mark Nero out as especially or unusually outrageous. Bad behaviour in the theatre, on the part of both actors and members of the audience, appears to have been seen as similarly fashionable – until, that is, it got too seriously out-of-hand.[55]

When assessing Nero's more outrageous, and sometimes cruel, behaviour, we must, as Champlin has shown,[56] place it into the context of the celebration of the festival of *Saturnalia* and its importance to the young Emperor. The festival was held to coincide with the winter-solstice in December. In the Roman household it was an occasion when the traditional social rôles were reversed, and when the king of the *Saturnalia*, chosen by lot, was expected to encourage outrageous talk and behaviour by telling jokes and often aiming insults at, and scoring points over, others who were present. The exchanges between Nero and Britannicus, cited above, occurred at the celebration of December, AD 54, when Nero had been chosen as king. Although, in the event, Britannicus' contribution on this occasion proved to be his undoing, it would seem to have been well within the normal customs of the occasion.[57] Nero evidently saw this particular kingly rôle as capable of being extended outside the bounds of the *Saturnalia-*

celebration itself to other areas of life; hence, for example, his nocturnal adventures. For him, this provided a means to the creation of a populist image, thus reinforcing the bonds between the Emperor and his ordinary subjects. These were increasingly important to Nero and were later to be demonstrated in Nero's shows and parties and in the building and use of the *Domus Aurea*[58] as a 'People's Palace'.

For his part, Nero evidently identified his mother as the principal impediment to the development of his life and reign in the manner that he wished; it was she who wished to constrain his pleasures and to interfere in his life. Indeed, he is said on occasion to have contemplated abdication on account of it.[59] Nero had also come to have less trust in the good offices of Seneca and Burrus on the grounds that not only were they his mother's protégés, but had also supported the idea of a limited reconciliation between himself and her. It is said[60] that Seneca had to intervene to persuade Nero not to remove Burrus as Praetorian Prefect, although in the event the Emperor drew back from taking this step.

If, then, Agrippina's influence was diminishing from the early weeks and months of the reign, where did power really lie? To some degree, this is linked with the question of turning-points in the reign. Tacitus, for example, places a turning-point in AD 58, by recounting, at the close of *Annals* 13, the story of the ominous withering of the *ficus Ruminalis*;[61] he then opens his account of the events of AD 59 with the words, 'Nero ceased delaying his long-meditated crime' – that is, the murder of his mother.[62] That this was an appalling crime, that struck at the heart of Roman morality, there can be no doubt, although its effect upon government may have been less tangible. In its aftermath, Tacitus[63] seems to lay stress on the *personal* release that it represented for Nero, as he talks about the Emperor plunging into improprieties from which his mother's influence appears formerly to have restrained him.

There seems, however, to have been another perceived turning-point – the death of Afranius Burrus in AD 62;[64] Tacitus observes that the death of Burrus broke the power of Seneca. Thus, AD 62 seems to represent the final loss of the sounder influences that had been available to Nero in his earlier years. As we have seen, there are differing views regarding early influences on Nero's reign. Dio Cassius[65] says that Nero left policy-decisions to others, although Tacitus seems to be closer to the truth in arguing that, whilst Nero did involve himself in governing, he was largely keeping to an agenda laid out by Seneca and Burrus. Tacitus' own sources for this included historians, such as Cluvius Rufus and Fabius Rusticus, both of whom were active in Nero's reign – the latter as an associate of Seneca.

To many, at the time of his accession, Nero seemed affable and cultivated – indeed, almost a Messianic figure, if we believe the comments of contemporary authors. As we have seen, the poet, Calpurnius Siculus,[66] specifically hailed the advent of a new 'golden age' and the bliss that surrounded the coming of the youthful prince. With rather less taste – and perhaps with tongue in cheek – the epic poet, Lucan,[67] the nephew of Seneca, in his account of the civil war between Pompey and Julius Caesar (*Pharsalia*), extols the war on the ground that it represented the only available means to bringing about the Principate of Nero. Such eulogy, if it is regarded as sincere, closely matches the effusive views expressed on the accession-papyrus from Egypt.[68] Indeed, many of the characteristics for which Nero was later to be detested seemed at first like manifestations of this 'golden age': a *princeps* of poetic and artistic culture, a *princeps* who shared the pleasures of his subjects.[69] Indeed, Seneca praised Nero for his musical talent,[70] hailing him as the equal of Apollo for his singing and lyre-playing – a status which Nero claimed for himself on his coinage.[71] Whilst such a view was not shared by all, the claim itself clearly and sharply illustrates the delicate balancing-act which Seneca felt it necessary to perform in order to retain the ear of his young protégé.

Ever since its establishment by Augustus, the Principate had obviously been a system of government in which personality counted for a great deal. In describing Emperors contemporary to himself, Nerva (AD 96–8) and Trajan (98–117), Tacitus[72] pinpointed the central issue as the relationship between *principatus* (the position and rôle of *princeps*) and *libertas* (liberty, and specifically that of senators). Principate and liberty were not perceived by Tacitus as abstract concepts, but their harmonisation represented the Emperor's ability and willingness to co-operate with the Senate through his respect for its traditions and for its members as a body and as individuals.[73] Again, since Nerva and Trajan were seen by Tacitus as the first Emperors to achieve this harmonisation, the reconciliation of Principate and liberty meant the rejection of the dynastic principle of succession in favour of Emperors 'emerging' through their own passage along the senatorial career-structure (*cursus honorum*). In that way, the Senate's standing could again be perceived as real and meaningful.

Augustus had tried to operate a system of government that was outwardly diplomatic, in that as much influence as possible was seen to reside with the Senate. Claudius, on the other hand, was no less assiduous in his enthusiasm for government or for the Senate having a stake in it. However, perhaps because of the growing complexity of government, he was seen overwhelmingly as an Emperor who drew an increasing amount of control towards the centre – to the detriment of magistrates and such bodies as the Senate. Thus, despite Claudius' readiness to work with the Senate – he even fined members for non-attendance – he was seen as an Emperor who, in practice, undermined it. The situation was made to look even worse by the fact that Claudius was dominated by the influence of the womenfolk and freedmen of the imperial court. This was naturally resented by the Senate, particularly when it saw its own members as the principal victims of the actions of that court.

As we have seen, when Servius Galba, in the last troubled days of his short reign in January of AD 69, sets out to choose a successor, he is represented by Tacitus as attempting an analysis of the problems of exercising power. In the first place, clearly reflecting on the relationship between Principate and liberty, Galba saw the effects of a dynastic system of succession as extremely damaging and leading to a situation in which Rome and its Empire had, in effect, become the property of the Julian and Claudian families. At the same time, however, he saw that the system needed an accountable person at its head; accountability, a cornerstone of the Old Republic, had been lost during the early Principate. He also recognised the pitfalls inherent in the personal relationships between rulers and ruled. He talked of the corruption bred by success and seems to have meant that, however virtuous a *princeps* might be, the constant sycophancy of those around him threatened to overwhelm those virtues: 'to persuade an Emperor of what he ought to do is a laborious task; but to flatter him whatever he does is easy, and indicates a lack of affection and sincerity.' Without these, the system devised by Augustus could not work and, in their different ways, the governments of Tiberius, Caligula and Claudius had all demonstrated the truth of this.

What, then, could be expected of an Emperor who, at his accession, was not yet seventeen years of age – especially one whom his mother fully expected to use as a vehicle for her own continued domination? As we have seen, Nero was inexperienced rather than ignorant, but was certainly not lacking in ideas. His youth, however, put other considerations on his agenda. His advisers, Seneca and Burrus, were essentially conservatives in the matter of governmental principle; they had little time for the new methods of Claudius, but rather, it seems, wanted to see a return to an approach that was more reminiscent of Augustus Caesar. Some confirmation of such an approach is to be seen in the use of an Augustan motif on the early gold and silver coinage of Nero's reign[74] – the oak-leaf crown on the reverse, enclosing the legend, OB CIVES SERVATOS ('for having saved the citizens'); further, the use of EX S C ('by decree of the Senate')[75] on the reverses of the gold and silver coinage from AD 54 to AD 64 indicates that Nero's government was (or, at least, was affecting to be) serious in the matter of working with the Senate.

As we have seen, there was little hope of achieving this whilst Agrippina remained at the centre of affairs; thus, although she had stage-managed Nero's path to power, his instruction and guidance in his early days in government were obviously rôles for his mentors – especially his former tutor, Seneca. In the accession-speech, which Seneca reputedly composed for him, Nero, by highlighting the importance to him of the Senate and the army, laid stress on a prospectus for government that essentially looked back to Augustus.

Everything was being done by Nero and on his behalf to indicate that the accession of the new *princeps* ushered in not only a 'golden age', but a new beginning that encapsulated best practice as it was perceived at the time. Of course, Nero's two predecessors had inaugurated their reigns by giving voice to very similar sentiments, although, in the event, their performances were seen as falling well short of their undertakings. The reasons for this were perhaps more worrying. Caligula clearly had temperamental problems which vitiated whatever he may have promised to do, whilst Claudius had to acknowledge that the government of such a large Empire called for a great deal more centralisation than was palatable to many. This emphasises the fact that attitudes had to be flexible, not only on the Emperor's side, but on the Senate's too. So was there any realistic prospect that Nero's undertakings would (or could) have a sounder outcome?

Seneca and Burrus were clearly determined that they should; indeed, in an effort to keep the righteous path before Nero's gaze, Seneca published in the first months of the reign his treatise *De Clementia* (On Clemency). This set out, in Hellenistic tradition, the qualities to be expected of the good ruler; its base-point, however, was that the imperial power was absolute.[76] The clear implication of this, of course, was that ultimately Nero could not be kept in check by any external – that is, legal – devices. Thus, it was crucial to build upon the new Emperor's better characteristics – and one, in particular. Nero liked to be popular, and appreciated that a generous disposition on his part could help to secure this. Indeed, Suetonius[77] informs us that 'Nero never lost an opportunity to display his generosity, clemency and affability'. It is made clear that Nero's clemency would mark the beginning of a new age, when 'no longer will the wretched Senate-chamber be empty and the prisons full';[78] further, Seneca[79] provides an example of this when he quotes Nero as having said, in the context of signing an execution order, that he wished that he had never learned to write.

In reality, however, although the notion of clemency might sound comfortable and reassuring, it was, in fact, a highly dangerous virtue. This had been demonstrated as early as the reign of Tiberius, who also prized his *clementia*.[80] In his case, it seems to have related chiefly to his behaviour in trials for treason; for, ultimately, it was Tiberius' choice whether or not to invoke his *clementia*, and not the legal process, which determined whether defendants were condemned or not.[81] *Clementia*, then, presupposed that the Emperor was the source of all good things – rather as the Egyptian accession-papyrus explicitly claimed. Further, in the opening of *De Clementia*,[82] Seneca imagines the indissoluble connection in Nero's mind between the absolute power that he held and the generosity that it enabled him to bestow and to which the whole of humanity looked. It was, of course, a hopelessly idealised picture and would have taken a man of immense personal discipline, strength of character and soundness of judgement to keep within bounds – a man rather as the later Emperor, Marcus Aurelius (AD 161–80) in his *Meditations*, was to portray his father-in-law and predecessor, Antoninus Pius.[83]

Nero, however, was never, in his late teens, a 'prototype' of Antoninus Pius, and would never become one; the Roman world was to discover in time how Nero would react to indications that his real or imagined beneficence was not appreciated in the way and on the scale that he wished and expected. A notable example of this can be seen in the threat that he made, on hearing a piece of particularly unfavourable news during the rebellion against him in AD 68, to release wild beasts into the streets of Rome.[84] It can also be seen in his extravagant reaction to news of conspiracies against him.[85] In such circumstances, the price that had to be paid for having a ruler who was governed by his own whims and who was subject to no legal checks or mechanisms to ensure accountability would be very high indeed. Further, it has to be said that the very extravagance with which Nero's accession was greeted in AD 54 helped only to fuel his expectations and make such a situation worse. For Seneca, clemency may have represented the foundation-principle for a Principate proceeding in the footsteps of Augustus, with an Emperor governed by his own self-discipline. It has, however, to be borne in mind that Augustus' powers were subject to review-dates when he would be held to account for what he had done. In Nero's case, *clementia* came to represent carte-blanche to act as he pleased. Thus, in the final analysis, even if his chief aim was to please, the outcome could be no better than tyranny.

Whatever the reasons and the influences upon him, Nero's early involvement with government showed signs of a desire to be conciliatory towards the Senate; although it annoyed and alarmed Agrippina, the ghost of Claudius needed to be laid in the Senatorial Order. Thus, as we have seen, the model of government, that had originally been both Augustan and Claudian, became decidedly more Augustan. Yet Nero could not afford, in the interests of the legitimacy of his own position, to disown Claudius; he might join in the jokes about his adoptive father's deification, and he certainly came to neglect it but he did not annul it. An example of this is the destruction of the Temple of the Deified Claudius which Agrippina had started to build on the Caelian Hill in Rome and that Nero removed to make way for part of his extensive palace-complex, the *Domus Aurea*.[86] Some official records continued to include in Nero's titulature 'Son of the Deified Claudius'.[87] His continued piety towards Claudius was due to the Claudian basis of his position; without it, he would have been more vulnerable to the claim made in AD 55 by Agrippina, on behalf of Britannicus and to men, such as Faustus Sulla, the husband of Claudius' older daughter, Antonia.[88] Her continued significance may be gauged from the apparent plan to link her name with the conspiracy of Gaius Piso in 65.[89] It also explains why Nero's marriage to Octavia lasted for as long as it did;[90] he did not rid himself of her until after the removal of Britannicus (murdered/died in AD 55), Rubellius Plautus and Faustus Cornelius Sulla (both exiled in AD 60 and murdered in AD 62). Nero was plainly increasingly sensitive regarding men with impressive pedigrees.

In his earlier years, Nero's government displayed a tendency, in making appointments to the consulship, to favour men who were descended from members of the nobility of the Old Republic or whose families had been raised to senatorial status by Augustus. In each of the first six years of the reign (AD 55–60), although Nero himself held a consulship in four of these, at least one of the *ordinarii* – consuls who took office at the opening of the year and thus gave the year its official title – looked back to ancestors of late-Republican nobility – Lucius Antistius Vetus (AD 55), Publius Cornelius Scipio (AD 56), Lucius Calpurnius Piso (AD 57), Marcus Valerius Messala Corvinus (AD 58), Gaius Fonteius Capito (AD 59) and Cossus Cornelius Lentulus (AD 60). Subsequently, this tendency diminished, although, like Augustus, Nero refused a permanently reserved annual consulship for himself and, after AD 60, held the office only once (in AD 68). Yet the numbers of men of aristocratic distinction reaching the highest office decreased in the AD 60s; the consulship, of course, represented the pathway to senior – and sensitive – military commands, and, by that time, Nero evidently no longer felt that he could trust such men in senior military commands.[91]

In the earlier years of the reign, Nero enjoyed relatively cordial relations with the Senate. Although, since the time of Augustus, there had been a growing tendency for the Senate to content itself with empty flattery of the Emperor,[92] there seems to have been a sense of genuine contentment with Nero's early performance, following his inaugural speech, even if it was on occasion expressed in extravagant terms.[93] His government evidently appeared to the Senate to be moderate and conciliatory. Although, as we have seen, Nero, in AD 54, had taken most of the powers of the Principate *en bloc*, he probably gained in the eyes of senators by his refusal – at first, at least – to accept the title of *Pater Patriae* (Father of the Fatherland). He also rejected honours that he plainly regarded as extravagant and unnecessary. These included to make the Emperor's birth-month (December) the beginning of the year, and others that he should assume a permanent consulship, and that his statues, in silver and gold, should be erected in public places.[94] Such moderation well accords with the likely advice of Seneca and Burrus.[95]

Nero avoided the imposition of crippling burdens and, much to his mother's annoyance, cancelled a requirement introduced by Claudius that quaestors-designate – that is, young men in their early twenties and on the threshold of a senatorial career – should stage gladiatorial shows at their own expense.[96] The Emperor also made it easier and less embarrassing for senators who had fallen on hard times to apply for and receive financial assistance that would restore their fortunes to the level of the senatorial wealth-qualification, and thus obviate any need for them to forfeit their senatorial status.[97]

A wide range of social issues was addressed, particularly pertaining to the security and well-being of Italy that, by the mid-first century AD, was beginning to show signs of the social and economic stress that was to become serious by the second half of the next century.[98] A major contributor to these problems sprang from depopulation, as young men who, recruited from Italy into the legions, in increasing numbers, chose – or were required – to take their retirement in the provinces in which they had served, in order to accelerate the process of Romanisation.[99] Although colonial settlement in Italy may have been losing much of its attraction,[100] this problem of depopulation seems to have prompted a renewal of the programme, as at Pompeii and Puteoli (Pozzuoli)[101] on the Bay of Naples. Such foundations, however, may be indicative of other problems: it is possible, for example, that the decision to found a *colonia* at Pompeii may have been connected with the outbreak of hooliganism in AD 59 in the town's amphitheatre. This was recorded by Tacitus and is depicted on a surviving wall-painting, now in Naples Archaeological Museum.[102] Alternatively, it may have been an attempt to reinvigorate the town after the damaging earthquake of AD 62, from which Pompeii had evidently not fully recovered by the time of the disastrous eruption of Vesuvius in AD 79.[103]

It is evident, too, that law and order were becoming issues of concern in the mid-first century. Ironically, whilst Nero himself, as we have seen, contributed to the lawlessness on the streets of Rome by night, during the day we find him cooperating with the Senate to handle disturbances that had been precipitated by fear of local corruption.[104] More famously, the outbreak of hooliganism in the amphitheatre at Pompeii, mentioned above, was punished with a ten-year closure of the building, a measure clearly intended to be both punitive and preventative. Lawlessness had been a developing problem both in Rome and, more widely, in Italy. A feature of the complaint raised in AD 54 against Nero's aunt, Domitia Lepida, was that she had failed to exercise proper control over the slaves on her country-estate in Calabria.[105] Periodic outbreaks of hooliganism continued; in AD 62, Poppaea Sabina claimed that gangs in support of Nero's wife, Octavia, were rampaging through the streets of Rome, destroying her statues;[106] in AD 64, a gang of gladiators tried to escape at Palestrina (Praeneste).[107] Earlier (in AD 55), Nero had experimented with reducing the police-cover at the games, but had had to reverse the measure in the following year, because of riots between gangs of rival-supporters.[108]

The concern for Italy exhibited by Nero and his advisers may have been intended as a palliative for senators after what had been seen by some as Claudius' excessive concern for the provinces.[109] The wording of senatorial complaint at that time indicates clearly that senators felt that Italy was in distress; that distress stemmed from the growing signs of social and economic decline. Similarly, the undoubted growth of prosperity in the provinces, that Nero, as we shall see, attempted to foster, was leading to an increase in the number of those from outside Italy who could satisfy the financial criteria to take up office in Rome. Whilst this was beneficial to the integration of the Empire, it was bound to lead to an impression that Italy was being neglected. Thus, the interest in Italy shown by Nero's government was probably intended to reassure.

Care is also demonstrated in Nero's early handling of judicial and financial matters. Suetonius attests[110] the great concern shown by the Emperor in hearing cases and in weighing and taking into account the *written* views of his assessors. His decisions were also published clearly and in writing – an obvious attempt to allay fears of any return to Claudius' secret trials, that had been conducted in private (*intra cubiculum*).

Although detail is lacking regarding Nero's financial management, it is clear that, like his predecessors, he gave subventions to the state's main treasury (*aerarium Saturni*) from his personal resources that were, in any case, buoyant because of the developing practice amongst wealthy Romans of including the Emperor amongst the beneficiaries in their wills. The purpose of this, however, apart from the obvious flattery, was to try to buy security for their personal bequests, and does betray a growing fear of imperial greed. Further, in a much-publicised example in Britain in AD 59–60, Prasutagus, the leader of the tribe of the *Iceni* and a 'client-monarch' of Rome, failed to protect his family from the rapaciousness of imperial officials, despite leaving part of his fortune to the Emperor – hence, as we shall see, the rebellion of his widow, Boudica.[111]

Another aid to more transparent financial management – as well as being intended to undermine the position of Agrippina – was the dismissal in

AD 55 of Pallas, Claudius' chief financial aide.[112] Perhaps, also, greater efficiency was sought by replacing the two quaestors, who had traditionally been in charge of the main treasury, by two *praefecti* who had already held the praetorship – usually, therefore, relatively senior men in their mid- to late-thirties. Whilst this helped to keep financial management close to the palace, it was also more realistic to have men of some seniority in such positions.

There was also an attempt to set up radical changes in the area of taxation, although the fact that it was not, in the event, put into effect has, of course, diminished our chance of understanding what lay behind the idea. In AD 58,[113] Nero suggested the abolition of indirect taxation (*vectigalia*) across the Empire; this *may* have been one of the Emperor's characteristic outbursts of generosity, or he may have been attempting to reduce the opportunities for profiteering available to the tax-gatherers (*publicani*). Much had been done since the corrupt times of the late Republic to curb the activities of these men, especially through the appointment to each province of a senior official of the equestrian order (*Procurator Augusti*) who, as his 'job-title' suggests, was responsible directly to the Emperor. Yet, greed and corruption remained – as the events that precipitated Boudica's rebellion showed. Further, in AD 62, Nero himself established a commission, consisting of three former consuls, to investigate the whole range of the state's financial activities. Even so, when, in AD 77, Gnaeus Julius Agricola became governor of Britain, we are informed by Tacitus[114] that he still found major areas of corruption in the collection of the grain-tax that required his attention.

It is just possible that Nero and/or his advisers had in mind what would have constituted a major reform: the removal of taxes on the movement of goods may have been intended to free-up trade. In this way, more people would have become wealthier and would thus have satisfied the financial criteria for attempting to hold local or imperial office – more encouraging for them and a stimulus to more extensive Romanisation in the provinces. It is, indeed, worth noting that Dio Cassius, in his account of Romanisation along the Rhine in the time of Augustus, lays stress on the notion that trading activities had the effect of 'making people different without knowing it'.[115] Ultimately, the state would not have lost, as, in time, not only would the Empire have become more effectively integrated, leading to the spread of Roman citizenship, but also increased wealth would have facilitated a greater 'take' from direct taxation upon personal wealth.

Thus, it is perfectly reasonable to suppose that Trajan might have characterised Nero's first five years as a period of good government, dubbing the period the *quinquennium Neronis*,[116] always accepting, of course, that the observation by the fourth-century author, Sextus Aurelius Victor, has any historical validity at all.[117] As we have seen, the period that it embraces does approximate to that which came to an end at the turn of AD 58/9, a period that Tacitus, too, appeared to separate as of better quality than what followed. However, how much of this was due to Nero and how much to the influence of his advisers remains unclear; in any case, it must not be forgotten that this same period was tainted with crime – the deaths of Marcus Junius Silanus and Narcissus, the probable murder of Britannicus and the forcible marginalisation of 'rivals' such as Rubellius Plautus and Faustus Sulla, not to mention the intrigues that surrounded Agrippina and Nero's treatment of Octavia.

In other words, the period perhaps held promise of a return to an Augustan Principate, but was also flawed by crime – in all, a rather shabby *quinquennium*. If Trajan really did make the observation attributed to him, perhaps he was referring to another period in Nero's reign. Indeed, in view of Trajan's interests in building and in imperial expansion, it is, at least, possible that he had specifically in mind such activities in the *final* five years of Nero's reign.

Chapter Five

The End of the Beginning

As we have seen, Tacitus clearly regarded the turn of the years, AD 58 and 59, as a significant point in Nero's reign. The thirteenth book of the *Annals*, alone amongst the surviving Claudian and Neronian books, comes to a close with the ending of a year, a point in time that was itself marked by the portent of the withering of the ancient tree, the *Ficus Ruminalis*.[1] Although the tree sprang back to life, this was a sign that was taken to be both momentous and disturbing.

The reason, of course, is not far to seek: *Annals* 14 opens with an account of Nero's murder of his mother. This was a crime that will have caused revulsion in the Roman world, for the mother was that most sacred of icons within the Roman family.[2] For Tacitus, this deed was plainly made worse by the degree of premeditation that he noted on Nero's part and by the bizarre farce into which it turned. It represented to many contemporary Romans – even if they were afraid to admit it – the depth to which the Emperor had sunk. Further, consciousness of what he had done remained to haunt Nero, and the matricide was cited by Gaius Julius Vindex in 68 as a principal reason for the raising of his rebellion against Nero.[3] So why did the young Emperor embark upon a crime of such appalling magnitude?

The official reason[4] was that Agrippina was involved in a plot to assassinate Nero; this, it was said, was deduced from the fact that one of her freedmen had been discovered with a weapon. Indeed, the story of incest between mother and son, for which Tacitus cites Cluvius Rufus, is said to have been an indication of Agrippina's desperation, as she felt her influence over Nero evaporating, to maintain some kind of a hold over the Emperor.[5] Further, it was then alleged that Agrippina herself had committed suicide from a sense of guilt. The method of Nero's attack on his mother was planned by his freedman and former tutor, Anicetus, who was now the Prefect of the fleet at Misenum, on the Bay of Naples. Agrippina was to embark at night[6] on a boat for a trip across the Bay of Baiae. This boat, however, had been sabotaged so that it would collapse, and as a consequence Agrippina would drown in what would look like an accident. Unfortunately for Nero, Agrippina was an accomplished swimmer, and managed to reach the shore, from where – feigning ignorance of the truth – she sent a message informing her son of her lucky escape from a freak accident.

Nero, not surprisingly, panicked and called on Seneca and Burrus to help him out of his mess. Tacitus says[7] that it was uncertain whether they had prior knowledge of Nero's plans, although Dio Cassius[8] says that writers 'whom he trusted' had alleged that it was Seneca who put the idea of murdering Agrippina into Nero's head. The explanation that he gives for this unlikely version is that Seneca hoped that the crime would occasion such disgust that it would lead to Nero's downfall. It is hard to credit this, particularly since, from the point of view of Seneca and Burrus, by AD 59 Agrippina could not have appeared any longer as an overwhelming problem, although, given her past record, she might understandably have continued to be regarded as a 'lighted fuse'. It remained, however, for Nero to finish what he had started. Burrus doubted whether the Praetorian Guard could be persuaded to inflict violence on the daughter of Germanicus, thus, it was left to Anicetus, with officers of the fleet, to complete the crime. Dio tells us that Agrippina, realising why they had come, exposed her abdomen, telling her attackers to strike the womb that had carried Nero. The tradition plainly contained stories of rather perverted behaviour on Nero's part towards his mother's dead body;[9] Tacitus, perhaps following a source slightly more sympathetic towards Nero – perhaps, Cluvius Rufus – was clearly not convinced by this.[10]

Why, then, did the young Emperor decide upon so drastic a course of action that, potentially, was extremely damaging to himself and his reputation? As we have seen, the early years of his reign were dominated by three people – Seneca, Burrus and Agrippina. Although by AD 59 he plainly did not retain the same level of confidence in Seneca and Burrus that had once been the case, he had also shown that ultimately he did not feel able to do without them. Agrippina, however, although marginalised in the hierarchy of advisers, continued to irritate him. Probably, like Livia in the case of her son, Tiberius, Agrippina was obtrusively insistent on the debt that she maintained Nero owed to her in return for his rise to power. To be reminded constantly of a debt that could not be repaid went beyond the irritating to become a cause of real fear and suspicion. Hence, perhaps, Nero was the more easily able to convince himself that Agrippina was undermining him – even to the point of plotting against him. Her past ability to switch her allegiance to Nero's rivals will have made her continued existence appear even more alarming.

In retrospect, however, historians needed an explanation for the matricide that seemed to be consistent with Nero's character; hence the anachronistic introduction of Poppaea Sabina, the 'arrogant whore' (*superba paelex*) and the Emperor's future wife, as the reason for Nero's decision not to delay any further the crime that he had long contemplated.[11] It is clear that a number of versions existed of Nero's relationship with Poppaea, which differed considerably in detail.[12] Despite the fact that her father was Titus Ollius, whose career had been undermined by association with Sejanus, Poppaea preferred to use the more distinguished name of her mother's family.[13]

Poppaea's maternal family appear to have been leading citizens of Pompeii, where the family had property-interests; the residence known now as the 'House of the Golden Cupids' belonged to a Gnaeus Poppaeus Habitus, and the 'House of the Menander' to a Quintus Poppaeus.[14] Pompeii was evidently a place where Nero and Poppaea enjoyed considerable popularity,[15] and it is possible that the grant of *colonia*-status to Pompeii in AD 63 was made, in part at least, as an honour to Poppaea and her daughter, who was born in January of AD 63. In addition, Poppaea herself is known to have owned a brickworks near Pompeii, and the extensive villa at Oplontis,[16] that was also consumed in the eruption of AD 79. She was thus wealthy and regarded, as was her mother, as one of the leading beauties of the age, although socially she was considerably the inferior of Agrippina and Octavia.

Poppaea was probably about six years older than Nero, and had early on been married to Rufrius Crispinus, Prefect of the Praetorian Guard under Claudius, until Agrippina had him dismissed in AD 51; the couple had a son whom Nero was to remove some time after the middle of AD 66.[17] At some stage before AD 58, it appears, Poppaea divorced her husband and married Nero's friend, the future Emperor, Marcus Salvius Otho. Poppaea proceeded to flirt with Nero, whilst taunting him that she would not leave her husband for the Emperor, since he was in thrall to his slave-mistress, Acte.[18] An alternative version is that Nero was already inflamed with passion for Poppaea whilst she was still married to Crispinus, and entrusted her to Otho to look after until he (Nero) was in a position to marry her himself. According to Plutarch,[19] he did this out of respect for Octavia. In either case, the relationship between Nero and Otho became extremely fraught, as Otho's passion and Nero's jealousy grew.[20] In AD 58, Nero sent Otho to be governor of the province of Lusitania,[21] where he remained until the Emperor's death. This move can be construed either as an effective banishment or as a diplomatic ruse, perhaps organised by Seneca,[22] to get Otho out of harm's way. Despite this, however, Suetonius indicates that Otho assisted Nero in the plot to murder his mother.

In short, therefore, it would appear that the only serious obstacle to Nero's development of a relationship with Poppaea prior to AD 59 would have been his continued marriage to Octavia; the removal of Agrippina did not, in fact, do anything to ease the way for Nero to marry Poppaea. Indeed, of greater relevance was his fear of rivals, especially Faustus Sulla and Rubellius Plautus, and the fact that it was his marriage to Octavia that constituted the chief factor that provided him with legal superiority over them.[23] It seems that it was not until the death of Burrus in AD 62[24] – whether from natural causes or Nero's intervention was unclear – and the consequent loss of influence by Seneca[25] that Nero at last felt able finally to rid himself of Sulla, Plautus and Octavia and to marry Poppaea.

It may well have been the influence of Burrus and his continuing conviction of the importance, in legal terms, of Nero's marriage to Claudius' daughter that not only caused an increasing strain in his relationship with the Emperor, but also prevented Nero from taking the step of eliminating Octavia at an earlier stage. It was, therefore, the events of AD 62 that finally cleared the way for Nero's divorce from Octavia and his marriage to Poppaea Sabina. It is because of this that some have come to regard Nero's relationship with Poppaea Sabina as having had no direct relevance to his decision to remove Agrippina, suggesting that the affair with Poppaea may have been anachronistically relocated in the tradition so as to provide a more obvious (and damaging) explanation for Nero's crime. Indeed, this has led to the suggestion[26] that the relationship between Nero and Poppaea may not have started much before AD 62.

If there is no real hint that Agrippina was actually intriguing against Nero in the last months of her life, we can conclude only that he found her presence so irritating and intimidating, and her attitude so domineering, that he could see no alternative to his drastic plan. In short, the problem for Nero may be summarised by suggesting that he knew that he needed Agrippina, but that he was at the same time afraid of the fact that he needed her. Perhaps Agrippina's disapproval of his actions represented to Nero the voice of his own conscience; such a powerful personality as hers might well have come close to rendering Nero unable to act on his own behalf. It is significant that his plan for her removal involved no direct action on his part, but was to have been initiated, as it were, at a distance that, he hoped, would appear to absolve him from responsibility for the act.

It may also have been that stories[27] of Nero's rather unorthodox relationship with his mother stemmed simply from his own realisation of the enormity of what he was planning to do, and from his appreciation and fear of the strength of her personality. Tacitus, for example, indicates at the end of his description of the episode that Agrippina's mere continued existence prevented him from doing things that he wanted to do – such as appearances in chariot-races and the institution of the games known as the *Juvenalia*, that were to offer a stage for the demonstration of his own theatrical aptitude.[28] Whatever Nero's motivation for such plans – whether it was simply a matter of self-indulgence or whether he wanted positively to bring pleasure into the lives of his ordinary subjects – he will have known well enough that such extravagances, whilst perhaps increasingly in tune with changing times and fashions,[29] would find no favour with those who wanted a traditional Principate on the Augustan, or even the Claudian, model. This assessment on Tacitus' part makes it clear that, despite all that had happened, and despite the ebb and flow of his relationship with his mother, Agrippina's approval or disapproval of him had remained of great – perhaps, too great – importance to Nero.

The Emperor now had to decide how to survive this act, naturally so repugnant to contemporary opinion. Tacitus recounts[30] that the Emperor spent the remainder of the night of the murder in a state of panic, expecting that the coming of daylight would usher in the end of him. Instead, however, at the instigation of Burrus, officers of the Praetorian Guard came to offer their congratulations to Nero on his deliverance from extreme danger, and gradually people emerged to give thanks to the gods that so great a crisis as a plot by Agrippina had been thwarted before it could achieve its end.

As a consequence, Nero's confidence began to return, and Tacitus recounts how the Emperor's acting-skills came to the fore in his response to the popular mood, although the sight of the landscape in which the deed had been done kept bringing Nero's conscience and fear of reprisal back to the harsh reality.[31] A letter to the Senate was composed, supposedly by Seneca,[32] in which Nero sought to justify what he had done by detailing Agrippina's malevolence and crimes, both in the recent and the more distant past, and making out that his mother had been an enemy not only to him, but also to the soldiers, senators and equestrians. Indeed, the letter said that matters would have been far worse had the Emperor not intervened.[33] The opportunity was even utilised by Nero to blame his mother for everything that had been wrong with Claudius' Principate.

Nero's version of events had, from his own point of view, the desired effect, as senators competed in offering thanks for the escape which had been engineered by the intervention of *Good Fortune*. The decrees that were passed were as outrageous as Nero's own explanations; one proposal was that a golden statue of the Goddess, Minerva, should be erected in the Senate-house, with one of Nero beside her, whilst another suggested the celebration of games each year on the anniversary of Agrippina's death, that had fallen during the period of the *Quinquatria* (19–23 March), a festival sacred to Minerva.[34] In AD 59, at any rate, lavish games were organised, presumably in the *Circus Maximus* (after the fashion of the *ludi maximi*), to celebrate Rome's and Nero's deliverance from the plots of Agrippina.[35] Dio,[36] in a tone of considerable revulsion, goes into some detail of the performances involved, and says that the events took place over several days in five or six theatres at once.

At the time, only one senator made clear his disgust at all of this: the Stoic, Publius Clodius Thrasea Paetus, who was to become a beacon of opposition to Nero for the next six years, until his trial and execution in 66,[37] made his protest by saying nothing and then walking out of the Senate-house.[38] Tacitus observes – rather churlishly, it might appear – that this failed to set an example to others, but merely created danger for Thrasea Paetus himself. It can, however, be seen elsewhere[39] that the historian entertained suspicions of the motives of such apparently self-advertising acts of opposition. Not surprisingly, Agrippina's violent death was followed by a crop of unfavourable omens.[40]

Still, however, Nero delayed his return to Rome, uncertain of the nature of his reception. He need not have worried, however, as the crowds of senators and ordinary citizens greeted him in celebratory mood, as if, Tacitus says, they were out to view a triumphal procession. Nero rose to the occasion; as Tacitus describes the scene:

> *Hence it was as a haughty victor over the servility of the people that he approached the Capitol, repaid his debt of gratitude, and released himself into all the lusts which, though ill-curbed, had nevertheless been retarded by such respect as he had had for his mother.*[41]

The formality of a procession to the Temple of Jupiter Capitolinus, like the celebration of the *ludi maximi* in the *Circus Maximus*, was traditionally part of the pomp and ceremony associated with the celebration of a triumph. Tacitus' language, referring to Nero as the 'haughty victor' (*superbus victor*), makes it clear that he saw this 'show' as a parody of a traditional triumph.

As on other occasions, Nero reacted big-heartedly to signs that his actions had met with public approval. However, although he showed some reciprocal generosity by restoring to Rome a number of people who had been driven out at the instigation, he claimed, of Agrippina, he also exhibited greater fear than before of some whom he regarded as political rivals. Already, in AD 58, the harmless Faustus Sulla had been sent from Rome to live in Massilia (Marseilles); Sulla was the son of Nero's aunt, Domitia Lepida, by her second marriage.[42] Now, the Stoic, Rubellius Plautus, following the appearance of a comet, that was interpreted as an indication of a coming change of ruler, was required to retire to his family-estates in the province of Asia. Undoubtedly, Nero feared him because of his blood-connection with Augustus, and perhaps also because, in the light of recent events, he was seen as a decent man with a proper respect for tradition.[43]

Following his account of Nero's return to Rome and release from the constraints that he felt that his mother had placed upon him, Tacitus informs us of the Emperor's development of his enthusiasm for chariot-racing and singing. It is at this point that we are made sharply aware of Nero's philhellenism through his argument that chariot-racing was traditionally a royal pursuit and one that was celebrated by the poets of old.

There is little doubt that he was referring to the Greeks of the heroic age whose deeds were captured in Homeric song. In Italy, Nero's philhellenism exhibited itself, it was said, by his love for the resort of Baiae on the Bay of Naples,[44] that gave rise to the allegation that, also in AD 59, he had poisoned his more elderly aunt, Domitia, in order to acquire her estate and fishponds there.[45] The Emperor's interest in the god, Apollo, also became more overt from this time; he observed that Apollo was the god of music, and that his statues were everywhere to be seen in the form of the lyre-player, *Apollo Citharoedus*, whose image was later (in AD 64) to be prominently displayed on a coin of Nero's, a development that was sufficiently noteworthy to be remarked upon by Suetonius.[46] For some, it may have begun to seem but a short step to the interchangeability of Emperor and god.

In an attempt to maintain some measure of control over the Emperor, Seneca and Burrus conceded his wish to race chariots: a circus, started by Caligula, was completed in the valley alongside the Vatican Hill, initially in the hope that it might provide a secluded location for Nero's enthusiasms.[47] However, Nero also commissioned a new bridge across the river Tiber, the *Pons Neronianus*, to provide ease of access to the new stadium for his public. Clearly, the intention was that spectators should be invited to attend, and they rose to the occasion just as Nero undoubtedly hoped that they would; people delighted in observing that their Emperor shared their own pleasures.

Tacitus strongly criticises[48] Nero's involvement of other members of noble families in these spectacles, on the ground that it sprang from a desire to humiliate them. In fact, the argument lacks logic; for if, in Nero's mind, participation in such events elevated the Emperor, so too it did those who took part with him. On the contrary, Nero's motivation again probably derived from his admiration of the Greek heroic age, when leaders and heroes competed for honour in sporting contests. Indeed, as we have seen, on the evidence of Juvenal,[49] it seems that chariot-racing, even on the streets of Rome, was a popular – and highly dangerous – pastime of the young in the later-first century. It is further worth noting that, whilst his mother was still alive, Nero erected a temporary stadium in the *Campus Martius*, probably close to the site in the Piazza Navona where a stadium was later laid out by Domitian, and a temporary amphitheatre that was renowned for lavish and exotic decorations of the types that looked forward to what were later to adorn the *Domus Aurea*.[50]

From such developments as these came the games known as the *Juvenalia*, in which men and women of all classes and ages enrolled to compete in poetry and song. The location was at 'Augustus' Pool', and the venue developed in a manner that might, it seems, be likened to a Pop Festival/'Love-In' of the 1970s.[51] The particular propriety of the location, that must have appealed to Nero, was that this site had been laid out by Augustus in 2 BC in honour of Gaius and Lucius Caesar and their elevation to the title of *principes iuventutis.* Nero himself appeared, much concerned that his performance should be of the highest order. Tacitus adds that a 'sorrowing Burrus' also attended the proceedings. This was evidently the first occasion on which Nero enrolled young members of the equestrian order as his personal attendants or cheerleaders (the *Augustiani*), who led the applause for the Emperor and who were noted for their outlandish dress and hair-styles.[52]

In the following year,[53] Nero introduced another set of games and competitions, known as the *Neronia*, that were to be celebrated every five years.[54] Nero did not compete personally on this first occasion, but did at the second celebration in AD 65. However, although he had not competed, the Emperor was nonetheless declared the victor. It appears that, despite doom-laden predictions, there was no disorder at the celebrations of AD 60. It is further worth noting that, if we can rely on Tacitus' account, beyond the celebration of the *Neronia*, the year AD 60 was characterised by wars in Britain and the East,[55] and by a continuation of the 'good housekeeping' in which, as previously, Nero and the Senate cooperated.

Two years later, however, in AD 62, there does appear to have been another turning-point in the reign: the period from AD 59 to AD 61 had seen Nero survive his mother's assassination; indeed, the nature of his reception after it must have gone a long way towards convincing him that the gods were, after all, on his side. He had followed his own whim with the inauguration of the *Juvenalia* and *Neronia* and, although these certainly contained features that traditionalists found unsavoury, they had not proved to be a public disaster. To his own mind, Nero had demonstrated his sense of culture through his love of all things Greek, and the imperial beneficence involved had been widely welcomed: so far, the reciprocity of imperial generosity and public gratitude seemed to be in tune. Further, Nero had rid himself of people whom he regarded as dangerous – his mother, who had frowned on his pursuit of his own tastes, Faustus Sulla and Rubellius Plautus who, as a Stoic, had seemed to be an embodiment of the traditions which Nero was so keen to modernise.

The events of AD 62, however, represented the beginning of changes that ultimately were to carry Nero beyond what was broadly regarded as acceptable. As if he was consciously introducing the turning-point, Tacitus notes at the opening of his account of AD 62 the renewal of operations under the law of treason – Augustus' *Lex Julia de Maiestate*, that, years before, had removed any credibility from Tiberius' attempts to cooperate with the Senate.[56] It had been a feature of his early attempts to show a conciliatory face to the Senate that Nero had, at the opening of his reign, suspended operations under this law that, in the past, had proved particularly oppressive to senators,[57] demonstrating as it did the complete dependence of senators on the goodwill of the *princeps*. Tacitus divined, probably correctly, that Nero's motive was not – at first, at least – the securing of the ruin of people whom he considered dangerous, but rather the provision of opportunities for displays of imperial clemency. In this respect, Nero's motive appears to have been similar to that attributed by one senator to Tiberius.[58] It will also have emerged as significant, however, that the informer in the first reported trial, Cossutianus Capito, was the son-in-law of Tigellinus who made his appearance in this year as a Prefect of the Praetorian Guard.

Indeed, the greatest contribution to the change that was to characterise Nero's later years was undoubtedly the death of Afranius Burrus, who had occupied the command of the Guard since his appointment by Claudius and had acted as one of Nero's two closest advisers.[59] Tacitus, albeit with some doubts, reports that it was generally believed that Burrus' death was due to poison administered on behalf of the Emperor. The loss of Burrus from Nero's counsels was a severe blow, that was accentuated by the quality of his replacements: Nero reverted to the system whereby the command[60] of the Praetorian Guard was shared by two men – on this occasion, Faenius Rufus and Ofonius Tigellinus. Tacitus contrasts the 'sluggish innocence' of the former and the 'blazing outrages' of the latter; Nero, it is said, shared with Tigellinus a passion for horses and had long admired his immorality and infamy; Tigellinus thus, as a consequence, exercised the greater influence over the Emperor, pandering to his 'most intimate lusts'. It would appear that, in Nero's mind, the logic that lay behind this particular dual command was that Tigellinus would be his unprincipled fixer, whilst the perceived honesty and popularity of Faenius Rufus would help to maintain an acceptable image for Nero.

Unsurprisingly, Seneca's enemies were quick to take advantage of his new isolation to attack and further undermine him;[61] the chief area of this attack was the vast wealth that Seneca had undoubtedly amassed during his period as Nero's adviser, but with hints, too, that there was something sinister about Seneca's behaviour. In any case, it was said, at twenty-five years of age Nero no longer required a tutor. Seneca, sensing the danger, sought of Nero leave to retire, offering to place a substantial portion of his wealth under the Emperor's supervision. Whilst offering his old tutor, in return, the opportunity to remain associated with him, Nero affably allowed Seneca to step aside. In reality, the Emperor must have felt that he had moved beyond the need for lectures on such subjects as clemency; he now had a markedly different lifestyle in his sights.

Tigellinus lost no time in setting about the undermining of his colleague, Faenius Rufus, suggesting that Rufus had been a friend of Agrippina;[62] comparing himself favourably with both Faenius Rufus and Burrus, Tigellinus assured Nero that he had no divided loyalties. In reality, he wished to ensure that his own skill in evil practices would commend him to the Emperor. The Prefect also excited anew Nero's suspicions about Faustus Sulla, now in exile in Marseilles, and Rubellius Plautus in Asia, pointing out that the former enjoyed physical proximity to the legions on the Rhine, whilst the latter was close to the armies of Domitius Corbulo, Nero's commander in the East.[63] Hints of possible armed insurrection prompted Nero to make a move: the executions of both men were ordered, and their heads brought to the Emperor. Without reporting their deaths, Nero advised the Senate of the dangers that both Sulla and Rubellius Plautus continued to pose; ironically, senators voted that both men, although already dead, should be removed from their order!

The Emperor was now sufficiently emboldened to make the move that was the most important to him – the removal of his wife, Octavia, and marriage to Poppaea Sabina, who was evidently pressing Nero to facilitate this. Once again, Nero found himself under pressure from a strong-willed woman. Nobody will have been much surprised at Nero's desire to divorce Octavia, since she had borne him no heir and, in any case, he never appears to have had any affection for her. However, whilst divorce in Rome was common enough and, in this case, Nero might be considered to have had acceptable grounds for it, there remained the fact that Octavia was Claudius' daughter and, as Burrus had consistently maintained, this provided the principal feature of the legitimacy of Nero's succession. Indeed, Burrus is on record[64] as having said, whenever Nero raised the matter with him, 'Give her back her dowry' – meaning, of course, the Roman Empire. It should be noted that not only did the death of Burrus make the divorce from Octavia less fraught, but so, too, Tigellinus' persuasion of Nero to put Sulla and Rubellius Plautus to death beforehand effectively removed any potential anti-Neronian rallying-points.

Twelve days after his divorce, Nero married Poppaea Sabina; it was probably her apprehension that caused Nero very quickly to remove from Octavia Burrus' house and Plautus' estates, that had recently been granted to her, and to banish her under armed guard to Campania. This led to protests[65] and to the popular overturning in Rome of images of Poppaea and their replacement by those of Octavia. According to Tacitus,[66] Poppaea's anger and fear forced Nero into sterner action: he alleged that Octavia had been having an adulterous affair with Anicetus, the Prefect of the fleet at Misenum and the murderer of Agrippina; Anicetus connived at this untruth to provide Nero with the justification for his actions against Octavia. Nero stiffened the terms of her banishment by sending her to the barren island of Pandateria, where she was executed on 9 June, AD 62 – ironically, six years to the day before Nero's own death; her head was paraded before Poppaea. People pitied Octavia's fate, recalling that of the Elder Agrippina under Tiberius,[67] but there were no further disturbances. The anonymous play, *Octavia*, often wrongly attributed to the pen of Seneca, but which seems to have been published shortly after Nero's death as part of the posthumous demonisation of the late Emperor during the Flavian period, provides a bitter attack on Nero's failings and, in its 'canonisation' of Octavia, refers to Poppaea as the Emperor's 'haughty mistress'.[68]

Thus, Nero had freed himself from his mother, his wife and his advisors – not to mention those whom he considered to be his rivals for power. He had survived, to all intents and purposes unscathed. However Tacitus' closure of *Annals* 14,[69] with its forward-looking allusion to the conspiracy of Gaius Calpurnius Piso in AD 65, indicates that the last of the Julio-Claudians was yet to 'reap the whirlwind'.

Chapter Six

Nero and the Empire

One of the criteria by which a Roman Emperor may be judged lies in the quality of the appointments that he made to senior posts, especially those that carried with them a military responsibility and the *de facto* command of legions. Until his later years, at least, Nero's appointments were generally sound – men such as Gaius Suetonius Paullinus (Britain) and Gnaeus Domitius Corbulo (the East). In his last few years, however, the Emperor appears to have preferred in senior military commands men who may not necessarily have been less efficient, but whose social status, it was evidently hoped, would rein in their political ambitions.[1]

At a more junior level, too, he had shown himself to be prepared, as were other Emperors, to fast-track promising candidates into jobs for which, presumably, they were regarded as especially suited. For example, there are cases in Nero's reign where men approaching the praetorship were permitted to omit that office in order to make them rapidly available for the important military post of legionary commander (*legatus legionis*).[2] Contexts are not lacking in Nero's reign in which such promotions could have been valuable.

Under Augustus, the provinces of the Roman Empire were basically of two types – the imperial provinces and the so-called public (or senatorial) provinces. The Emperor was legally the governor of the former group, although he delegated his authority to senior senators (entitled *Legati Augusti Propraetore*) who were chosen by him for their loyalty and reliability.[3] The public provinces were governed by *proconsuls* who were chosen by lot from suitably-qualified former magistrates (ex-consuls and ex-praetors). Most of Rome's military forces were disposed in the imperial provinces,[4] in this way emphasising their direct connection with the Emperor as their commander-in-chief (*imperator*). By the close of Nero's reign, the principal imperial provinces were those along the Danube and Rhine rivers (Dalmatia, Moesia and Pannonia, and Upper and Lower Germany), the 'Three Gauls' (Belgica, Aquitania and Lugdunensis), Britain, Spain (Tarraconensis and Lusitania), Syria and Judaea. The chief public provinces were Asia, Africa (the only such province containing legionary troops), Macedonia/Achaea, Crete/Cyrenaica, Bithynia/Pontus, Sicily, Spain (Baetica) and Gaul (Narbonensis) (Figure 6.1).

The only major exception to this distribution was the former kingdom of Egypt: following the deaths in 30 BC of Marcus Antonius and Cleopatra (Egypt's last monarch), Augustus declared the territory to be his own personal property – a reflection of its material and agricultural prosperity. It was governed for the Emperor by a *praefectus* of equestrian standing, an appointment that constituted the pinnacle of the equestrian career-structure. Nobody was permitted to enter Egypt without the Emperor's expressed permission and, as we have seen, Tacitus records[5] Tiberius' rebuke to Germanicus Caesar for overlooking this Augustan convention. Augustus undertook building-work in the territory, including (in 15 BC) the temple at Dendur (Tutzis in Nubia), that was dedicated to the goddess, Isis of Philae, along with an enclosure-wall and wharf.[6]

From the points of view of both the military security of western Europe and the Emperor's own political security, the most sensitive of the military spheres were the areas on either side of the rivers Danube and Rhine. These were eventually, in the later-first and early-second centuries, to form a continuous European frontier, consisting of the *limes Raeticus* and the *limes Germanicus.*

The tribes of Gaul and Germany had long been objects of interest, even of fear, amongst Romans. In the late-second century BC, two of them, the Cimbri and the Teutones from northern Germany, had swept south through Gaul and had even penetrated northern Italy. For a time, it was as if Rome was about to experience a repeat of the legendary Gallic invasion of 390 BC,[7] that was to remain deeply embedded in the Roman memory for generations. Successive Roman commanders had lacked the competence

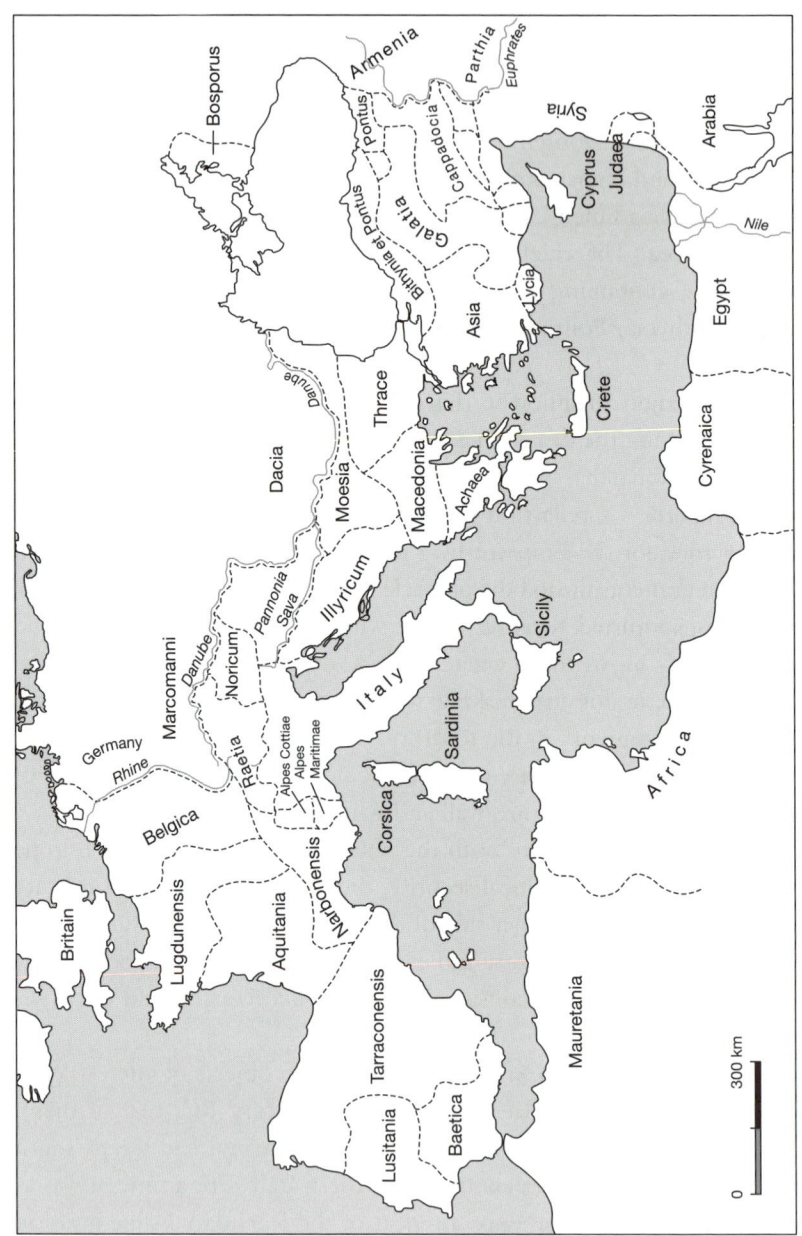

Figure 6.1 Map of the Roman Empire in the mid-first century AD. Author's own.

or the will to deal with these incursions until, in 104 BC, Gaius Marius, employing his reformed army-structure and carrying his reputation for winning where others could not, effectively saved Italy – for the time being, at least.[8]

The reason for these and other later tribal movements in central Europe was generally land-shortage caused by the gradual encroachment westwards of people whose homelands were much further to the east. In the mid-first century BC, Julius Caesar was sent to Gaul to put a brake on such movements. He, more far-sighted than many of his contemporaries, realised that a longer-term solution was dependent upon the organisation of people up to the river Rhine, at least, and in time probably beyond. The south of Gaul (Gallia Transalpina (Narbonensis); modern Provence) had been a Roman province since the 120s BC, but Caesar added three further Gallic provinces – Lugdunensis, Aquitania and Belgica – that extended Roman territory up to the Rhine.

The Emperor, Augustus, sought a solution on a wider front, and attempted to incorporate territory as far east as the river Elbe. However, almost continuous campaigning under such generals as Marcus Agrippa, Nero Claudius Drusus (Nero's great-grandfather) and the future Emperor, Tiberius (Nero's great-uncle) failed to achieve Augustus' objective. Indeed, all was brought to a shattering halt when, in AD 9, Publius Quinctilius Varus lost three legions (XVII, XVIII and XIX) in the treacherous forests and marshes of the Teutoburgerwald.[9] This defeat was one of the worst to have been suffered by a Roman army, and it was made worse (and more worrying) by the fact that its architect, Arminius (chief of the tribe of the Cherusci), was a German who had been regarded as Romanised, and thus safe and trustworthy.

The disaster had a terrible effect upon Augustus,[10] who seems to have decided that, as a result, the Roman frontier would be based upon the Rhine; territory on the west bank was formed not into provinces, but into military districts (Germania Superior in the south, and Germania Inferior in the north)[11]. Eight legions were disposed along the Rhine under Augustus and Tiberius (at Xanten, Neuss, Cologne and Bonn in Germania Inferior, and at Mainz (double fortress), Strasbourg and Windisch in Germania Superior). From the latter years of Augustus' reign military activity was scaled down, although Nero's grandfather, Germanicus Caesar, took expeditions across the Rhine, officially for punitive purposes, but perhaps in the hope of reviving Augustus' dream of reaching the Elbe.[12] These expeditions were finally called off by Tiberius in AD 16,[13] who regarded them as too costly in terms of risk, money and manpower for the small results that were being achieved. Indeed, as if to emphasise the propriety of the Emperor's judgement, it should be recalled that Germanicus' army had, in AD 15, very nearly become embroiled in a disaster similar to that which had destroyed Varus six years previously.[14]

It is hardly surprising that Romans were sensitive to the dangers posed by the German tribes, some of whom were to create further difficulties in the Gallo-German War that broke out soon after Nero's death. The Roman sensitivity inspired a considerable literature on the matter in antiquity. One of Germanicus' officers, Albinovanus Pedo, wrote an epic poem on Germanicus' campaigning, a short extract from which, dealing with the storm recounted by Tacitus, has been preserved by the Elder Seneca;[15] in the reign of Vespasian (AD 69–79), the Elder Pliny published his *German Wars*, which were to constitute a major source for all subsequent writers, whilst, in AD 98, Tacitus published his *Germania*, a treatise on the German tribes.[16] Such writings seem to have carried the implicit warning that the tribes to the east of the Rhine were not to be trusted, together with some from the west, also. Romanisation was attempted in the Julio-Claudian period by enrolling tribal groups as auxiliary units of the Roman army, although the events of AD 68–70 in the region showed that, in the short term at least, such a policy had met with only limited success.[17]

During the early part of Nero's reign, a plan to complete a flood-protection embankment on the Rhine started by Nero's great-grandfather, Nero Drusus, led to disputes between Roman officials[18] in the German military districts and in neighbouring Gallia Belgica. Further, there was some trouble amongst the tribes of the east bank, in which the Frisii took over land allocated for Roman veteran-settlement – presumably because of land-shortage – but it was prevented from getting out-of-hand by effective sabre-rattling on the part of local Roman commanders and (probably) by the Germans' habitual inability to co-operate with each other.[19] Nonetheless, Seneca, whose brother-in-law (or possibly father-in-law), Pompeius Paulinus, was *legatus* of Germania Inferior at this time, was moved to write about the martial prowess and ferocious toughness of the German tribes.[20] Throughout the latter years of the Julio-Claudian period, a programme of stabilisation was pursued, with the rebuilding of the legionary fortresses in stone, and the development of settlements (*vici*) outside the forts and fortresses.[21] There was also a slight reduction in the overall size of the Rhine-garrison in Nero's later years, due presumably to the extra requirements necessitated by the hostilities with the Parthians and Jews. The governors for Nero's last eight years were the brothers, Scribonius Proculus (Superior) and Scribonius Rufus (Inferior), men of aristocratic background, who were, in AD 67, invited by Nero to commit suicide, presumably on suspicion of involvement in the plot of AD 66.[22]

For their part, the Danube lands were not yet providing the Roman government with the problems that would become acute later in the first century. There were six legions in the Danube provinces, and there were already hints of the tribal turmoil on the north bank amongst the Daci, Roxolani, Sarmatae and Iazyges. One governor of Moesia, Tiberius Plautius Silvanus Aelianus,[23] who had received the 'triumphal insignia' in Claudius' reign for his services in Britain as a member of the Emperor's entourage, is on record as having allowed 100,000 tribesmen to cross the Danube, pay homage to Rome and settle on the Roman side of the river. This was intended to defuse the pressure on land that must have been creating the instability; it was necessary, too, because of the loss from the area of legions, that were transferred to fight in the Eastern war. The problems of this area were to come to the fore in the Flavian period, and Plautius Silvanus was to receive a second consulship from Vespasian in AD 74, perhaps in recognition of his earlier work on the Danube, and perhaps too as a way, on Vespasian's part, of underlining the importance of a region that he regarded as having been neglected under Nero. It is perhaps significant, in any estimate of the region's contemporary status, that no Roman official from the Danube provinces was evidently regarded as a credible candidate for power during the disturbances of AD 68–9. The honour to Plautius Silvanus may provide a further indication[24] that Vespasian looked back to Claudius' reign for inspiration, regarding Nero's as something of an aberration to be allowed to slip into oblivion.

In the West, the most active theatre of operations was in Britain;[25] the conquest and consolidation were proceeding smoothly enough during the AD 50s, and it is likely that, in many parts,[26] the local tribes were welcoming the social and economic opportunities that the presence of well-paid Roman troops offered. In the south of Britain, in particular, urban and rural development were proceeding; in the north, too, Cartimandua, the leader of the tribe of the Brigantes whose territory still lay outside the province, was evidently content to maintain good relations with Rome. Her husband, Venutius, however, seems to have had reservations about a pact with Rome and to have become more of a nuisance; it is possible that Cartimandua's refusal of sanctuary to Caratacus, the leader of Rome's enemies in Britain, was a step too far for Venutius.[27] As a consequence, Roman military intervention was required during the AD 50s and AD 60s to keep the neutrality of the Brigantes intact.[28] Indeed, the recent discovery at Silsden (in Yorkshire) of a hoard of British gold coins, mainly of the Catuvellaunian leader, Cunobelinus, may point to the pressure that was exerted by Catuvellaunian warlords on Cartimandua in an effort to persuade her to set aside her treaty with Rome.[29]

It was clearly not Nero's policy at this stage to advance the conquest of Britain further in a northerly direction; in the event, he had two problems in the province that appear to have become interconnected. Initially, the chief of these problems was represented by the Druids of north Wales, and of Anglesey, in particular. Just as Watling Street (the 'Roman A5') provided a route of penetration for the Roman army from its chief base at Wroxeter, so the same route, but viewed in reverse, gave the Druids a line of infiltration into the province, that evidently went back to the pre-Roman past. In this way, just as Druids had probably been able, at the time of the conquest in AD 43, to radicalise young tribal leaders in the south-east, such as Caratacus, so the same influence was perhaps able to be brought to bear in the troubles that emanated in the AD 50s and beyond from discontent amongst the Iceni and the Trinovantes of East Anglia and Essex.

In addition, a particular problem arose out of the arrangements that had been made at the time of the conquest for the governing of Icenian territory: Claudius, who favoured the use of client-kings, had recognised Prasutagus as the pro-Roman ruler of the Iceni. However, as this was evidently a personal arrangement between Claudius and Prasutagus, it was never likely that it would be allowed to continue after their deaths. Claudius, of course, had already died in AD 54; thus, when Prasutagus died in AD 59, even though he had taken the common precaution of including Nero amongst the beneficiaries named in his will, the remainder of the will was crudely set aside, and the Roman financial officer (*procurator Augusti*), Decianus Catus,[30] moved in to dispossess Prasutagus' widow, Boudica, and her daughters of their inheritance.[31] No attempt was made to do this with any dignity or consideration: the women were brutally maltreated, and the tribe, joined by the Trinovantes who had their own complaints against Roman officials over the way in which land had been confiscated for the establishment of the veteran-*colonia* at Camulodunum (Colchester),[32] rose in revolt. Further, many of those Britons who had accepted the Roman presence may have felt unsettled by rumours that Nero might decide to evacuate Britain. Suetonius[33] says, without providing a date or a context, that the Emperor contemplated this course of action, and such a rumour may well have prompted Roman financiers, such as Seneca, who had lent considerable sums of money[34] to Britons who wished to buy into Roman culture, to consider calling in those loans. However, whilst Dio clearly links the recall of loans to the outbreak of Boudica's rebellion, Suetonius' failure to provide a date for the rumour of Nero's proposed evacuation of the province leaves it uncertain whether the rumour and the recall of loans should be placed before, during or after the rebellion.

Boudica's moment was well chosen, and may point to collusion between her and the Druids: the provincial governor, Gaius Suetonius Paullinus, himself a distinguished senator and military leader, was engaged at full stretch in an attempt finally to bring the Druids of north-west Wales to heel. The Icenian queen's progress was electrifying: according to Tacitus,[35] some 70,000 people were killed in the ransacking of Colchester, St Albans and London; Colchester was attacked with especial venom, and the imperial cult centre there destroyed as a symbol of the alien domination.[36] An altar to *Victoria* was smashed down, and a bronze head of the Emperor, Claudius, that had evidently been wrenched from a statue or bust, was thrown into the river Alde in Suffolk, presumably as an offering to a local deity.[37] In the course of Boudica's progress, legion IX *Hispana*, that was under the command of the future provincial governor, Quintus Petillius Cerialis, was cut to pieces. However, once Paullinus reached the scene with reinforcements, the issue did not remain in doubt for long, and the rebellion was put down.

Not surprisingly, on the Roman side recriminations soon began as to who was to blame for the disaster. The *procurator*, whose share in the blame was obvious and considerable, had fled the province, to be replaced by Gaius Julius Alpinus Classicianus, a mature man of Treveran origin, who was clearly fitted to soothing bruised sensibilities within the province.[38] Inevitably, questions were asked as to whether Paullinus should have committed so many of the province's troops to his campaigns in the west. There must have been some prior intelligence over the situation as it had affected the Trinovantes, although the involvement of the Iceni may have come as a surprise.[39] In all, the governor could have been viewed as an official who had failed to pay equal attention to the totality of his responsibilities; on the other hand, Petillius Cerialis, the commander of legion IX,[40] was to gain a deserved reputation for recklessness, and may have been culpable in the manner of his response to the crisis. It is evident, in any case, that the episode had created bad blood between members of the Roman hierarchy in the province.

Nero, at any rate, decided that the whole affair required an independent investigation, and sent a commissioner to Britain to conduct an enquiry. He gained few friends, however, by choosing for this delicate task Polyclitus, an ex-slave; senators could not be expected to see anything edifying in the presence of an ex-slave delving into their disputes;[41] nor, according to Tacitus, were the Britons impressed either. Before long, Suetonius Paullinus was replaced as governor by Publius Petronius Turpilianus, a relative of Britain's first Roman governor, Aulus Plautius.[42] This relationship was clearly expected to win the confidence of the Britons, whilst the fact that Petronius was one of the consuls of AD 61 demonstrates the Emperor's faith in his abilities. His orders and those of his successor, the elderly Trebellius Maximus,[43] were clearly to do nothing that could be interpreted as provocative, and so allow passions to cool.

Even so, disputes continued on the Roman side and, by the end of Nero's reign, we find Trebellius Maximus, the governor, in conflict with the commander of legion XX *Valeria-Victrix*, Marcus Roscius Coelius.[44] This became sufficiently serious by AD 69 for Trebellius Maximus, who may well have been in his late-60s or early-70s, to desert his post. In all, therefore, whilst we might say that Nero had been prepared to be flexible, even innovative, in his handling of Britain, this was not a happy period for the province.[45] Whilst it is unlikely that the orders to treat Boudica in such a harsh and undignified manner had emanated from Rome, the episode serves to highlight the dangers of policies that changed abruptly from one Emperor to another.

Although, as noted above, Suetonius does not provide a date for Nero's alleged consideration of the possibility of permanent evacuation of Britain, a point in the aftermath of Boudica's rebellion might seem a plausible suggestion; such behaviour by provincials might have been interpreted by this Emperor, who thrived on his subjects' expressions of gratitude for his beneficence, as signs of their ingratitude. On other occasions, a perception on the Emperor's part of such ingratitude might precipitate imperial tantrums; this was by no means the only occasion upon which Nero reacted (or threatened to react) impetuously and dramatically in such circumstances.[46] However, as on other occasions, Nero appears to have calmed down, and to have set in train the process of rebuilding after the destruction caused by Boudica.[47]

If Britain provided Rome with one of its most testing episodes during this period, affairs in the East highlighted the dangers of long-running unresolved problems. This is evidenced in serious downturns in Nero's reign in Rome's relations with both Parthia/Armenia and Judaea.

In essence, Rome's problems with Parthia went back to the 60s BC and Pompey's involvement of the Parthian king in his efforts to deal with the long-lived and troublesome King Mithridates of Pontus.[48] Since that time, there had been periodic increases of tension between Rome and Parthia, that hinged on the status of Parthia's northern neighbour, the kingdom of Armenia, that had been less than helpful during Rome's disputes with Mithridates. On two occasions – in 53 BC and 36 BC – fighting had broken out in which Roman armies had lost a number of their precious legionary emblems, the 'eagles'. These were eventually returned in the reign of Augustus (in 20 BC), following Roman initiatives that consisted of a combination of diplomacy and military threats.[49]

Thereafter, the sticking-point in this theatre turned on the question of whether the throne of Armenia should be filled by a Roman or a Parthian nominee. Both parties were naturally sensitive on the matter, as Pompey's settlement of the East in the late-60s BC had relied on creating a Rome-orientated Asia Minor by turning the coastal regions into full provinces and the lands of the interior into pro-Roman monarchies (client-kingdoms). The settlement also, of course, had the effect of bringing Roman and pro-Roman territory in the region up to the western borders of the Parthian kingdom. Hence, the significance of, and sensitivity over, the status and political inclination of Armenia.

Throughout the remainder of the reign of Augustus, Rome and Parthia managed to keep the peace; however, early in Tiberius' reign, the agreement faltered[50] and the Emperor sent Germanicus Caesar, Nero's grandfather, to restore the situation. This he did by installing Zeno (Artaxias) on the Armenian throne – a solution that maintained the peace until the latter's death in AD 32. In the vacuum left by this, however, the Parthian king,

Artabanus III, threatened to take over Armenia and 'drive the Romans out of Asia Minor'.[51] He was dissuaded by the prompt action of Tiberius in sending out as governor of the province of Syria the energetic Lucius Vitellius,[52] who was later to become a powerful and influential courtier under Caligula and Claudius and a supporter of the cause of Agrippina and Nero. Generally, the difficulties arose because kings of Armenia chosen by Rome tended to be too Romanised for local taste, whilst those chosen by Parthia were often too pro-Parthian to satisfy Rome. As we shall see, Nero should take at least some credit for eventually installing a king who was acceptable to both parties.

Once again, in the latter years of Claudius' reign,[53] the area fell into political turmoil: in AD 47, at the request of the Parthians, Claudius sent Meherdates to become their king; however, lacking tangible Roman support, Meherdates soon fell and the area returned to feuding. He was replaced by Vologaeses who made his intentions clear by installing one of his brothers as king of Media and, in AD 52, set out to make the other, Tiridates, king of Armenia. Taking advantage of the opportunity provided by the fall of the current king of Armenia (Mithridates), Tiridates was imposed upon the Armenians by armed Parthian intervention and without any consultation of Rome. This contravened the old agreement between Rome and Parthia and had the effect of joining Armenia firmly to the Parthian Empire. Clearly, this state of affairs could not be tolerated by Rome.

The chief Roman province in the area was Syria, in which four legions were based; its governor was regarded as the military commander of Rome's Eastern provinces and client-monarchies. At the opening of Nero's reign, there were no legions in any other eastern territories. This, then, was the disturbed and dangerous situation that greeted Nero on his accession in AD 54. Within a very short time, Nero's government, obviously eager to make a powerful and effective impact in the region, sent Gnaeus Domitius Corbulo,[54] the most impressive general of the day, to take over Cappadocia and Galatia to which three of Syria's legions were transferred. His brief was simply to restore the integrity of Armenia as an independent state. To ensure that the military strength and balance of the area was not compromised, Syria's full garrison was restored by transfers from other provinces. There was evidently no question of altering the Empire's overall military balance by raising new legions; thus, risks had to be entertained in the other theatres from which transferred legions had been drawn.

The appointment of Corbulo,[55] whom Tacitus notes as a stern and old-fashioned disciplinarian, provides a good illustration of the fact that, in its early days, at least, Nero's government had no qualms about placing strong men of high profile in military commands.[56] In this job, however, Corbulo was clearly under orders to give diplomacy a chance: for, in AD 58, he tried, albeit unsuccessfully, to persuade both Vologaeses and Tiridates that Rome would accept the position of Tiridates in Armenia provided that both men submitted a formal petition for Nero's agreement. When this proposition was rejected, Corbulo was left with no alternative but to remove Tiridates from Armenia, installing the pro-Roman Tigranes in his place.

In the meantime, Corbulo was made governor of Syria, and he requested that Armenia be made a separate command. According to Tacitus,[57] much that followed was diplomatic posturing, as neither Corbulo nor Vologaeses wished to go to war over the matter. In the course of this, Tigranes, who was proving unpopular in Armenia because of his Romanised ways, was dropped by Rome; in return for this, Vologaeses accepted the possibility of Corbulo's original proposal by agreeing to enter into negotiations for Roman recognition of Tiridates as king of Armenia.

For reasons that are not now fully understood, these negotiations faltered, and Roman policy changed again: in AD 62, Lucius Caesennius Paetus, who had been consul in the previous year, was sent to Cappadocia, claiming that his brief was to bring Armenia to the status of a Roman province.[58] Even so, Paetus, who had no great military reputation, does not appear to have set out to provoke the Parthians into warfare; further, although the blame for the resumption of hostilities lay with the Parthians, they do not appear to have wanted the catastrophic defeat of the Roman army that they achieved at Rhandeia, a defeat that was principally due to Paetus' incompetence. The defeat, in fact, led to a resumption of negotiations in which the Parthians agreed to petition for Roman acceptance of Tiridates' status, but still refused to countenance the proposition that he should himself go to Rome and receive his kingly diadem personally from Nero.

This irritation led to a further adjustment of Roman policy: Corbulo[59] was to be given an overriding Eastern command (*maius imperium*) of the sort that, under previous Julio-Claudian Emperors, had been enjoyed only by members of the imperial family. The message conveyed by this was clearly that the Roman intention now was, indeed, the reduction of Armenia to provincial status; at this, Vologaeses and Tiridates agreed that the latter should put his diadem aside, to resume it only from Nero's hands in Rome.

The whole episode had lasted for the best part of a decade; in the end, the Parthians had effectively agreed to what had been offered by Corbulo at the outset. To achieve this, however, Nero's government had not stuck stubbornly to an immutable policy; flexibility and some sensitivity to local feeling had been shown. Despite the length of time that had been taken, Rome had not seriously lost face; even the defeat at Rhandeia could be conveniently blamed on Paetus' incompetence. Tacitus entertained certain misgivings about Corbulo's arrogance and his occasional failure to cooperate with colleagues;[60] yet, in Corbulo, Nero had made a strong appointment whom he continued to support. For his part, Corbulo probably had misgivings over the appointment of Caesennius Paetus, though he will have realised that Paetus' obvious failings brought more power to his own image. Corbulo adhered – perhaps rather pompously on one occasion[61] – to the policy of diplomacy backed by the threat of armed force, a reapplication of the formula that had first been used by Augustus and Tiberius in 20 BC to retrieve the legionary 'eagles' that had been lost with Marcus Crassus at Carrhae in 53 BC and Decidius Saxa in 36 BC. Nero's policy, then, had achieved the desired result, and it is evident, from their eventual compliance, that Nero and Corbulo had talked a language that was understood by Vologaeses and Tiridates. Besides the desired result, that was by any standards a stunning achievement, Nero had also managed to demonstrate that there was amongst the Parthians no real appetite for all-out war with Rome.

The Neronian solution lasted, until it was effectively put aside for no very good reason by Trajan half-a-century later; its strength was ably demonstrated by the fact that it was possible between AD 67 and AD 70 to divert substantial numbers of troops from the legionary garrison of Syria to the problems of Judaea, to conduct rearrangements amongst the client-kingdoms in the area and, in the event, to ride out the disruptive forces that both precipitated and followed upon Nero's fall in AD 68. Not only this, but after Rome's civil war, Vespasian was able with impunity to carry out far-reaching reorganisation in Asia Minor.[62] The significance of Nero's peace, therefore, should not be lightly dismissed.

Events around the Empire over the next half century were to put the stability of Nero's arrangements to the test, and they measured up to that test. Further, the effort expended by Nero and his very persistence in securing stability in the East may well have dissuaded the Parthians from further military and political adventurism. In its turn, this will have greatly helped the process of Romanisation in the East, a policy that was to become a major preoccupation of another philhellenic Emperor, Hadrian. Indeed, perhaps Nero, like Hadrian, appreciated that Rome had two rivals to fear for dominance in the eastern half of the Empire – the Parthian Empire and the Jewish people; both Emperors tried, through the Greek provinces and the Hellenistic kingdoms, to offer an alternative that was firmly based in the Classical world of the Mediterranean.

Nero, then, had achieved peace across the world, and unsurprisingly lost no time in proclaiming the fact – from coin-issues to triumphal monuments on the Capitoline Hill.[63] In AD 66, the coinage in Rome duly proclaimed the message in an imaginative way typical of Nero – by showing the temple of Janus in Rome with its doors shut, a traditional symbol of peace across the world. If anyone missed that message, then the coin's reverse legend made it thoroughly clear: world-peace had been achieved. It was totally characteristic of Nero that he should try to extract a full measure of favourable publicity for what he had achieved – and at a time, as we shall see,[64] when his image was in need of a boost. It is possible that the *Ara Pacis* coin-issue of AD 64,[65] recalling the altar erected by Augustus was also intended to refer to success in the East, unless, at a sensitive time, a more general reassurance was intended.

Totally characteristic, too, was this Emperor's method of maximising the impression that he made. In an extremely theatrical[66] – and excessively costly – round of ceremonial, Tiridates duly came to Rome; this included, according to Dio, gladiatorial games put on in Tiridates' honour in the amphitheatre at Puteoli.[67] He was accompanied by Parthian and Roman nobility, that included Corbulo's son-in-law, Annius Vinicianus, to receive personally from Nero's hands the kingly diadem that he had laid aside at the time that agreement with Rome had been reached. The opening of Tiridates' address is preserved for us by Dio Cassius: 'Master, I am the descendant of Arsaces, brother of the kings Vologaeses and Pacorus, and your slave. I have come to you, my god, to prostrate myself before you, as I do before Mithras'.[68]

This designation is of interest, as it well accords with forms of address, such as 'The New Apollo' and 'The New Sun', that were readily applied to Nero in the eastern portion of the Empire; further, such designations also raise the question of whether or not Nero, by this stage of his reign, entertained a real desire for self-deification,[69] or whether he simply saw it as an enhancement of his image. A further point of interest relating to the Mithraic reference is the fact that, at the conclusion of the Pisonian conspiracy in the previous year, especial thanks had been offered by the Senate to Sol (the Sun-god), both because the failed assassination attempt was to have taken place near to the temple of Sol and because the god was thought to have shed light on the conspiracy leading to its detection.[70] After the 'coronation', Nero is said to have sung in public to the accompaniment of the lyre and to have taken part in a chariot-race. According to Dio Cassius,[71] Tiridates was disgusted at the way in which Nero made such a spectacle of himself, and expressed surprise that Corbulo could serve such a master. In this, however, Dio may have been intending to point a moral equally applicable to his own 'third-century agenda'.

The day on which Tiridates received his diadem in Rome was, for Nero, a 'golden day'; the tag evidently derived from the almost-complete covering of gold that the Emperor gave to the Theatre of Pompey – just for the one day.[72] Champlin notes the dazzling effect of the reflections of the sun as its rays hit all this gold. It is also important to observe that the presence of the shining sun was, for Nero, a vital ingredient of the day.[73] Indeed, Suetonius notes that the ceremony with Tiridates had been set for an earlier day, but had been postponed at the last minute because the sky was cloudy. The equation of gold with the light of the sun needs no emphasis, and the gold reflected by the sun represented the equation of Nero with Helios-Apollo.

Tiridates' salutation of the Emperor as Mithras was clearly no accident. Of course, Nero's obsession with gold was not restricted to the events of the 'golden day'; all around the city, all of the time, work on the 'Golden House' (*Domus Aurea*) proceeded. It is little wonder that bystanders, such as Seneca, were depressed to see how far Nero had departed from the principles enunciated in *On Clemency*, that had been published at the beginning of the reign, just over ten years previously.[74]

An immediate dividend of peace with Parthia was, as we have seen, Rome's ability in the last years of Nero's reign to turn its attention to developing problems in Judaea, that erupted into open warfare in AD 67. The contemporary problems were not new, and whilst they were not *caused* by any specific failing in the quality of the province's government in Nero's reign, their timing on this occasion may have been.

Contrary to what is sometimes alleged, the Romans were not specifically anti-Semitic; indeed, appreciating some Jewish sensibilities, Rome excused the Jewish people from Emperor-worship and from service in the Roman army. Most anti-Jewish activity in the Empire was actually the result of feuding between Greeks and the Jews of the Diaspora. As at Alexandria in the reign of Caligula,[75] this arose principally out of jealousy on the part of the Greek community that the Jews enjoyed more privileges than they did. Although Caligula clearly did not have the patience to introduce effective solutions to the difficulties, a letter of Claudius (dated 10 November, AD 41) survives which firmly laid out the political realities to both communities.[76]

Many Jews, however, looked not just to independence from Rome, but to domination of the world by themselves, a fact that was later to bring them into disastrous conflict with the Emperor, Hadrian, as he sought to bring greater stability to a Romanised East. In his description of the Jewish people, Flavius Josephus[77] divides them into three groups – the Sadducees, the Pharisees and the Essenes. The latter were a separatist group that formed an ascetic monastic community and, in response to apocalyptic visions, retreated into the wilderness of Judaea, especially in the region of Galilee.

Judaea had been a province under a *procurator* of equestrian status since the time of Augustus, with the exception of a brief return, between AD 41 and AD 44, to a client-monarchy under Claudius' friend, Herod Agrippa. The *procuratores* tended to work through the Sadducees, although feuding within this group made them rather ineffective. For their part, the Pharisees were more concerned with their desired destiny of a Jewish state, particularly the most extreme of their group, the Zealots, whom Josephus regarded as robbers and bandits,[78] who would bring destruction upon their own people. The Dead Sea Scrolls, which many regard as a reflection of Essene opinion, offer us some insight into the forces that lay behind their hatred of Rome. Independence from Rome was the principal hope that the Jewish people entertained of their Messiah; one of the Dead Sea Scrolls, *The War of the Sons of Light Against the Sons of Darkness*, envisaged a final war against the Roman occupiers, in which it was ordained by God that the Romans would be defeated.[79]

It is likely, therefore, that the troubles that came to a head late in Nero's reign had more to do with what might be called 'the philosophy of Judaism' than with individual instances of bad government on the Roman side. Nevertheless, despite the fact that, in their own eyes at least, the Romans had tried hard to reach compromises through concessions to Jewish principles, there had been unfortunate episodes in the recent past. Caligula's decision to have his statue erected in the Temple at Jerusalem had caused immense anger until it was rescinded, and must have left a sour legacy in relations.[80] Tacitus alleges[81] that Antonius Felix, the *procurator* between AD 52 and AD 60, had behaved high-handedly, although it may be that the historian's attitude had more to do with the fact that Antonius Felix was the brother of Claudius' influential and much-feared freedman, Pallas.

However, the immediate cause of the trouble in AD 66 seems to have been the decision of the current *procurator*, Gessius Florus, to defile the Temple sanctuary by taking from the Treasury money that was 'due to Caesar'.[82] It has to be said that Gessius Florus was not one of Nero's better appointments; indeed, he seems to have owed his position principally to the fact that his wife was a friend of Poppaea Sabina, who was regarded by some as sympathetic towards Judaism. However, as Griffin points out, the description used of her by Josephus seems to indicate a respect for religion in general rather than for one specific cult.[83] It is also worth noting, in respect of this appointment, that, given the level of hostility between Greeks and Jews in the Diaspora, it was probably not sensitive to appoint as *procurator* of Judaea a man who was himself Greek and who had a Greek wife.

Rioting broke out in Jerusalem, and a fortress at Masada[84] ('Mountain Fortress') was taken and its garrison annihilated; simultaneously with this, there were disturbances amongst the Jews of the Dispersion, causing the Prefect of Egypt, Tiberius Julius Alexander, to use legionary troops to quell rioting in Alexandria. The region was on the brink of war; but that war became inevitable when Cestius Gallus,[85] the elderly governor of Syria, brought into Judaea troops lent to him by Corbulo, who had remained Rome's Eastern supremo; Cestius Gallus was attacked and heavily defeated; he died in the winter of AD 66–7.

Corbulo may, indeed, have been expecting an extension to his special position in the East to enable him to take command in dealing with the Jewish revolt. Instead, in AD 67, he was summoned to attend upon Nero, who was in Greece for the literary festivals and, along with the Scribonius brothers who were *legati* in the two Germanies, was 'invited' by the Emperor to commit suicide.[86] Nero, as we shall see, was probably, by that stage, hypersensitive to criticism and suspicious of disloyalty following the conspiracies against him in AD 65 and AD 66; it appears that Corbulo's son-in-law, Annius Vinicianus, was involved in the latter of these, leading Nero to the conclusion, perhaps correctly, that Corbulo and senior army commanders had turned against him.

The new Judaean command was given to Titus Flavius Vespasianus (the future Emperor, Vespasian); Vespasian was of Italian stock, and a first-generation senator; his father was an Italian tax-collector.[87] Vespasian's career had had its blemishes: as an aedile, he had been given a salutary lesson by Caligula for failing to keep the streets of Rome clean;[88] later, whilst accompanying Nero on his tour of Greece in AD 67, he had fallen asleep during one of the Emperor's performances.[89] On the positive side, he had served well as a legionary commander during Claudius' invasion of Britain. It may be that we see in Vespasian's appointment another glimpse of Nero's growing reluctance in his later years to give important military commands to men of elevated social status. In his mood of the later-60s, Nero could readily imagine such men as potential rivals. It is worth noting that, after Vespasian became Emperor at the end of AD 69, there were those who clearly felt that he was not fully up to the job, and needed advice.[90]

Another key command was the appointment of Licinius Mucianus to succeed Cestius Gallus as governor of Syria. Mucianus, too, had rather unimpressive social credentials, and Nero may have felt relief that Vespasian and Mucianus did not at this stage enjoy a cordial relationship. Indeed, Griffin has suggested that Mucianus, who had been a legionary commander under Corbulo, may have suspected Vespasian of poisoning the Emperor's mind against Corbulo.[91] In such circumstances, Nero may well have believed that the Jewish War and the mutual hostility of the governors of Judaea and Syria would provide him with a greater measure of political security.

With three legions, Vespasian worked his way systematically through Judaea and, by the summer of AD 68, he was in a position to lay siege to Jerusalem. This was, however, interrupted by news of Nero's death, at which point Vespasian and Mucianus laid aside their personal hostilities, in order to consult about the political future of Rome and the Empire, and their places in it. They will have been anxious that the destiny of Rome appeared to lie entirely in the hands of the Western army groups and their commanders.

As a result, it was agreed that Vespasian should make a bid for power; to facilitate this, he handed over effective control of the siege of Jerusalem to his elder son, Titus. Jerusalem fell in AD 70, and the Temple was destroyed, presumably in an effort to break the heart of Jewish nationhood. The struggle, however, was continued by a small band of Zealots, who held out at three fortresses – including Masada – until AD 73, when they were finally defeated by the new governor of Judaea, Lucius Flavius Silva.[92] Beyond that, the funds that Jews had traditionally given to the Temple were transferred to *Jupiter Capitolinus* in Rome; other than that, the long-standing privileges enjoyed by the Jewish people remained in place. The Roman victory was celebrated in Rome, and contemporary scenes from those celebrations can still be seen on the Arch of Titus, that was erected at the southern end of the *Via Sacra*, the road leading towards the Roman Forum; spoils from the war were put towards the building of the Flavian Amphitheatre (Colosseum), a project which was intended to return to the people at least part of the land used by Nero for his *Domus Aurea*.[93]

As we have seen, after the conclusion of the agreement with Parthia and Armenia in AD 66, Nero ceremonially closed the gates of the Temple of Janus in Rome, signifying that the world was at peace. This peace, however, was interrupted not only by the disturbances that led to the Jewish War, but also by the preparations that Nero was beginning to make for a military expedition down the Danube and into the region of the Black Sea and beyond – the so-called 'Caspian Gates' project. From AD 66 onwards, Nero was moving and raising forces for this; troops were taken from the Rhine and from Illyricum; the latter, indeed, were still in the area when Vindex's rebellion broke out in AD 68.[94] Legion XIV *Gemina Martia Victrix*, together with its Batavian auxiliaries, was moved into the region from Britain.[95] In addition, Nero raised a special new legion in Italy – I *Italica*;[96] each of its soldiers was six feet in height, and it was proposed to nickname it 'the Phalanx of Alexander the Great'.[97]

What, then, might Nero have had in mind? It is difficult to achieve absolute certainty on this, because the expedition was superseded first by the Emperor's Greek tour of AD 67 and subsequently by Vindex's rebellion, and perhaps, in the event, by Nero's lack of natural interest in military matters. However, some suggestions may be made: the nickname given to the men of legion I *Italica* prompts the theory that it may have pleased the Emperor to project himself in the rôle of a successor to Alexander the Great,[98] operating in a region that had witnessed the Macedonian king, a monarch of learning and culture, perhaps thought to carry within him a spark of divinity and defending the Classical world. In this way, Nero might have enjoyed the idea that he was inheriting a mantle that had intrigued many Roman leaders in the past, including his grandfather, Germanicus Caesar.[99]

There may, however, be more down-to-earth explanations to hand: although Rome's problems with the tribes living on the north bank of the Danube did not come to a head until the reigns of Domitian and Trajan in the late-first and early-second centuries, there had already been clear signs of impending troubles. As we have seen,[100] the governor of Moesia, Tiberius Plautius Silvanus Aelianus, is on record as having had to resettle one hundred thousand Sarmatians on the south side of the Danube in *c*. AD 62. This was due to the westward and southward movement of populations away to the north and east in central Asia, that was bringing confusion to the lives of the Daci, Roxolani and Lazyges – Sarmatae – as well as to Rome as the imperial authority.

Nero was then possibly planning an expedition to the passes of the Caucasus mountains (Caspian Gates) in an effort to stop the latest invaders from the East, the Alani, a Sarmatian group, from encroaching further west. This objective, incidentally, would have been equally valuable to Parthia and Armenia, who had also suffered the effects of these population-movements.[101] The Alani appear for the first time in Latin literature as a threat in *c*. AD 64–5.[102] Tacitus, however, appears to suggest[103] that the object of these preparations was the tribe of the Albani, who had failed to support Rome during the recent dispute with Parthia; however, the scale of what Nero had in mind seems far too large to have been directed against this small tribe. As a consequence, it was suggested long ago that *Albani* should be emended to *Alani* in Tacitus' text.[104] Classical writers, such as the Elder Pliny and Ptolemy, seem to have been somewhat confused over the geography of the region, although it should be noted that Corbulo had reconnoitred and drawn up maps of the area.[105] In part, the problems of interpretation stem from the loss of the text of Tacitus' *Annals* at this point and from the consequent confusion over the nature of Nero's plans, that appear to have been directed to the passes through the Caucasus, giving access to the Alani.

Perhaps connected with all of this was the process of Romanising the Black Sea area; in the early- and mid-60s, the rulers of Pontus and Bosporus had ceded their kingdoms to the Romans who had then organised them as provinces.[106] The tribes around the Black Sea were thus kept under surveillance by Roman provinces, a legionary detachment and a permanent naval presence on that 'hitherto savage and unnavigable sea'.[107] Such activities, that had been in train over a longer period than the preparations for Nero's expedition also suggest the possibility of a growing Roman interest in the commercial potential of the region.

There is also the possibility that, in the later years of his reign, Nero was contemplating extending warfare into Ethiopia (effectively, modern Sudan). The Emperor was planning a visit to Egypt, but appears to have been deterred by what were seen as bad omens, but that may, in fact, have been anxieties concerning his health.[108] There were certainly some military preparations, although it remains unclear whether the true motive for these was the winning of cheap success, or whether they may have been concerned with the developing crisis in Judaea; alternatively, Nero may have been looking here, too, for possible commercial gains in the region. Yet another possible objective could conceivably have been centred on pure research – to discover the source of the Nile, and thus reflect glory onto the Emperor for the achievement.[109]

Although Nero seems never to have been much concerned to maintain contact with his troops, through his appointments and the policies that he required his commanders to follow, and the degree to which he evidently felt able to trust them, Nero's record as *imperator* is not unimpressive. What perhaps is more questionable, in some instances at least, is the quality of the provincial government, which in some cases precipitated the military crises.

In his opening address to the Senate,[110] Nero had guaranteed to the Senate control over its 'ancient functions', and had indicated that this included Italy and the public provinces (the so-called senatorial provinces). He himself would look after the armies, although, in fact, there is no sign that he ever visited his troops or, indeed, that he showed any real interest in them.[111] Suetonius even alleges[112] that Nero's financial difficulties left him unable to pay his soldiers and give the veterans their bonuses, although he provides no details of this. It may be that here, as elsewhere, the biographer was generalising from a specific incident. Nero's guarantee appears to suggest that the Emperor was promising to restrict his direct interventions to the imperial provinces. Evidence, however, certainly survives to show that Nero intervened in provinces of all types, as can be seen in his moves to curtail the activities of the tax-farmers.[113]

Nero succeeded an Emperor who had been concerned for the integration of the Roman Empire, and the policies required to achieve it, and we have already noted his rebuke to the Greeks and Jews of Alexandria for their divisive behaviour. Nevertheless, the establishment of *coloniae* and grants of Roman citizenship were not pursued uncritically. Rome and Italy remained at the heart of Claudius' thinking, and defending their integrity was the cornerstone of his policy; there was certainly no question of downgrading Italy – as happened later – in favour of provincial advancement. In particular, as surviving documents show,[114] citizenship was extended to those thought to have merited it, whilst those who did not show sufficient commitment were not so privileged.[115] As a consequence, most of Claudius' grants were in the West, although many from the East, too, must have attained it through military service. As he showed in his speech[116] on the admission in AD 48 of Aeduan Gauls to senatorial membership, Claudius believed that talent, whatever its origin, should be harnessed, and that those who had a contribution to make should be empowered to make it. Taking examples from history, he held that restrictive attitudes over the granting of such privileges were ultimately self-defeating; Claudius no doubt appreciated that a willing Empire would be easier and more economical to govern, with benefits accruing to all.

Not everyone in the Senate, however, agreed with what they regarded as a diminishing of what it meant to be Roman,[117] and Claudius met opposition to his proposal regarding the Aeduan Gauls. Perhaps, as a consequence, although Nero's government continued with the policies of enfranchisement and *colonia*-foundation, it was less open-handed and perhaps, as at Pompeii, tied to particular objectives. Even the Emperor's much-proclaimed Hellenism did not lead to major advances of this kind in the East – except perhaps in Greece itself, and even then these appear to have been largely tied to Nero's visit to Greece in AD 67.

Advances in the Romanisation of the West continued; wealthy aristocrats from Spain and Gaul could make an impact locally and, perhaps subsequently, on the wider imperial stage. We should not forget, for example, that Nero's two principal advisers in his earlier years, Seneca and Burrus, came respectively from Spain and Gaul. In Britain, archaeological evidence shows that, during Nero's reign, local people, particularly in the south, were being drawn into villa-ownership and aspects of urban life. Yet Romanisation needed to develop solidly and further before major advances for large numbers of people became a realistic prospect; many, although not necessarily hostile to Rome, were naturally reluctant to lay aside traditional ways. Thus, in the West, tribal loyalties remained important, as is shown in a positive way by the establishment of the *civitas*-system of selective local government, and in a more negative way during the Gallo-German uprising of AD 69–70. For easterners, traditional city-life remained a magnetic force.

The growth of wealth, therefore, was a key to Romanisation: the Roman army, with its requirements for supplies and services, was an important element in wealth-creation and thus Romanisation, as the money of indivual soldiers and whole units could purchase at local level much of what was required. As is dramatically shown by the writing-tablets from Vindolanda,[118] that date mostly to the turn of the first and second centuries AD, Roman soldiers and local people could start to build an economy and a culture that was Romano-British. Dio Cassius' observation[119] regarding the nature of Romanisation amongst the German tribes in the Augustan period has a clear relevance to Britain also.

We have noted already that, early on in Nero's reign, the government apparently conceived a plan that could effectively make more people wealthier through changes in the system of taxation, which would, in its turn, have freed up trade. After all, insufficient wealth was a major obstacle in the paths of those who wished to advance themselves in the Roman world. Although the proposal fell, perhaps seen as too radical by some, a measure of improvement could be effected by curbing the exactions of the Emperor's financial agents in the provinces (*procuratores Augusti*). Britain, as we have seen, provides a good example of this through the damaging effects of the poor behaviour of the *procurator* towards the tribe of the Iceni in AD 60, and Nero's determination subsequently to discover the root of the problems. Yet again, a little later, Tacitus notes[120] that Agricola, as governor, put a stop to certain, obviously lucrative, types of official corruption in the collection of the grain-levy. Thus, perhaps Nero's government saw the advantage of progress towards Romanisation that was slower, but ultimately more sound.

There was also a readiness on the government's part to come down hard on officials found guilty of extortion, although it has to be said that Nero's own behaviour in his later years over the acquisition of works of art to adorn the *Domus Aurea* and other buildings in Rome was little short of extortion itself. However, in the earlier part of the reign, where cases of extortion were proved, punishments could be severe, as in the case of

Cossutianus Capito in the province of Cilicia in AD 57: Capito was expelled from the Senate (although later reinstated through the influence of his father-in-law, Nero's confidant, Tigellinus).[121] Satisfaction at seeing the punishment of a malefactor, however, was one thing, but restitution to a province of its losses was quite another, particularly because it remained expensive for a province to bring a prosecution itself.[122] Nero also dealt with other forms of corruption, such as the taking of bribes for favours and the promotion of shows that led to heavy financial burdens on provincials.[123] He further required that provincial governors should give precedence to the hearing of cases brought against the 'farmers' of indirect taxes (*publicani*).[124] Also outlawed was the practice on the part of some provincial governors of covering themselves with favourable references from corrupt and oppressive local grandees.[125] Added to this, as we have seen in Britain in the aftermath of Boudica's rebellion, there was a greater readiness than had sometimes been shown in the past to enquire into the heart of problems.

Against this background, prosperity did grow: Josephus[126] refers to Gaul as 'flooding almost the entire world with its products'. In Ostia, we can see the international face of trade through the mosaics that characterise each of the offices in the 'Forum of the Corporations'. By AD 68, the province of Africa was sufficiently prosperous and important to Rome as a food-supplier to allow Lucius Clodius Macer, the commander of legion III *Augusta*, to pose a real danger to Italy by threatening to cut off grain-supplies.[127] Indeed, by the second and third centuries AD, north Africa was fast becoming one of the most prosperous areas of the Empire, as is shown by the magnificence of its surviving buildings.

In some senses, the tangible results of an increasing care for the provinces during the Julio-Claudian period can be seen in the years following Nero's reign; for example, in the AD 70s, of those senators whose origins are known 80 percent were of Italian origin and 20 percent provincial; by the early-second century, 65 percent were of Italian origin and 35 percent provincial. Of the known provincial senators, in Vespasian's reign 70 percent were from western European provinces and 30 percent from elsewhere. By Trajan's time, those with a western European background had fallen to 55 percent. Such figures, whilst based inevitably on incomplete information, nevertheless provide a general indication of trends.

Thus, the record of Nero's government in the Empire does not occasion the opprobrium attaching to some aspects of his behaviour at home; it is less clear, however, whether this state of affairs came about because of Nero, or because he was little interested in what went on in the provinces, but left this area of administration to advisers who had more of a vested interest. This may provide an explanation for the fact that most of our evidence for positive attitudes to the provinces derives from the early part of the reign, when Seneca and Burrus were more influential. However, the continued absence of clear signs of provincial discontent in the later years makes it likely that the lack of documentary evidence is due more to changing pre-occupations on the part of the historians than to any dramatic deterioration in the quality of provincial government.

It is worth noting, too, that before we dismiss totally Nero's reputation with his armies, we should remember that, when the Emperor's crisis came in AD 68, his armies were not straining at the leash to desert him. As we shall see, some provincial governors and army commanders had had enough of Nero's wayward conduct, but they did not find it easy to persuade their troops to follow them in a crusade against him. The army of Verginius Rufus, for example, marched to Vesontio (Besançon) to defeat Vindex and his Gauls in the name of Nero; for his part, Tacitus observes that Nero was, in the event, overcome more by rumours of desertion than by actual armed force.[128] In spite of everything, the rebellion against the last of the Julio-Claudians was in no obvious sense a popular movement.

Chapter Seven

The Imperial Builder

❧❧❧

One of the most frequently-quoted dying remarks of any Roman Emperor is Nero's *qualis artifex pereo* (usually translated as 'What an artist dies with me'); as we shall see,[1] Champlin has offered an alternative interpretation that relates specifically to Nero's attempts to prepare his own grave prior to his suicide in AD 68. Whilst this seems perfectly plausible, it does not alter the fact that the contribution of Nero's reign to the development of Roman architecture was considerable, and that a building, such as the 'Golden House' palace (*Domus Aurea*), so often held up to criticism and ridicule because of its extravagance, not only provides a valuable insight into Nero's mindset, but was also ground-breaking in structural terms.

Roman politicians down the ages – and especially since the second century BC – had appreciated the contribution that public building projects could make to their own image-creation. The politicians put up the money, and the resultant buildings constituted a permanent reminder of their contribution to the growth of Rome. It tells us a great deal about priorities in the Roman state that, whilst the names of those who sponsored buildings are in many cases well-known, that is seldom true of the architects – unless, of course, like the Emperor, Hadrian, they were both architect *and* political leader.

In the last two centuries of the Old Republic, imperial growth often placed large sums of money and gangs of prisoners-of-war/slaves at the disposal of those seeking immortality through bricks and mortar. As a result, buildings became more lavish and extensive, and appearances changed as new materials, such as marbles, from the expanding Empire became available. In the second century BC, three notable families – those of the Porcii Catones, the Sempronii Gracchi and the Aemilii Paulli – sponsored public halls (*basilicae*) in the area of the Roman Forum in the heart of Rome. Some traditionalists perhaps regretted the abandonment of the older traditional materials of timber and terracotta in favour of marble and concrete but, as the poet Horace pointed out in the context of literature,[2] it was essential for Roman writers to study their Greek originals 'by night and by day'. This necessity of studying Greek originals, however, extended way beyond poetry because, as Horace put it elsewhere,[3] 'captive Greece took captive her savage captor, and introduced the arts to rustic Latium'.

Such buildings as were erected, therefore, provided public or religious space, represented work for the city's population and were a memorial to those who sponsored them. Thus, long before Rome came under the rule of Emperors in 31 BC, a precedent had been established that the Emperors readily continued to utilise for their own image-creation both in Rome and in the Empire. As Augustus was to put it, 'I found Rome a city of brick and left it a city of marble',[4] and in so doing worked to make Rome's appearance worthy of her imperial rôle.[5] Further, because of the fact that Rome's wars were generally being fought in the Emperors' names, they could use the material spoils of victory, as Vespasian did in the case of the spoils from the Jewish War that he had, of course, fought in the name of Nero, to outdo all other citizens in the provision of buildings. Indeed, the last recorded involvement of a private citizen in financing a public building-project in Rome occurred in AD 22, when Tiberius allowed his friend, Marcus Aemilius Lepidus, to restore at his own expense the *Basilica Aemilia*, his ancestral monument in the Forum.[6]

The breadth of the Emperors' control over the Roman state gave them unlimited opportunities for this kind of patronage: through their *imperium proconsulare* (proconsular power) they were the commanders of Rome's armies; through their *tribunicia potestas* (tribunician power) they inherited the rôle of the tribunes of the Old Republic as the people's defenders and champions; as *pontifex maximus* (chief priest), the Emperor was the head of the Roman state religion. Thus, triumphal arches, public halls, theatres, amphitheatres, circuses and temples all featured on the imperial building-agenda. Nor should we overlook the fact that these buildings provided more than simply facilities, vitally important though these were;[7] as the Emperor, Vespasian, is on record as having observed, part of the purpose of such building-projects was served by the construction-work that they provided for ordinary people.[8]

As we have seen, Augustus' early political activities had been none too salubrious; he concentrated, therefore, in his propaganda on creating a more traditionalist image. The poet, Virgil, in his *Aeneid*, wrote of Aeneas' – that is, Augustus' – piety (*pietas*), whilst his contemporary, Horace, in his 'Roman Odes', emphasised the need to restore respect for tradition, especially in the field of religion – again, *pietas*.[9] In his account of his life and reign (*Res Gestae Divi Augusti*), Augustus highlighted the number of temples that he had built or rebuilt.[10] *Pietas*, however, embraced duty to family, the core of Roman society, as well as to the gods; so Augustus' completion of the *Forum Iulium* (Forum of Julius Caesar) and of Caesar's unfinished public hall in the Roman Forum (*Basilica Iulia*), together with his building of the Forum of Augustus,[11] with its temple to Mars the Avenger (*Mars Ultor*) – a thank-offering to Mars for the avenging of the murder of Julius Caesar – all highlighted aspects of Augustus' *pietas* (Figure 7.1).

With the vast collection of building-work that he undertook, Augustus effectively created an imperial architecture fit for an imperial city; it is perhaps best described as a harmonisation of the best of Roman tradition with the grace of Greek building – a product that directly followed Horace's prescription; the change from brick to marble represented only the surface of Augustus' revolution. It is fitting, too, that he should announce his greatest political achievement – the harmonisation of the Old Republic with the new governmental imperatives – with a building – the Altar of Augustan Peace (*Ara Pacis Augustae*), that was dedicated in 13 BC and completed four years later.[12] Thus, Augustus had used his opportunity and his obligation well to produce a physical entity that mirrored the image that he was creating for himself. In view of his studied emulation of Augustus, it will not have been insignificant that Nero chose to commemorate this monument on his coinage.[13]

So, what of Nero? It is clear that he had, along with his other artistic interests, a passion for architecture; alongside this, he was possessed of the generosity of spirit that led him to want to provide for his people. It has been pointed out[14] that the attraction for him of the winter-solstice festival of the *Saturnalia* lay not simply in its encouragement of outrageous humour,

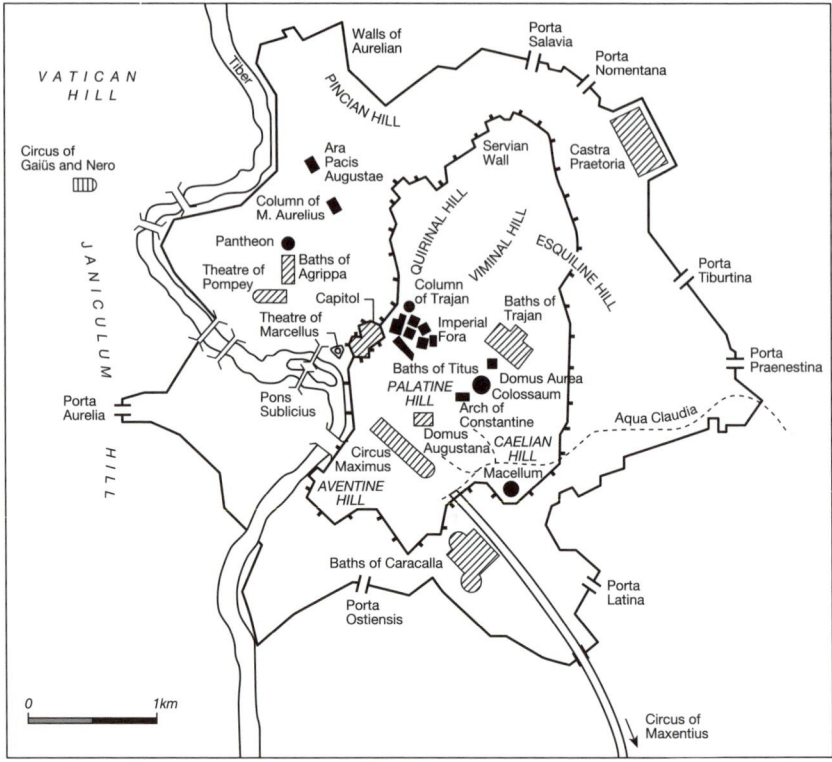

Figure 7.1 Rome in the Imperial period. Swan Hellenic Cruises 2002. Swan Hellenic does not hold any responsibility for the accuracy of the information in the figure above.

but also in the opportunity that it offered for him to level himself with the interests of his ordinary subjects. His buildings, too, point him up as a public benefactor who gladly shared his subjects' enthusiasms.

His architectural interests seem to have started early in his life, as he is credited with the reworking of the villa at Antium (Anzio),[15] in which he was born, into a substantial sea-side residence of the type that he was to grow to admire on the Bay of Naples, and particularly at Baiae.[16] Amongst his early building-activities in Rome was the completion of the Circus which Caligula had started alongside the Vatican Hill;[17] it was a place where Nero intended to perform and to which the people were invited as spectators to their Emperor's prowess – if that is the true implication of the new access-bridge across the Tiber (*Pons Neronianus*). The Circus was eventually destroyed by the Emperor, Constantine I, to make way for the first Basilica of St Peter,[18] that was evidently built to respect the tomb in the Vatican

Plate 1 Head of Agrippina the Younger (c. 16–59), (marble) by Roman, (1st Century AD)/Louvre, Paris, France/Girandon/The Bridgeman Art Library. Nationality/copyright status: out of copyright.

Plate 2 Nero as a child, Musée du Louvre, see Griffin, M. T., *'Imago Vitae Suae'*, pp. 1–38 in Costa, C. D. N. (ed.), Seneca (London, 1984), plate 1. Photo: akg-images, London/Erich Lessing.

Plate 3 Villa of Poppaea Sabina at Oplontis: rear (north) façade, author's own.

Plate 4 Villa of Poppaea Sabina at Oplontis: wall decoration in the *Atrium*, author's own.

Plate 5 Villa of Poppaea Sabina at Oplontis: wall decoration in the *Triclinium*, author's own.

Plate 6 Villa of Poppaea Sabina at Oplontis: wall decoration in the *Viridarium*, author's own.

Plate 7 Pompeii: The House of the Golden Cupids: Peristylium, author's own.

Plate 8 Pompeii: The House of the Golden Cupids: Wall decoration showing a scene from Egyptian religion, author's own

Plate 9 Pompeii: The House of the Menander: Peristylium author's own.

Plate 10 Pompeii: The House of Lucius Caecilius Iucundus: household altar showing buildings tottering during the earthquake of AD 62, author's own.

Plate 11 Pompeii: The arena of the Amphitheatre, author's own.

Plate 12 Pompeii: The Amphitheatre: exterior view, author's own.

Plate 13 Pompeii: wall painting of the Amphitheatre depicting the rioting of AD 59, Naples Museum. The Bridgeman Art Library. Nationality/copyright status: out of copyright.

cemetery thought traditionally to have been that of the Apostle, following his martyrdom in the Circus.

In the same vein, Nero is said by Tacitus[19] to have constructed in AD 57 a temporary wooden amphitheatre on the Campus Martius on the site of a stone amphitheatre that had been erected in 29 BC by Augustus' friend and general, Titus Statilius Taurus. Although it is said by some to have been remarkable for the lavishness of its decoration, other references do not appear to suggest that it was a particularly exceptional monument.[20] This decoration evidently included a great deal of amber from the Baltic that, presumably because of its gold colour, became very fashionable in Nero's reign. Such lavishness, of course, looked forward to the *Domus Aurea*.[21] This arena was evidently flooded for the staging of a sea-battle between the Athenians and the Persians, as well as being used for Greek war-dances and games that included gladiatorial contests involving senators and equestrians, but at which no deaths were permitted.[22] It has been suggested[23] that this may have been the structure, the remains of which were identified beneath the Stadium of Domitian in the Piazza Navona in Rome.

Another monument for which Nero was responsible early in his reign was a triumphal arch (or arches) on the Capitoline Hill; its erection was voted by the Senate, along with other honours for Nero, in recognition of a victory of dubious significance won by Corbulo in the East in AD 58.[24] Despite the fact that the arch will have seemed to many to be a rather hollow honour in view of the way in which the campaign ended in 62,[25] construction work continued. The arch, that was celebrated on the coinage,[26] appears to have been a highly-decorated single-span construction. No trace of it has been found, and it is possible that it was completely destroyed after Nero's death. In the field of public utility, the Emperor added improvements to the city's water-supply, taking a branch-aqueduct (*Arcus Caelimontani*)[27] from the *Aqua Claudia* to the Temple of Claudius on the Caelian Hill; this was later extended to take water on to the Palatine, Aventine and Transti-berine regions.

After his mother's death in AD 59, as part of his programme of activities to salve his conscience and to retain public sympathy, Nero dedicated on the Caelian Hill an elaborate market-place of two storeys under a domed roof (*macellum*), that he proceeded to advertise on his coinage;[28] it is possible that the moving of markets from the centre of the city to the periphery may have been part of a policy to make the heart of Rome more hygienic and noble.[29] Similarly portrayed on the coinage, in one of the most artistic presentations of the first century, is the new harbour at Ostia that was opened by Nero, but actually completed under Claudius.[30] It remains unclear whether Nero was falsely claiming the credit for this work, or whether the coin may have represented an act of *pietas* to the memory of his adoptive father. Perhaps, however, Nero's view of Claudius is better reflected by his incorporation of the *Claudianum*, a temple to the Deified Claudius, that had been undertaken by Agrippina, into the complex of the *Domus Aurea*. It is worth noting that Vespasian, who entertained a favourable view of Claudius, having served under him in Britain in AD 43, rid the site of its Neronian features and completed the temple as begun by Agrippina.[31]

In AD 62, Nero completed what can be regarded as a trend-setting building – the Neronian Baths, that were constructed on the Campus Martius to replace, or supplement, the Augustan baths of Agrippa. This building, that was highly regarded in antiquity,[32] set the pattern for the great imperial bath houses of the second and third centuries AD – those of Trajan, Caracalla and Diocletian – showing structural confidence in the use of concrete vaults and domes to roof over large areas of public space. Significant, too, was the incorporation of Greek features, such as a gymnasium, with its capacity for social and educational activities. In this way, Nero may be regarded as having taken a step towards developing the Roman bath house in the direction of the modern leisure-centre. It is said that there was free entry into Nero's baths and complimentary body-oil for all who used it.[33] This gymnasium was regarded as the most magnificent in Rome:[34] it was erected in AD 60,[35] opened officially in AD 62,[36] but destroyed by fire in that same year following a lightning-strike, in which a bronze statue of Nero inside the building was melted into a shapeless mass.[37]

It is, however, for the opulence of his own living-arrangements that Nero has been most commented upon and frequently criticised. He inherited from his father a house on the *Via Sacra*,[38] that perhaps suggested to him the desirability of linking it together with imperial properties on the Palatine and Esquiline Hills by means of what he called the *Domus Transitoria* (The Passageway).[39] Effectively, this was Nero's first palace, although only fragments of it have survived the posthumous condemnation that embraced all things Neronian, not to mention the ravages of the Great Fire of AD 64.

Of these two fragments, two are accessible and serve to provide some idea of Nero's conception: first, beneath the *Domus Augustana* (the Palace of Domitian)[40] on the Palatine Hill, a fragment of a fountain-court (*nymphaeum*) remains in place, because it was incorporated into the foundations of the Flavian palace. The cascading fountain faced onto what was essentially a pavilion for private dinner-parties, and the whole was flanked by suites of barrel-vaulted rooms that were richly decorated with marble-paving, marble-stucco, semi-precious stones, glass and painted scenes, presumably executed by Famulus,[41] who was noted for his eccentric habit of painting in his best clothes. The style of painting that he adopted was that of fantasised architectural scenes, that in the context of Pompeii and Herculaneum became known as the 'Fourth Style'. Griffin[42] has pointed out that everything that is known of this painter – his dress, his subject-matter, even his name – suggests that he was a man of Italian rather than Greek origin, providing a corrective to the view that everything artistic in which Nero became involved exhibited his obsession with Greece.

The other surviving feature of the *Domus Transitoria* is a long, semi-subterranean corridor, known as the *cryptoporticus*, that ran across the Palatine Hill towards the Esquiline; it was decorated with scenes from Virgil's *Aeneid*, executed in marble-stucco, and would have afforded Nero access between the palace-complexes without having to be seen in public, perhaps, therefore, reflecting a stage in his life when unguarded public appearance was beginning to make him more nervous.

Work on the *Domus Transitoria* was started in AD 64, but the complex was largely destroyed in that same year by the Great Fire, that started in the *Circus Maximus* and spread across the Palatine and Caelian Hills to the Esquiline. The Temple of Vesta, one of the most sacred buildings in Rome, and the *Regia* (the official residence of the *pontifex maximus*) in the Forum may also have been burned; at any rate, the Temple of Vesta is commemorated on Nero's coinage of AD 65–6.[43] This commemoration of the Goddess of hearth and home might also have had something to do with Nero's conscience over the carnage for which he had, over the years, been responsible within his own household.[44] Rome was at that time divided into fourteen regions; of these, three were totally destroyed in the blaze and only four left unscathed.

Nero was away at Antium when the fire broke out; he was, of course, accused of having started it – some saying that he wanted to destroy the old city and rebuild it as *Neropolis*, a monument to himself,[45] whilst Tacitus[46] writes – rather more guardedly – that Nero 'capitalised on the ruins of his fatherland' with his extravagant plans for rebuilding. Others, again, suggested that it was a means of providing a crime of which to accuse the Christian community in Rome; certainly, although Suetonius[47] does not directly connect the attack upon the Christians with the fire, the punishments inflicted upon them – being burned alive and being used as human torches – are consistent with a charge of incendiarism.[48]

Suetonius and Dio unhesitatingly accuse Nero of the crime of arson, although Tacitus is far more cautious about it;[49] he does, however, say that one of the members of the Pisonian conspiracy in AD 65, Subrius Flavus, explained that his involvement in the plot to remove Nero was due to the fact that Nero was an arsonist.[50] Our sources differ on the matter of Nero's conduct: according to Suetonius,[51] Nero watched the 'beauty of the flames' from the *Tower of Maecenas* (on the Esquiline Hill) and, putting on his tragic costume, sang his poem on 'The Fall of Troy' in its entirety. Dio, on the other hand, agrees that the Emperor sang the poem, but from a vantage-point on the Palatine Hill, whilst Tacitus indicates the venue as a private stage, but has doubts about the whole story. These differing versions point to a clear lack of reliable evidence, but show simply that Nero was viewed in such a way that people believed him capable of this enormity. In fact, when Nero returned to Rome from Antium, he attempted to put in place measures to stop the fire, that might have worked, had not the wind changed direction and strength.[52] He involved himself in clearance-work, forbade looting and opened a relief-fund for those made homeless, although both Tacitus and Suetonius suggest that the fund-raising bore down very heavily on some communities.

The phoenix that rose from these ashes, of course, was Nero's new palace, the 'Golden House' (*Domus Aurea*) (Figure 7.2).[53] This building, that was much reviled in antiquity, in fact deserves to be regarded as of major significance in the development of Roman construction. Like the *Domus Transitoria*, the *Domus Aurea* encompassed a considerable area of the city, prompting the quips[54] about 'Rome being converted into a villa' and spreading as far as the neighbouring town of Veii. In fact, it spread over the Palatine, Esquiline and Caelian Hills, together with the intervening valley, which subsequently became the location of Vespasian's new amphitheatre, the Colosseum, that was constructed on the site of a large artificial lake, a major feature of the landscaping that took place. Neronian work has been identified largely by studies of the brick and concrete employed in the

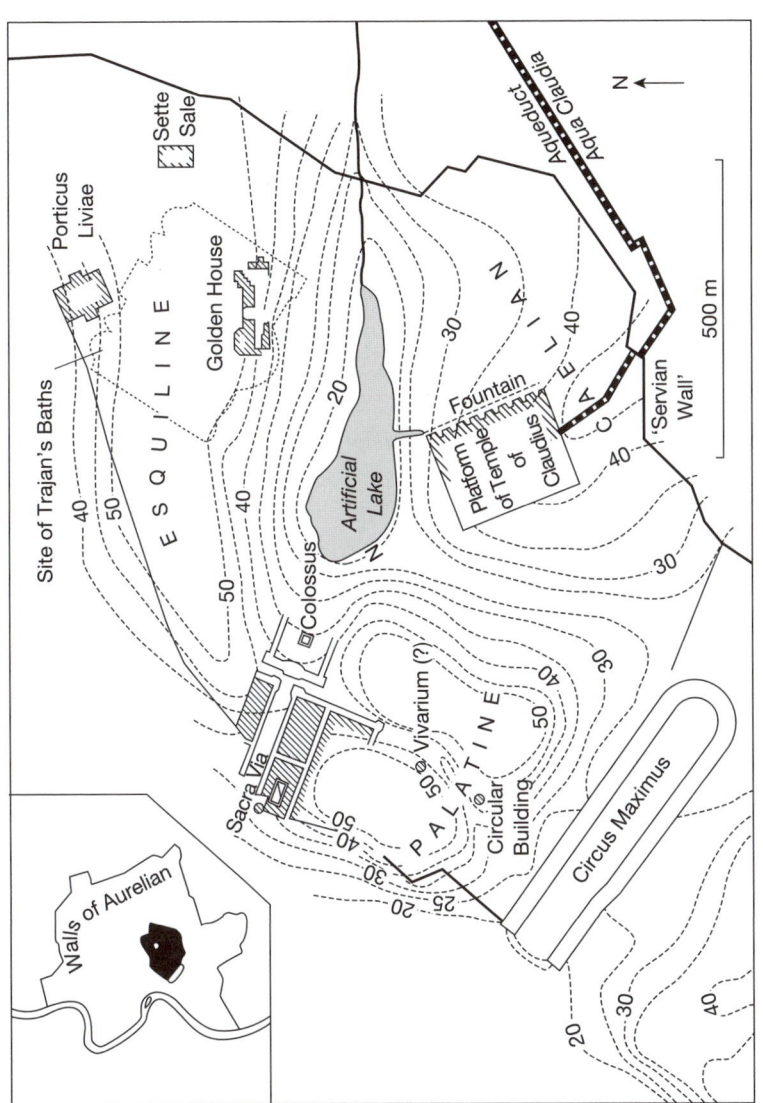

Figure 7.2 Nero's Domus Aurea. Boethius, A. and Ward-Perkins, J. B., 'Etruscan and Roman Architecture' (1970), London, Penguin Books, p. 215. Copyright © the Estate of Axel Boethius, and J. B. Ward-Perkins, 1970. Reproduced by permission of Penguin Books Ltd.

remains that have been excavated, although in one place (on the western side of the Palatine Hill) a caricature of Nero was found scratched into a wall, along with other graffiti.[55]

In assessing the project, we must bear in mind the fact that, other than Nero himself, its creators were two engineers, Severus and Celer, who seem to have been exceedingly adept at devising schemes involving water, and with whom the Emperor appears to have become entangled at this stage in his life.[56] Tacitus, indeed, implies that Nero was carried away by the grandiose nature of their ideas:

> *But Nero profited by his country's ruin to build a new palace. Its wonders were not so much customary and commonplace luxuries like gold and jewels, but lawns and lakes and faked rusticity – woods here, open spaces and views there. With their cunning, impudent artificialities, Nero's architects and engineers, Severus and Celer, did not baulk at effects which Nature herself had ruled out as impossible.*[57]

Tacitus adds that another scheme of theirs, in which they had involved Nero, was the digging of a canal from Lake Avernus to Ostia to accommodate large transport-vessels. This would have avoided the potentially dangerous sea-journey from Puteoli to Ostia, and so created a more reliable route for the carriage of Rome's food-supplies, that had at times in the recent past encountered problems.[58] In other words, the plans of Nero, Severus and Celer for a canal across the isthmus at Corinth were not as outrageous as has sometimes been supposed, but indicate an Emperor who was concerned with social and economic considerations.[59]

The fullest description of the *Domus Aurea* in antiquity is that given by Suetonius in his *Life of Nero*:

> *The most wasteful of all his activities was his building-programme: he built a house which stretched from the Palatine to the Esquiline, which he called the* Domus Transitoria. *When it was later burnt down, he rebuilt it with the new name,* Domus Aurea. *The following details will provide some idea of its size and opulence: its entrance-way was large enough to accommodate the* Colossus, *a statue of himself which was 120 feet high; so spacious was the site that there was a triple colonnade running for a whole mile. There was a lake which was so large that it resembled the sea, and was surrounded by buildings which were constructed to look like whole cities; moreover, there*

were rustic areas which were landscaped with ploughed fields, vineyards, pastures and woods, in which great herds of every kind of domestic and wild animal roamed around.

In the house itself, all surfaces were covered with gold leaf, and encrusted with precious stones and pearls; the dining-rooms had fretted ceilings fitted with panels of ivory, which were movable and equipped with pipes so that flower-petals and perfumes could be showered on those below. The main dining-room took the form of a rotunda which revolved day and night in synchronisation with the heavens. The baths had a constant supply of sea-water and water from sulphurous springs. When the decoration of the house had been completed in this fashion, Nero dedicated it, adding approvingly that he could now at last begin to live like a human being.[60]

Despite difficulties in interpreting the meaning of our sources in all respects, undoubtedly there were here elements that were extravagant and self-indulgent; but was Nero's purpose inherently as shallow as it has often been made to sound?[61] It has been suggested that the completed complex would have been a microcosm of the Roman Empire, with the artificial lake representing the Mediterranean Sea.[62] It has frequently been assumed that Nero intended, through the very extent of the *Domus Aurea*, to shun the public and to court privacy; but is such an interpretation consistent with an Emperor who loved to perform in public and bask in public applause?

Shortly before the fire of AD 64, Nero had staged a party for the people, in which rôles were reversed, as at the *Saturnalia*-celebrations, that was deliberately suggestive of the pleasures of the Neapolitan resort of Baiae. It has, indeed, been argued[63] that, through his engineering projects, Nero sought to bring to Rome that traditionally aristocratic resort. The great difference, however, between the real Baiae and Nero's creation was that the Emperor wanted to make its pleasures available to the people. Recent excavations near the Arch of Constantine and the Colosseum have revealed a colonnaded pool,[64] the *stagnum Neronis*, which imitated Nero's lake at Baiae and the *stagnum Agrippae* on the Campus Martius. The implication of this appears to be that Nero intended that his new house and the rebuilt city of Rome should be one – the home of the people and of himself, their Emperor, Protector and Entertainer. It may thus be that the observation that the whole of Rome was 'becoming a villa' originated not as a criticism of Nero, but as an expression of his concept for Rome, its Emperor and its people.

The living-accommodation of the *Domus Aurea* is itself of considerable interest. Coastal villas on and around the Bay of Naples[65] and elsewhere had over the years become increasingly lavish in the early-imperial period. Indeed, the Augustan poet, Horace, and others[66] complain about the practice of building them on piers, projecting into the sea and thus robbing the fish of their living-space! Contemporary wall-paintings provide some idea of the style and scope of villas in the area, and one that seems particularly relevant to the *Domus Aurea* is to be found on a painting from the House of Lucretius Fronto at Pompeii: this depicts a villa with a polygonal sun-court similar to that identified in the *Domus Aurea*.[67]

This sun-court and octagonal domed hall in the east wing of the *Domus Aurea* have been described as representing the 'breakdown of the tyranny of the right angle' in Roman architecture[68] – a process taken much further by Hadrian's extensive villa at Tibur (Tivoli) and by Maximian's at Piazza Armerina on the island of Sicily. Such structures are seen as concentrating less on the mass of the building than on the spaces created in them. The *Domus Aurea*, then, may have been criticised for its extravagance; its significance, however, is not to be denied.

As we saw in Suetonius' description, a dominant feature of the complex was the giant statue – or, more precisely, a column capped by a statue – that has been known as the *Colossus*.[69] Many uncertainties surround the *Colossus*: for example, it remains unclear whether the *Colossus*, a column of 120 feet crowned by a statue of Nero himself, that was fashioned by the sculptor, Zenodorus, was erected during Nero's lifetime; nor is it clear where it was initially placed or intended to be placed, although it has been suggested that it was to be placed in the entrance-way to the house that is thought to have been Nero's father's house on the *Via Sacra* and which had been incorporated into the *Domus Aurea* complex. Was the crowning statue a representation of Nero himself, or Apollo – or perhaps 'Nero Apollo'? Nor is it certain whether the Elder Pliny[70] refers to the Neronian form of it as a completed piece of work or as an on-going project in Zenodorus' workshop. Vespasian evidently changed the crowning statue to one of the Sun, although he may simply have added a radiate crown to the original statue of Nero.[71] Hadrian, to make room for his great temple of Venus and Rome,[72] moved the *Colossus* from its original site to one closer to the Colosseum, where its base has in recent years been excavated. Again, Commodus replaced the statue[73] with one of himself as Hercules.[74] After Commodus' death in AD 192, however, it was restored as a statue of the Sun.[75] Although its name is regularly applied to the adjacent Flavian Amphitheatre, there is, however, no evidence of this having happened before *c.* AD 1000.[76]

When Nero died, the *Domus Aurea* was still unfinished, particularly in the matter of its decoration. In January AD 69, Nero's erstwhile friend, Marcus Salvius Otho, became *princeps* in succession to Nero's conqueror, Servius Galba. Having found that his power-base was fragile, Otho set about trying to capitalise on Nero's popularity with ordinary people, styling himself 'Nero Otho', a formulation that, according to the historian, Cluvius Rufus, appeared on official documents.[77] A further move by Otho to win popular support, that incidentally shows that the *Domus Aurea* was not unpopular with ordinary people, was to earmark fifty million *sestertii* for the completion of Nero's palace, a sum which, in his very short reign, Otho appears not to have had sufficient time to spend.[78]

Otho's successor, Aulus Vitellius, attempted to use the *Domus Aurea*, but gave up because he felt that the building was lacking in comfort.[79] The Flavians,[80] for obvious reasons, had no wish to be associated with favourable attitudes towards Nero's memory; Vespasian, therefore, set about dismantling parts of the *Domus Aurea* and either returning them to their original purposes or changing them to popular uses of a different kind – for example, the Flavian Amphitheatre that replaced Nero's large ornamental lake. The works of art that Nero had pillaged from around the Empire were placed in Vespasian's 'Temple of Peace',[81] although as late as AD 79 the Elder Pliny refers to having seen a statue of Laocoon[82] in the house of Titus, Vespasian's elder son and successor.[83] As we have seen, parts of Domitian's new palace on the Palatine Hill (*Domus Augustana*) utilised surviving features of the earlier Neronian palace (*Domus Transitoria*) as foundation-material.

In AD 104, another fire in Rome destroyed more of the *Domus Aurea* and prompted the Emperor, Trajan, to construct his baths on the site; some of the rooms and corridors of Nero's palace are still filled with the rubble put there by Trajan's builders to make them a sounder foundation for the baths. Ironically, however, Trajan's baths followed the design-model that had been adumbrated in Nero's extensive bath-suite. The vestibule, in which the *Colossus* either stood or was to have stood, that was situated adjacent to the *Via Sacra* and close to the Arch of Titus was, by AD 121, finally demolished by Hadrian to make way for his new Temple of Venus and Rome.[84]

That Nero was not, however, living in a complete fantasy-world with his new palace, as has sometimes been alleged, can be seen from another consequence of the Fire of AD 64. Not only had many public buildings been destroyed, but so too had large areas of the city's housing and business-accommodation. In many cases, what had been destroyed was built of timber and situated on narrow, winding, streets;[85] these characteristics had contributed substantially to allowing the Fire to have the devastating results that it did. Nero was determined[86] that old mistakes should not be repeated, and effectively created new building-regulations: the city should have regular, wide, streets, with porticoes protecting the frontages of buildings. A maximum height of seventy feet was put in place for all buildings, which reinstated a ruling of Augustus that had come to be ignored.[87] Trajan was to reduce this maximum by a further ten feet.[88] Nero also enacted that all houses should be structurally disengaged from their neighbours, that the use of timber should be kept to a minimum and that fire-resistant building-stone should be used.[89]

It may never have been intended to re-name Nero's Rome *Neropolis*, but it was a new, safer, city that emerged from the ruins of the Fire, one that was in every way fit for purpose. It was, in fact, a city divided into orderly blocks (*insulae*) of the kind that can still be seen in the remains of Rome's port of Ostia.[90]

Nero, like many members of the Roman nobility before him, was particularly fond of the Bay of Naples,[91] especially Naples itself, where he would spend long periods of holiday – for example, in AD 65, AD 66 and AD 68, when he first heard news of the rebellion of Vindex in Gaul.[92] In AD 66, as we have seen,[93] the Emperor devised a lavish entertainment at Puteoli for the Parthian, Tiridates, who had come to Italy to receive the diadem of rulership of Armenia personally from Nero.[94] Baiae was another of Nero's favoured places in the region,[95] and he had acquired there the properties of his aunt, Domitia, and of Gaius Calpurnius Piso who, in AD 65, unsuccessfully conspired against him.[96] Nero initiated two major engineering-projects in the area: first, he and his architects, Severus and Celer, planned to dig a canal from Lake Avernus to Ostia, partly, at least, to facilitate the transportation of food and trade from Puteoli to Ostia,[97] without running the risks inherent in a journey by sea. Nero's appreciation of the importance of Puteoli to Rome is made clear by its elevation to the status of *colonia*.[98] It appears that, for the greater part of Nero's reign,

Puteoli remained the main port of entry for Rome's corn-supply, most of which was coming from Egypt and north Africa.[99] As we have noted before, a similar plan of Nero's to dig a canal through the isthmus at Corinth had far more to recommend it than many ancient critics allowed. The second major work of construction in the area of the Bay of Naples was a covered pool (*stagnum*), extending from Misenum to Lake Avernus,[100] thus creating a continuous waterway that was to run from the mouth of the river Tiber to the Bay of Naples, and that thus afforded Nero easy and luxurious access from Rome to his favourite part of Italy. Commenting on this scheme, Tacitus[101] describes Nero as a 'lover of the incredible' (*incredibilium cupitor*). Presumably also a part of this extensive plan was the idea of linking Rome with its port of Ostia with a continuous double wall, evidently to emulate the walls by which Athens, in the fifth century BC, had been linked with its port of Piraeus.[102]

Nero may have been much criticised in antiquity for the extravagance and inappropriate nature of his buildings. However, we can detect a clear, and often very practical, logic in most of them: he regarded his relationship with the ordinary people as of prime importance to him – his generosity reciprocated by popular gratitude. Thus, it was natural that he should contrive schemes that not only guaranteed work ('bread') for the people, but also provided places for their entertainment ('circuses'), which were also places where his special relationship with his people could be recharged and clearly demonstrated. One such expression of his special relationship with his people, as we have seen,[103] can be recognised in the party that he organised in AD 64 at Agrippa's Pool (*stagnum Agrippae*) on the Campus Martius.[104] This event, that appears from the surviving description by Tacitus to have resembled a 'love-in', reached its climax with Nero, as the bride, marrying his freedman, Pythagoras. What Poppaea, then pregnant for the second time, thought of this is not a matter of record. However, the most lavish expression of Nero's relationship with his people was to be seen in the *Domus Aurea*, where the 'father' and 'family' that comprised the city could be together; extravagant, perhaps, but not lacking in logic. The same might be said of his canal-schemes.

Further, we can see a concern for the dignity and hygiene of the imperial city in his moving of the main market from the area of the Roman Forum to the edge of the city, on the Caelian Hill. Finally, the same concern for good practice is clearly to be seen in the sound regulations that Nero put in place for the rebuilding of Rome after the Fire. Thus, the proper concerns were present – for health and safety, and for a decent lifestyle for the people; further, much of this was achieved in a manner that was architecturally ground-breaking. In short, those looking for signs of Nero's supposed madness will not find it here; his contribution to Roman construction should not be dismissed or underestimated in the shallow manner of many of his contemporaries. Here, writ large, is Nero the artist and popular provider – almost certainly the way in which he would have wished to be remembered.

Chapter Eight

The Beginning of the End

✣✣✣✣✣✣

Tacitus brought the fourteenth book of his *Annals* to a close on an ominous note:[1] by recounting Octavia's banishment and then her cruel and brutal death, the historian points up the sudden savagery of an Emperor who, although previously far from faultless, had generally refrained from such barbaric cruelty. The new depths that Nero now plumbed were symbolised[2] by the decapitation of Octavia and the presentation of the severed head to Poppaea Sabina. Even more depressing was the fact that the Senate greeted such an act with lavish expressions of gratitude, recalling the level of sycophancy that had once exasperated the Emperor, Tiberius,[3] and was to have the same effect on Nero's successor, Galba.[4]

It has been observed[5] that Nero was not previously noted for excessive cruelty, despite his sometimes rash and reckless conduct. The murder of Agrippina was shocking because it was an act of matricide, although aspects of it, assuming that they were not subsequently invented, were more bizarre than gratuitously cruel. Indeed, Nero's early years as Emperor had seen few deaths that were unequivocally attributable to him. Besides Agrippina, the most obvious cases were those of Britannicus (if, indeed, he was murdered), Faustus Sulla and Rubellius Plautus; all of these Nero plainly came to regard with increasing anxiety as possible rivals and, in the cases of the latter two, he had at first tried to obviate those fears by exiling the two men. Again, although many had criticised the character – particularly the lack of dignity – of Nero's games and shows, he had concentrated on artistic and athletic contests, and had not allowed fights to the death.[6] Indeed, Nero's games were perfectly consistent with the growing philhellenism of the young Emperor.

There can be little doubt that, despite Seneca's efforts to inculcate a 'proper' notion of clemency and authority into his pupil, presumably in the hope that he might thus mould him into the 'philosopher-king', Nero's view of clemency was whimsical and essentially self-indulgent, as was highlighted by the trial in AD 62[7] of Antistius Sosianus for writing scurrilous verses directed at Nero. The Emperor was, of course, well aware, as Seneca reminded him, that he held the power of life and death over his subjects.[8] The trial of Antistius[9] was of considerable significance for a number of reasons: first, it represented the revival of treason trials that Nero, at the opening of his reign, had promised to abolish. Secondly, on this occasion, the initiator of the charges against Antistius was Cossutianus Capito, the son-in-law of Nero's new Prefect of the Praetorian Guard, Ofonius Tigellinus. Thirdly, a sycophantic Senate was on the point of endorsing the death-penalty when the outspoken Stoic senator, Publius Clodius Thrasea Paetus, intervened to propose a less drastic course of action. Fourthly, in an ending, that, in some ways, recalls the conclusion of the trial of Marcus Scribonius Libo Drusus, during the reign of Tiberius,[10] Nero indicated that, although he was displeased and hurt at Antistius' conduct, he would, in any case, have exercised imperial clemency. Although the eventual outcome for Antistius himself may have seemed satisfactory, in reality it showed only how dangerous and potentially tyrannical a path Nero was now treading, one on which he had to some extent been launched by Seneca's teaching.

Octavia's death was not the only one to disfigure the closing of AD 62: Doryphorus, the Emperor's freedman, was put to death for opposing the marriage to Poppaea Sabina, and Pallas, Claudius' freedman, met his death, supposedly for being too wealthy.[11] Such behaviour as is manifested in these examples must have seemed, even to those who were well-disposed towards Nero, far removed from the conduct of government whilst Seneca and Burrus retained their influence. Indeed, by a forward-looking allusion to the conspiracy of Gaius Calpurnius Piso,[12] that was still three years in the future, Tacitus is pointing out that, with such arbitrary conduct on Nero's part, the relationship between the Emperor's generosity and reciprocated public gratitude was under threat; the effect would inevitably be that the popularity which had been demonstrated to have been so important to Nero would desert him – with unpredictable results.[13] Thus, AD 62 represented a major watershed in Nero's reign: questions regarding his fitness to rule would inevitably intensify and, with them, a growing frustration on Nero's part, as he realised that he was increasingly the subject of criticism and declining popularity.

As we have seen, Gaius Ofonius Tigellinus[14] was to be a key-figure in the history of Nero's later years; the son of a Roman citizen of Sicilian origin, Tigellinus is said to have become overly close to Nero's mother and her sister, whilst their brother, Caligula, was in power.[15] Caligula exiled him, although it may be significant that he refrained from having him killed. Tigellinus probably lived by the rule commonly enunciated in the tag: 'let them hate me, so long as they fear me';[16] at any rate, the cruelty and criminality of Tigellinus were well-known in antiquity;[17] Tacitus perhaps summarises the situation to best effect:

> *A man of humble birth, vicious childhood and dissolute maturity, he had achieved among other things the command of the Watch and of the Praetorian Guard. These are normally the rewards of virtue, but Tigellinus found it quicker to win them by vice.*[18]

It appears that the young Nero first made the acquaintance of Tigellinus when the latter had been recalled from exile by Claudius, at the prompting of Agrippina. He evidently established himself in the business of horse-trading, which will have provided him with a shared passion with Nero, whose obsessive interest in chariot-racing had developed when he was very young. From an early stage, therefore, Tigellinus probably became an intimate member of Agrippina's household, enabling him to assess the strengths and, more importantly for him, the weaknesses of Nero's character. In particular, he will have come to understand Nero's belief that he was effectively untouchable, whatever he chose to do, and will have appreciated that geniality and generosity on the young man's part as the means to the earning of gratitude and popularity[19] were powerful features of Nero's character. Agrippina had perhaps taken too little notice of these characteristics, but Tigellinus was careful not to fall into the same trap. Indeed, he had an ideal rôle-model in Tiberius' Praetorian Prefect, Lucius Aelius Sejanus, whom Tacitus describes[20] as following the Emperor's whims, whilst appearing to show independence of judgement.

Freed from the constraints that had for so long been exercised by Seneca and Burrus, although Nero retained his earlier interests, his practice of them became more overt and, to many, more distasteful and unacceptable. This led to a higher level of dissension, particularly amongst the upper levels of Roman society. It is hard to believe that this more abrasive Nero, who continued to crave popularity even more avidly than before,[21] was not due to the influence of Tigellinus, or perhaps the combined influences of Tigellinus, Poppaea Sabina and their associates.

Tigellinus benefited from good tuition: as a client of Nero's mother, whilst the Emperor was coming of age, Tigellinus will have noted the methods employed by Agrippina in her effort to retain her control over her son, and will have assessed how and why she ultimately failed. Indeed, he appears to have become involved in major crime for the first time under her patronage when he acquired an inheritance under a forged will.[22] Tigellinus' first major post was as *Praefectus Vigilum*, the head of what was, in effect, Rome's Fire Brigade and Police Force; as such, he will have been under the ultimate control of Burrus, as Prefect of the Praetorian Guard. Here was another model to study for the art of controlling Nero and, as *Praefectus Vigilum*, he will have been aware of Nero's hooliganism during his nocturnal excursions onto the streets of Rome.[23] This post will have provided Tigellinus with the opportunity to strike a balance between exerting some control over the Emperor and giving him his head.

It is from this point that a degree of megalomania can be detected in Nero's behaviour; indeed, the removal of Octavia may have demonstrated to the Emperor – even if he had not quite believed it before – that he really could do what he wanted without fear of serious repercussions. Whilst there were certainly popular demonstrations in Octavia's favour, Nero seems not to have been unduly troubled by them. By contrast, as we have seen in the case of Agrippina's murder three years previously, Nero had relied heavily on the continuing help and support of Seneca and Burrus in circumstances that highlighted the depth of his felt insecurity. So now, it seems, Nero had the confidence and the will to tread the path that he desired.

The most obvious and immediate indication of this was the marriage to Poppaea Sabina, that followed hard on the heels of Octavia's removal; greater urgency attended this, as Poppaea was pregnant, and neither she nor Nero will have wanted the child to be born out of wedlock, as this would have left its future status more questionable.

The Emperor's philhellenism, too, came more to the fore in this period. We saw[24] that a tension between Greek and Roman culture had long existed, but that Rome's conquest of Greece in the second century BC made it inevitable that the influence in Italy of Greek culture would grow: many of the prisoners taken in the Greek wars were men who were educated and who had cultural accomplishments. These were enthusiastically embraced by many members of Rome's noble families as teachers of their children and as their advisers and practitioners in aspects related to the new culture; although some members of the nobility decried this new culture, and claimed to find it demeaning to have their children educated by men who were by definition of servile status, most wanted to read and write in Greek and, by so doing, gain access to Greek literature. We saw in the last chapter how, under such influences, Rome's architecture moved away from methods and materials that owed most to early-Italian, principally Etruscan, culture to embrace what Greece had to offer. This showed itself most obviously in the adoption of the Greek orders of decorative architecture – the Doric, Ionic and Corinthian.

Gradually, through the second and first centuries BC, Roman attitudes moved away from hostility to and fear of Greek culture as a morally subversive influence on the Roman character – as was to be seen in the famous senatorial decree of 186 BC[25], outlawing the worship of the god, Dionysus – to the level of integration that is explicit in the Graeco-Roman culture of Augustan Rome. Augustus, of course, had come to power championing the cause of the moral integrity and superiority of Italian culture, especially in the fields of religion and family-life; yet, for him, his enthusiasm for aspects of Greek culture was something to be paraded, not kept private. There remained, however, a sense of both imperialist and cultural contempt for certain aspects of Greece – in particular, its people, who seemed to continue to bask in their glorious past. It is worth noting that when Nero's grandfather, Germanicus Caesar, undertook a commission in the East on behalf of Tiberius, his publicly-paraded enthusiasm for Athens had to be restrained by Gnaeus Calpurnius Piso, who warned him that this was not the Athens of old, but a city that was now the 'cesspit of the nations'.[26] Notwithstanding, a similar display of enthusiasm for Hellenistic culture is to be seen in the same man's reaction on stepping ashore in Alexandria a year later,[27] although this was directed principally to that city and its founder.

Later, in the early years of the second century, the satiric poet, Juvenal, imagined the thoughts of someone who had decided that he could stomach no longer the quality of life in the city of Rome, and expresses it with the exclamation, 'I hate this Greek city of ours'; he goes on to write of the Syrian river, Orontes, 'spewing its sewage into the Tiber'.[28] Yet, a little later in the second century, Hadrian, another philhellenic Emperor, was to encourage a physical revival of Athens, presumably to act as a bulwark of Classical culture against the feared westward encroachment of Rome's principal regional rivals, the Parthians and the Jews.

Augustus had, therefore, produced an acceptable *modus vivendi* for Greek culture in the Roman world; further, some, at least, of what Nero did was within those limits of cultural respectability – particularly aspects of Greek literary and religious culture. Perhaps a similar spirit of compromise (Graeco-Romanism) is to be seen in Nero's placing before the statue of Augustus of the awards he had received at the festival that inaugurated his new gymnasium in AD 62.[29] Less acceptable, however, by the first century AD was the practice, once regarded as Rome's traditional imperial right, of looting works of art from the Greek East for the adornment of the residences of the Roman nobility. In connection with his new palaces, Nero took this much further than was normal in his day.[30]

As we have seen, Nero wrote poetry, the quality of which provoked differing views in antiquity:[31] Tacitus, for example, accused the Emperor of plagiarising the work of his Greek companions, whilst Suetonius rebutted this, and saw evidence of taste and originality in the writings of Nero that he had seen. Although Suetonius will have lost his direct access to the imperial records when he was dismissed from the secretariat early in Hadrian's reign, he may well have already made notes in preparation for *Lives* that he had not yet written up.[32] In this case, his judgement on Nero's compositions may well be more reliable than that of Tacitus. There was certainly a literary clique around Nero, as there had been around Augustus. This contained some of the best writers of the day, Seneca's nephew, Lucan,[33] and the future Emperor, Nerva. Nero's best-known work was the *Troica*, an epic poem on the fall of Troy, in which the wayward Paris, rather than the dutiful Hector, was the hero – an unconventional twist that probably appealed to Nero. The Emperor also wrote occasional poetry after the manner of the Alexandrian School, which places him in a line of literary descent from Caesar's contemporary, Valerius Catullus. Thus, although he became Emperor before he could embark upon the normal final stage of education in the Greek East, he had obviously come to admire and empathise with things Greek through his wide range of artistic and athletic interests.[34]

Whilst, then, his private interest in the arts of Greece did not distinguish him from a great many of his contemporaries and class-peers, his desire to perform in public did; indeed, this was a step that appeared as an item in Vindex's catalogue of accusations against Nero, when he launched his rebellion in the spring of AD 68.[35] No Emperor before him had shared his obsession with appearing in public – whether it was as an actor in plays, singing to his own accompaniment on the lyre or participating in chariot-racing. The explanation for this obsession is not hard to find: the reciprocity that was vital to him between himself as the provider of entertainment and his public in its rôle as his adoring audience. It was due, as was so much that Nero did, to his endemic desire for popularity;[36] in this, he could not help himself, and by it he was set on a collision-course with traditionalists, especially those in Rome and Italy.

Tacitus[37] associates the beginning of this downward spiral with the death of Agrippina, and the removal of the constraint on her son that she represented. Nero's own public appearances encouraged (or compelled) some of his class-peers to follow his lead. As we have noted, however, Nero's desire to do this and his justification for it was his assertion that its precedent was to be found in the customs and deeds of the mythical Greek heroes of the distant past, as narrated by Homer and Pindar.

The degree of publicity that Nero sought and the stages of its development remain unclear; it is likely that his first performances were staged on his own properties, and before invited audiences – much as literary works were normally launched in Rome, and about which Juvenal complains so bitterly.[38] Perhaps, showing the diffidence that we have seen in others of his projects, Nero did not make his first properly public performances in Rome, but reserved them for Naples, in the Greek area of Italy that was so special to him.[39] Here, in AD 64, he sang in the theatre to his own accompaniment, and was sufficiently emboldened by the experience to repeat it at the celebration of the *Neronia* in Rome in the following year; despite the Senate's attempt to award him the victor's prizes without him actually having to perform, he joined the other competitors in the Theatre of Pompey.[40]

Nero's cultural interests had now become a matter of self-indulgence that was unacceptable to traditionalists; he obviously realised that what he was doing was unpopular with many, and made plans to take his performances where he thought that they would be truly appreciated – mainland Greece.[41] After some earlier abortive attempts to make the journey,[42] late in

AD 66 the Emperor and his entourage set off for Greece, so that he could take part in the great festivals – at Olympia, Delphi, the Isthmus and Nemea; at Nero's request, all of these – unusually – were held in a single year. Predictably, he won all the contests that he entered – and those that he did not. In the end, he had amassed 1,808 first prizes.[43]

Nero's gratitude to the Greeks for affording him the reception for which he had hoped was totally genuine; his response was dramatic and, on the surface, at least, lavish: he declared the 'Freedom of Greece', in an iteration of the ceremony of 196 BC when Titus Quinctius Flamininus had originally made such a proclamation, following the defeat of Philip V of Macedon.[44] Nero's oration on this occasion still survives in an inscription at the town of Acraephia (in Boeotia),[45] and shows the Emperor in a typically emotional and big-hearted mood, that is reminiscent of the public utterances of his grandfather, Germanicus Caesar.[46] Also extant is the official response of the local High Priest, Senate and people, in which Nero is styled 'Nero Zeus the Liberator' and 'Nero Apollo, the New Sun' – no doubt, gratitude on a scale that Nero will have regarded as fitting reciprocation of his generosity.

On the other side of the balance-sheet, however, it should be noted that, owing to the relative poverty of Greece at this time – due, not least, to the pillaging for which their Roman conquerors had been responsible over the years – this was not a gesture that would have cost the imperial finances a great deal, and certainly cannot be regarded as a substantial reason for the state of Rome's finances at the end of Nero's reign; the force of Nero's gesture was more symbolic and legal. Nonetheless, the principle behind what Nero had done – giving away imperial territory – could be regarded as setting a dangerous precedent. Immediately, the Senate was compensated for the loss of Achaea as a public province (that the liberation entailed) by the transfer of Sardinia from Nero's 'imperial provinces'.[47] The gift to Greece, however, was cancelled by Vespasian, on the ground that the Greeks were too quarrelsome and factious to have merited it.[48] According to Philostratus, Apollonius was so annoyed by Vespasian's action that he refused to meet him, accusing the new Emperor of 'enslaving the Greeks' and comparing him unfavourably with Nero.

The episode had won Nero considerable popularity in Greece, as Philostratus shows, although Greek writers continued to regard it as a compensation, in part, for the Emperor's other crimes, especially the looting of Greek artistic treasures with which to adorn the *Domus Aurea*. On a more practical level, Nero also used the occasion of his visit to inaugurate his plan to cut a canal through the isthmus at Corinth, a plan that had previously been contemplated by Julius Caesar and Caligula. The scheme would appear to have carried considerable advantages, as it would have avoided the necessity for shipping to use the long and dangerous route around the Peloponnese. The work was evidently undertaken by six thousand Jewish prisoners-of-war sent over by Vespasian, and supervised by soldiers of the Praetorian Guard.[49] One of those said to have been forced to work on this was the Stoic philosopher, Musonius Rufus, who had fallen foul of Nero as a result of the Pisonian conspiracy of 65.[50] An account of the inauguration of the project is contained in a work of the second century AD, that is usually ascribed to the satirist, Lucian, but which appears to have been written by the sophist, Philostratus, entitled *Nero, or the Digging of the Isthmus.* In it, we are told that the project was ceremonially opened by Nero himself, singing hymns to the gods of the sea and digging the first spit with a golden fork. For Nero, the tour of Greece must have seemed a great success in terms of public relations but, as we shall see, the Emperor's timing could not have been more ill-judged.[51]

The association of Nero with divinities, such as Zeus and Apollo, raises the question of whether he was coming to believe in his own divinity and, further, whether he was planning to change the structure of the Augustan Principate into a Hellenistic Monarchy, in which the ruler was regarded by his subjects as a god. Can we distinguish between genuine belief and excessive sycophancy?

Although rulers in the Hellenistic East had long been elevated to godly status by their subjects, such excess was not natural in the West; Julius Caesar had been accused of entertaining divine pretensions,[52] although his deification occurred only after his death, and set the pattern for the future of deifying dead Emperors who were thought to have served well. Although such deified former rulers became integral elements of the imperial cult,[53] the origin of the cult itself in the Augustan period was rather different.

Augustus' achievement in bringing peace out of chaos was viewed as little short of a miracle; some evidently thought that only a god could have achieved on this scale. Augustus was thus caught in a dilemma: he did not wish to attract the opprobrium that might attach itself to what could be regarded as excessive and ambitious claims but, on the other hand, it might be regarded as insulting and ungracious to appear to ignore popular enthusiasm. By instituting the cult of *Roma et Augustus* (Rome and Augustus), the Emperor was treading a traditional path; for, during the period of the Old Republic, it had been normal and acceptable to worship 'Rome and the Senate'. The personified goddess, *Roma*, was a natural object of worship by Romans. The place of Augustus in this, however, was more ambiguous. By associating Augustus with *Roma*, the cult provided a kind of national parallel to the situation that obtained in every Roman household, where the father was the intermediary between gods and men. In view of the fact that the Emperor was the head of the 'national family' through his title of *Pater Patriae*, the parallel appeared eminently suitable and safe, because it stopped short of treating the current Emperor as a living divinity.

Most of the earlier Roman Emperors entertained no pretensions in this direction: Tiberius was extremely unenthusiastic about allowing a temple to himself in Spain,[54] saying that his achievements as Emperor would be his 'temples'. The same Emperor also wrote in similar terms to the elders of Gytheum (in Sparta), saying that only the Deified Augustus was worthy of such honours, whilst he himself preferred honours that were moderate and appropriate to mortals.[55] Vespasian displayed a characteristically down-to-earth stance on the matter, when he is reported to have remarked on his death-bed, 'Woe is me! I think that I am becoming a god!'[56]

In the East, however, matters were rather different: there, as we have seen, the rulers of the Hellenistic kingdoms had been revered as gods, and the Emperor of Rome was essentially their successor. For the most part, Emperors accommodated this without difficulty; even Tiberius, who, as we have seen, turned down a request from Spain for permission to build a temple to him, allowed the province of Asia to build one in recognition of his beneficence following an earthquake in the region in AD 17.[57] Nero's grandfather, Germanicus Caesar, on the other hand, was less comfortable and, whilst in Egypt in AD 19, published an edict[58] instructing the people to refrain from showering him with divine honours, and warning that, if this was not heeded, he would be forced to restrict his public appearances. Yet, like Nero, he was personally enthusiastic over Greek culture and, indeed, incurred the censure of Tiberius for taking this too far.[59]

Nero seems to have made no attempt to restrain eastern enthusiasm, and the acclamations accorded to, even encouraged by, him became more extravagant: as we have seen,[60] decrees issued locally in Alexandria at the time of Nero's accession came close to treating him as divine; in other Greek cities, he was named as a god, or equated with particular deities – 'Nero Apollo' or 'the new Apollo' in recognition of his musical talent, 'Nero Zeus the Liberator' in return for his granting of freedom to the Greeks in AD 67, even 'Hercules Augustus'.[61] Hercules was a particular favourite of certain Emperors, a god who laboured for mankind appearing to be a particularly suitable image.[62] This may explain the discovery of a statue of Hercules at Corinth, that would seem to be particularly appropriate in view of Nero's inauguration of the construction of the canal.[63] Further, we are told that Nero[64] enjoyed playing the part of Hercules in the play, *Hercules Furens* (*Hercules Distraught*), in which the hero murdered members of his family whilst under the influence of the goddess, Hera, and gradually came to realise what he had done – perhaps an attempt on Nero's part to suggest that he was not in possession of his full faculties when he murdered his mother and his wife.

Perhaps more significantly, we can see a greater extravagance (or syco-phancy) in reactions to Nero. In AD 55, for example, the Emperor was given virtually equal standing with Mars the Avenger following a relatively minor success in Armenia;[65] a decade later, when Tiridates came to Rome to receive his kingly diadem from Nero, the Parthian hailed the Roman Emperor as 'Mithras' on what Nero regarded as 'The Golden Day',[66] that was also the 'Day of the Sun', a kind of climax within the 'golden age'. The later coinage also provides indications of Nero's stressing of his proximity to divinities: following the conspiracy of Piso in AD 65, a coin was issued showing *Iuppiter Custos* (Jupiter the Guardian),[67] whilst, during the same period, the Emperor's musical talents were being acknowledged on an issue depicting *Apollo Citharoedus*.[68] This issue was sufficiently striking to merit a comment from Suetonius.[69] On another, the Emperor is shown wearing the radiate crown of the Sun, with the legend AVGVSTVS GERMANICVS, presumably an attempt to link his own achievements in the East with those of his grandfather and his great-great-grandfather.[70]

Most of this can be dated to the period which showed a marked deterioration in the Emperor's relations with the Senate, and it is possible that, in his growing fear for his life, Nero sought, as an exercise in public relations and image building, to elevate himself in this way above the level of ordinary mortals. Suetonius[71] says that the Emperor had little time for religion; in view of this, whilst he may simply have enjoyed such acclamations, it might be seen as unlikely that he took his own divinity seriously. The use of religious sanction accords well with the notion of an Emperor who realised that, in practice, he could not be held subject to human law, and one who had come to the conclusion that it would be most effective – and safer for him – if he ruled as a king – in other words, a conscious decision rather than a flight of fancy.

This deterioration in the Emperor's relationship with the Senate brought in its train overt opposition, and even conspiracy.[72] Clearly, however, this decline had started earlier, even though it may have aroused little criticism at the time. He had easily survived the murder of his mother in AD 59 and, although, as we have seen, there were demonstrations at the time of Octavia's death in AD 62, Nero had dealt with these with no great difficulty. He had married Poppaea and, in January of AD 63, they had had a baby daughter, Claudia,[73] who, like her mother, received the title, *Augusta*. However, just three months later, Claudia died, leaving Nero distraught. Both of these events provoked excessive and sycophantic reactions: the whole of the Senate made the journey to Antium when the baby was born and, following her death, it was proposed that she should be officially deified. A significant hint, however, of problems to come was the fact that Thrasea Paetus, who had, over the years, been pointed in his criticism of certain of Nero's actions,[74] was not permitted to participate in the senatorial journey to Antium at the time of Claudia's birth. Clearly, Thrasea was deemed to have shown insufficient gratitude for the Emperor's earlier acts and was presumably regarded as unworthy to merit further imperial generosity and favour.

In the following year, AD 64, the Great Fire of Rome provides what might be termed a defining moment in Nero's Principate.[75] Major fires in the city were by no means unusual, because of both the materials used in the buildings and their overcrowding; Tiberius' reign, for example, had witnessed two. However, the fire of AD 64 assumed far more catastrophic proportions than these. It started in the *Circus Maximus*, and took hold rapidly because of the high inflammability of the booths there and their contents. Three of the fourteen Augustan regions into which the city was divided were completely destroyed, and only four escaped unscathed. The casualties included Nero's new palace, the *Domus Transitoria*.

As we have seen, Nero himself was at Antium at the time, but returned to Rome to take charge of vigorous relief-work; this did nothing, however, to check the spread of rumours that the Emperor had been responsible for the conflagration. Arsonists had supposedly been spotted and, in any case, it was believed that Nero entertained a wish to rebuild the city and rename it *Neropolis*. Also damaging to the Emperor's credibility was the fact that, after six days, the fire was waning, but a sudden change of wind strength and direction gave it new life. It was alleged that this resurgence had started near to property owned by Tigellinus. There were stories, too, that people had tried to interfere with the fire-fighting, although in reality these were probably looters. Of our main sources of information, only Tacitus introduces any note of doubt regarding the Emperor's responsibility for the disaster, and shows that it was due to the fact that he could not carry conviction with his protestations of innocence that he sought others onto whom he could shift the blame.

Tacitus, alone of our sources, specifically connects the attack on the Christians in Rome with the Emperor's search for scapegoats.[76] Of the later Christian apologists, Lactantius reports the attack, but connects it with the enormous growth of the religion during Nero's reign.[77] Indeed, contrary to the views of apologists, this was not a doctrinal persecution as such, as no items of dogma were involved; attacks on Christians on dogmatic grounds did not really begin until rules were laid down by the Emperor, Trajan, in his rescript to the Younger Pliny in Bithynia.[78] Although Tacitus makes it clear that the Christians were chosen as scapegoats, he also states that few were actually convicted of incendiarism, but rather of 'hatred of the human race', an observation deriving from the rumours that abounded of the Christians' alleged anti-social behaviour. The Eucharist, for example, was interpreted by some as cannibalism. Another doubt is introduced by the fact that Eusebius[79] appears to suggest most of the Christian deaths occurred in Nero's later years. It is said by Tacitus[80] that people tired of the savagery of the punishments, although it should be noted that the public punishment of criminals was normally exacted in a form thought to fit the crime.[81]

As we have seen, the Fire was followed by an explosion of expense, caused principally by the building-activity which included, of course, Nero's new palace, the *Domus Aurea*.[82] That the Emperor was faced by a growing financial crisis in the last years of his reign seems clear: at the conclusion of his account of the Fire, Tacitus[83] describes the rapaciousness with which Nero went about acquiring money and gold in Italy and the provinces – even to the point of plundering temples for their gold. Galba found a sorry financial situation when he reached Rome after Nero's fall in AD 68, and set about trying to recover some of Nero's lavish expenditure.[84] Amongst the measures that he put in place was the establishment of a commission, the membership of which included Tacitus' father-in-law, Gnaeus Julius Agricola (*praetor* in AD 68), in an attempt to recover misappropriated temple-treasure.[85]

Yet, in the earlier years of Nero's reign, finances had been handled more responsibly, although even at that stage expenditure was heavy; in AD 56, as noted above,[86] he had decided to replace the quaestors in charge of the public treasury (*aerarium*) by more senior men – *praefecti* of praetorian standing – and took action against rapacious provincial governors and tax-collectors.[87] The Prefect of the Corn-Supply (*Praefectus Annonae*), for example, had a primary duty to ensure that corn was neither spoiled through negligence nor lost through fraud.[88] Nero's payments into the *aerarium* were frequent and large, as were gifts to the people and donatives to the army, especially the Praetorian Guard, which received donatives after the murder of Agrippina in AD 59 and, again, after the Pisonian conspiracy in AD 65, as well as a monthly grain allowance.[89] Suetonius, indeed,[90] comments on the Emperor's generosity in his earlier years, whilst Tacitus[91] provides instances of Nero's generosity to individuals. Griffin[92] notes that, in AD 54 alone, Nero spent in largesse a sum (180,000,000 *sestertii*) that was one third higher than the donatives that Augustus had paid to all his veterans after the battle of Actium. On the other hand, his income in these early years was probably not great: he had his inheritance from his father that had been restored to him by Claudius, and presumably an inheritance from Claudius himself, together with access to Agrippina's wealth, so long as their relations remained amicable.[93] However, at that time there was little income from war-booty.

It is clear that such a level of generosity and expenditure, about which, as late as AD 62, Nero was constantly boasting,[94] when put together with what was spent on building-projects, games and shows, disaster-relief,[95] grain-subsidies, and a wide variety of hand-outs,[96] could not be sustained indefinitely. The Fire may have provided an opportunity for rebuilding the city of Rome, but the realisation will have dawned on Nero that the sums of money to accomplish this – not to mention the construction and decoration of the *Domus Aurea* – would be huge. It is worth noting here[97] that Otho required 50,000,000 *sestertii* just to complete the decoration of the palace.

It is little wonder that desperate measures became necessary, particularly since many of the handouts were politically too sensitive to discontinue.

Nero's need for gold seems to have become an obsession, linked perhaps to the growing importance in his mind of Apollo as 'god of the sun'. As we have seen, the 'golden age' demanded gold and, alongside it, the gold-coloured amber, that had been used to decorate the Emperor's amphi-theatre.[98] Nero even started a fashion in feminine hairstyling by referring to Poppaea's hair as amber-coloured. We should also note the bizarre episode in AD 65 when the Emperor became convinced by a rumour that the treasure of the mythical Carthaginian queen, Dido, still existed in north Africa, and could be retrieved.[99]

Another clear sign of Nero's growing awareness of the scale of his financial problems can be seen in his readiness to inflict and exact harsh taxes – a move in which a number of provinces are known to have suffered, including Africa, Britain, Egypt, Gaul, Greece and Judaea.[100] Dio records that, after the Fire, Nero deprived even Roman citizens living in Rome of their grain-allowance (*frumentum publicum*).[101] Added to this, he was more ruthless in his expectation of legacies; people came to the view that the only way in which they could seek protection for the interests of their true heirs was to leave a substantial legacy to the Emperor. In Britain, for example, as we have seen, the leader of the tribe of the Iceni included the Emperor in his will when he died in AD 59. However, this was not sufficient to protect the remainder of his legatees: the imperial procurator, Decianus Catus, seized the remainder, probably following instructions from Nero who, according to Suetonius,[102] was in the habit of saying to his officials, 'You know what my needs are; you and I must see to it that nobody is left with anything'. Nero would confiscate up to five-sixths of estates where the testators had failed to be sufficiently generous to him, a sign, as Nero characteristically put it, of their ingratitude. He also confiscated from those who had been condemned to death or exile.[103]

Perhaps the most noticeable sign of the deepening financial crisis was Nero's reform of the gold and silver coinage:[104] from AD 64–5, the weight of the *aureus* was reduced by approximately four percent, allowing forty-five coins to be struck from one pound of gold instead of forty, which had been usual in the Old Republic. This far exceeded the gradual weight-reduction, that had been normal under Nero's predecessors, in order to keep fresh coinage approximately in line with older and more worn issues. The weight of the silver *denarius* was also reduced, and the silver alloyed with copper, leaving the intrinsic value of the silver coinage at around five to ten percent below that of pre-reform issues.[105] The Elder Pliny[106] mentions the debasing of the silver coinage, but appears to direct the blame towards forgers rather than the Emperor.

A number of explanations have been offered for the coinage-reform, such as an attempt to accommodate eastern and western coinage-systems, or alternatively to check the flow of silver eastwards to the Middle East, India and China for the purchase of luxury items.[107] This does not, however, appear to have been seen as a problem when Nero, in AD 58, was proposing to cancel indirect taxation.[108] The most likely explanation, therefore, remains that the reform of the coinage at this time was intended to facilitate the payment of bills arising from the construction of the *Domus Aurea*. At the same time, the continued looting of art-treasures from around the Empire brought fresh criticism of the Emperor and hardship for his subjects. Unsurprisingly, Tacitus observes,[109] the year came to an end amidst omens and prodigies that were thought to presage a dire future; this was to manifest itself in conspiracies mounted against Nero in AD 65, AD 66 and AD 68, and in the Emperor's confrontation with the so-called Stoic opposition in AD 66. Given Nero's need to experience gratitude in return for what he saw as his magnanimity, such expressions of ingratitude will have alarmed and angered him. The result was predictable: an Emperor who behaved more tyrannically after these conspiracies than he had done before them. Such an outcome perhaps provides some justification for Tacitus' lack of enthusiasm for conspiracies:[110] the aftermath would often turn out to be worse than the state of affairs that the conspiracies had aimed to terminate.

As we have seen, relations between Nero and an admittedly sycophantic Senate had, up until AD 62 at least, been reasonably smooth. The advent of Tigellinus, however, had marked a change: under pressure from scurrilous lampoons circulating about him, Nero, as we have seen, reintroduced the treason law; the circumstances were similar to those that had led Tiberius to take the same course of action in AD 15.[111] The first case – that of Antistius Sosianus[112] – that, significantly, had been brought by Tigellinus' son-in-law, undoubtedly soured relations between the Emperor and the Senate; Nero, who later claimed that he wished to treat Antistius generously, found himself upstaged by Thrasea Paetus, who carried the Senate with him. This was, then, for Nero, yet another instance when his generosity had failed to produce the desired result. It was never likely, with Tigellinus having replaced Seneca and Burrus in Nero's counsels, that further friction could be long delayed. When it came, however, in the form of the conspiracy of Gaius Piso in AD 65,[113] relations will have deteriorated still further under pressure from the events of AD 64.

Although Piso's was evidently the first serious conspiracy against Nero, and although the incentives of some of its members could hardly be described as high-minded, the motives of a few, at least, will have had their roots in a culture of opposition that had, for more than a century, been developing around certain followers of the Stoic school of philosophy.[114] This culture of opposition, that had suffered one notable loss as early as the reign of Tiberius in the person of the historian, Aulus Cremutius Cordus,[115] had been represented in the earlier part of Nero's reign principally by Thrasea Paetus, who had been consul in AD 56.

Stoicism was a Greek philosophy that, over the years, had been embraced by many amongst Rome's upper classes; essentially, Stoicism was a moral rather than a political philosophy, although many Romans failed to observe a distinction between the two. A creed that talked of virtue and duty inevitably came to show how the moral man might serve the Republic and keep intact his dignity and freedom.[116] The moral code of Stoicism made a strong appeal to traditionally-minded Romans, and it came to be associated with that important concept, ancestral custom (*mos maiorum*), the most traditional expression of morality and virtue. The turbulent politics of the late Republic and early Principate demonstrated a widening gulf between morality and politics, and that gulf might be said to have reached new depths with Nero's murder of his mother. Because of its espousal of traditional virtues, Stoicism in Rome came to be associated with the Old Republic, and with those men who were perceived as its greatest champions – men such as Marcus Porcius Cato who, in 46 BC, committed suicide rather than live in 'Caesar's Republic', and Marcus Brutus, the leader of the plot to murder Caesar in 44 BC, and who died four years after Cato.

Opposition to the Emperor or the system was not, during the early Principate, obligatory upon Stoics;[117] Seneca, after all, managed to accommodate his Stoic beliefs with proximity to Nero,[118] arguing perhaps that the next best thing to a 'philosopher-king' was a king who was trained in the best governmental practices by a Stoic philosopher. Of course, it should be remembered that, a century after Nero, Rome had in Marcus Aurelius (AD 161–180) an Emperor who was himself a Stoic philosopher. Some Stoics in Nero's time, however, did not see things quite as Seneca did;

instead, they looked back in time for inspiration to the contests between Caesar and Cato. They even looked to Caesar's contemporaries, such as the historian, Sallust, such a comparison was valid and powerful.[119] Cicero, on the other hand, whilst he sometimes admired Cato's high-minded attachment to principles, could also dismiss him as cantankerous, obsessive and out-of-touch with reality,[120] standing in the way of the achievement of stable government. Cicero knew how Cato's intransigence, as much as anything, had forced the Republic into civil war in 49 BC; he knew, too, from personal experience, how the cantankerous obsessiveness of Cato had resented the participation of an outsider, such as Cicero himself, in what he termed 'our struggle'.[121]

Despite the reality as Cicero knew it, eulogies of Cato and his friends became an essential part of the hagiography embracing the spirit of the Old Republic in its struggle with absolutism, although there was nothing in Stoic doctrine that made such a stance inevitable. For some, then, in the early Principate, Cato, Brutus and Cassius (despite the fact that the latter two were not Stoics at all) were brought together as the antitheses of autocracy. As we have seen, the Tiberian historian, Cremutius Cordus praised Brutus and referred to Cassius as 'the last of the Romans'.

Tacitus, as we have seen, remained ambivalent in his views of Stoic politicians: both Thrasea Paetus and his son-in-law, the elder Helvidius Priscus, are accused of glory-seeking.[122] Helvidius went on to annoy even the patient and phlegmatic Vespasian beyond redemption, conducting a campaign designed principally, it seems, to aggravate.[123] Further, Tacitus lived through what appears to have been the final dénouement of this Stoic group – a conspiracy in AD 93[124] against the Emperor, Domitian, led by Helvidius' son and coming as the culmination of such acts of civil disobedience as the composition of eulogistic biographies of Cato. The historian did not relish the outcome and, in his *Life of Agricola*, proposed an alternative way.[125]

For Tacitus, as on occasion for Cicero, the behaviour of the Stoics seemed divorced from the real world; they were a closed, cliquey group, often bound together by close family ties and seeming to resent the intrusive support of outsiders. This was certainly true of many of the Stoics who were active in politics in the Neronian and Flavian periods. Their doctrines led to actions that seemed inopportune, as Tacitus shows in the case of the evangelical Gaius Musonius Rufus,[126] who tried to preach the blessings of peace to those involved in the civil war that followed Nero's death. Nor was it clear what they ultimately wanted to achieve, or upon what precisely their objections were based: did they want a *different* Emperor, or *no* Emperor? Did they advocate a return to the Old Republic? Did they object to materialism, immorality – or to monarchy *per se*?

Thrasea Paetus, who came from northern Italy, said much of which Tacitus would clearly have approved, particularly when he was attacking corruption in government or the bending of the laws. However, it was inevitable that a man who espoused older ideals and who, we may assume, will have approved of much, if not all, of the prospectus for government that Seneca laid out for Nero at the time of his accession, should come into conflict with an Emperor who, progressively from AD 59, seemed intent on forwarding the claims of a personal absolutism. For Thrasea, such acts as the deification of Nero's infant daughter in AD 63 and of Poppaea Sabina two years later[127] represented departures from tradition that, in some senses, were as unacceptable as Nero's murder of his mother and his former wife.

Yet, Thrasea was not himself a doctrinaire opponent of Nero nor, despite Tacitus' misgivings, did he take every opportunity for self-advancement. During his trial for treason in AD 66, he refused to command an open stage, nor would he allow a younger friend, the tribune Arulenus Rusticus, to risk his life and career by interposing his veto on Thrasea's behalf.[128] Indeed, much of what Thrasea said in the Senate on that occasion was calculated simply to expose and criticise corruption and corrupt people.

Relations between Nero and Thrasea Paetus had not been good since AD 59, and had reached a seriously low level four years later, when Thrasea had been refused permission, along with other senators, to 'greet' Nero's new daughter at Antium; this amounted to a renunciation of the 'imperial friendship'. Nevertheless, we should still ask why it was that Nero determined upon Thrasea's destruction, along with that of Barea Soranus, in AD 66 in what Tacitus called 'an assault upon Virtue itself'.[129] Tacitus alleges that the trial was timed to coincide with the arrival in Rome of Tiridates to receive his diadem of kingship from Nero, in the hope that attention would thereby be diverted by the ceremonial from this domestic outrage; possibly, however, Nero may have simply hoped to impress Tiridates by such a truly regal display of his power.

The trial[130] was clearly conducted in an exceedingly ferocious and intimidating manner: violent speeches of denunciation of Thrasea Paetus and Barea Soranus, encouraged by Nero himself, were made by Cossutianus

Capito (Tigellinus' eminently uncongenial son-in-law), Ostorius Sabinus and Eprius Marcellus. The first two of these were clearly motivated by personal animosity towards the defendants. Much was made of the connection of attitude between Thrasea and his friends and Marcus Cato and of Thrasea's sometimes ostentatious disapproval of Nero's behaviour:

> *As this faction-loving country once talked of Caesar versus Cato, so now, Nero, it talks of you versus Thrasea. And he has his followers – or his courtiers rather. They do not yet imitate his treasonable voting. But they copy his grim and gloomy manner and expression: they rebuke your amusements. He is the one man to whom your safety is immaterial, your talents unadmired. He dislikes the Emperor to be happy. But even your unhappiness, your bereavements, do not appease him. Disbelief in Poppaea's divinity shows the same spirit as refusing allegiance to the acts of the divine Augustus and divine Julius.*[131]

The substance, however, is hard to find: there is no indication, for example, that Thrasea, at least, had taken any part in the conspiracy of Piso in the previous year; nor does Tacitus' account of that event once mention him. Gaius Piso, as we shall see, was a shallow man of little consequence, and the motives of most of those involved are said to have been scarcely laudable. The only obvious Stoic connection seems to have been provided by Seneca's nephew, the poet, Lucan, whose motive for involvement appears to have been entirely personal,[132] and who subsequently tried to excuse his own conduct by inculpating his mother. Seneca himself, having retired from public life following Burrus' death in AD 62, was now required to commit suicide – perhaps simply an opportunistic excuse on Nero's part, or a case of guilt by association.[133]

The objective of the Pisonian conspiracy was to assassinate Nero, and replace him with Gaius Calpurnius Piso, a descendant of a famous Republican family, although, as Tacitus indicates, without naming alternatives, the plot evidently did not originate with Piso. Tacitus held no high opinion of Piso: an erstwhile friend of Nero's who had participated in some of Nero's projects, a man who enjoyed the comforts of the Bay of Naples and the excitement of performing on the stage. He appears to have been chosen because he was different from Nero – but not too different.[134] Tacitus, in his character-sketch of Piso, picks out the man's positive qualities, but concludes:

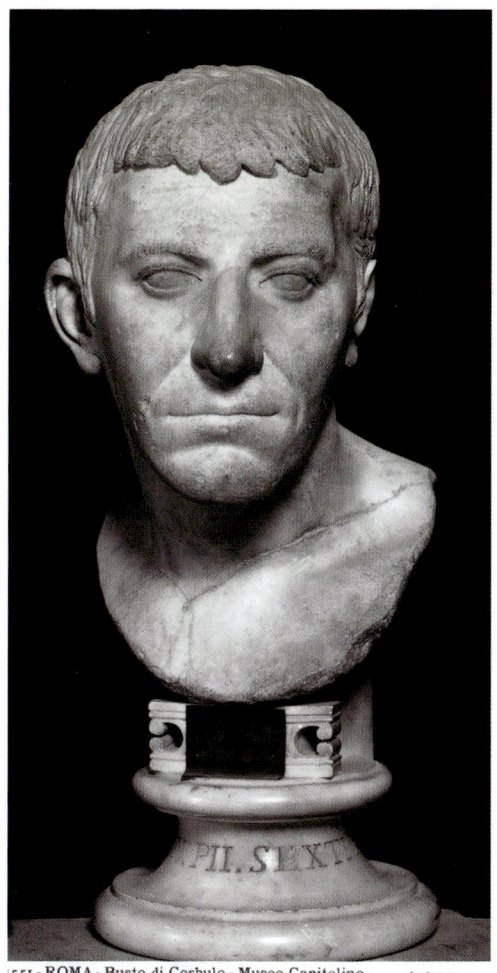

:551 - ROMA - Busto di Corbulo - Museo Capitolino -   *Anderson*

Plate 14 Bust of Gnaeus Domitius Corbulo, Museo Capitolino, Rome; Mansell Collection; see Griffin, M. T., '*Imago Vitae Suae*', pp. 1–38 in Costa, C. D. N. (ed.), Seneca (London, 1984), plate 5. ADA-F-001551-0000: Anderson/Alinari Archives-Florence.

Plate 15 Rome: The Arch of Titus, author's own.

Plate 16 Rome: The Arch of Titus: detail of the triumphal procession, author's own.

Plate 17 Rome: The Flavian Amphitheatre, author's own. (Photograph taken from the site of the *Donius Aurea* residence)

Plate 18 Ostia: Forum of the Corporations: office of the *Navi(cularii) Narbonenses*, a shipping company from Narbo (Narbonne in Provence), author's own.

Plate 19 Rome: Domus Transitoria: cryptoporticus with stucco decoration, author's own.

Plate 20 Rome: Domus Aurea: trompe l'oeil, author's own.

Plate 21 Pompeii: The House of Lucretius Fronto, showing a Villa with a 'sun-court', see Wheeler, R. E. M., *Roman Art and Architecture*, (1964, reprinted 1989), London, Thames and Hudson, p. 143, plate 126.

Plate 22 Pompeii: The House of Venus in a Sea-shell: wall decoration depicting a *Villa Maritima*, author's own. (The painting shows a villa which has been built out into the sea on a jetty).

Plate 23 Pompeii: The House of the Ancient Hunt: wall decoration depicting Helius-Apollo, author's own.

Plate 24 Rome: The Temple of Vesta in the Forum, author's own.

Plate 25 Nero: late portrait, see Malitz, J., *Nero* (Oxford, 2005), p. 96, fig. 8.
© The Art Archive/Corbis.

Plate 26 Castrén, P. and Lilius, H. (1970) Graffiti del Palatino, II, Domus
Tiberiana, *Acta Instituti Finlandiae*, 4, Helsinki, p. 121. Reproduced by kind
permission of P. Castrén.

But his character lacked seriousness or self-control. He was superficial, ostentatious, and sometimes dissolute. But many people are fascinated by depravity and disinclined for austere morals on the throne. Such men found Piso's qualities attractive.[135]

Galba was to warn his designated successor, Piso Licinianus, not to allow decent men to feel the loss of Nero.[136]

The membership of the conspiracy was wide-ranging, and included senators, equestrians, one of the Praetorian Prefects (Faenius Rufus) and some of his officers, and at least one woman, Epicharis, a freed slave. It appears that the motivations of many were personal and often quite trivial; Faenius Rufus had joined because he was afraid of the influence exerted upon Nero by his colleague, Tigellinus. A few joined for reasons of patriotism; these included Epicharis, whose behaviour throughout is noted for its honesty and courage. However, perhaps most striking of the patriots was Subrius Flavus, an officer in the Praetorian Guard, who, in the aftermath, said directly to Nero:

I hated you; and yet none of your soldiers was more devoted to you so long as you merited it. My devotion turned to hatred when you murdered your mother and your wife, and became a charioteer, an actor and an incendiary.[137]

These were, according to Tacitus, Flavus' exact words, and Nero was gravely affected by them; as we should expect, the Emperor was here brought face-to-face with what he will have regarded as the gross ingratitude of a subject.

However, whilst the driving-force behind the conspiracy may have been lightweight, there are signs that, at the same time, there was something more serious in the air. For example, there was a dispute over where the assassination should take place: some wanted it done in Piso's villa at Baiae where, at one time, the Emperor had been a frequent visitor. Piso, however, vetoed this, preferring a location in Rome in order to forestall any rivals who might use a power-vacuum to install themselves in Nero's place. In the event, the *Circus Maximus* was chosen, and Piso expected that, after Nero's assassination, he would be accompanied to the camp of the Praetorian Guard by Faenius Rufus.

One of the possible rivals to Piso was the consul, Vestinus Atticus, who was thought to entertain Republican sympathies; perhaps, however, a more serious figure was Lucius Junius Silanus Torquatus, a member of a family that, as we have seen, had not fared well at the hands of Claudius and Nero, and one who was the last living descendant of Augustus. Torquatus' name arises in a group of people who were punished in the months following the collapse of the conspiracy. Through this group, a connection, albeit tenuous, emerges with Barea Soranus, Thrasea Paetus' co-defendant in the trial that was to take place in the following year (AD 66).

Barea Soranus, by now an elderly man, was attacked by his accuser, Ostorius Sabinus, for his friendship with Rubellius Plautus,[138] and also on the ground that his daughter, Servilia, had consulted astrologers concerning Nero and her family. Such a course of action, even in calmer times, would have been viewed with considerable suspicion. As we have seen, Rubellius Plautus was a respectable, but rather dull, Stoic, who was descended from the Emperor, Tiberius. Earlier in the reign, Nero had been anxious about Plautus' association with Agrippina; he had been forcibly retired from Rome to his estates in the province of Asia and then, in AD 62, murdered on the instructions of Tigellinus. Nero had been principally concerned about Plautus' connections with the Julio-Claudian family; however, when Tigellinus had persuaded the Emperor to put him to death, he had hinted at a more serious revolutionary liaison with the commander of the eastern legions, Gnaeus Domitius Corbulo.[139] All of this prompts the suggestion that Plautus may have had connections with a group whose members, although not plotting at the time of Plautus' death, were concerned about the general state of affairs. It would not be at all surprising if such a group counted some Stoics in its number, some of whom may have progressed to conspiracy in AD 65 and AD 66.

As we have seen, the likely success of the conspiracy of Piso was undermined by the lack of coherence, even integrity, amongst many of its participants. In the event, however, the conspirators lost their 'cover' in April of AD 65, when two of their number, Epicharis and a senator, named Scaevinus, aroused suspicions through careless talk, and were informed upon to Nero.

Reprisals were rapid and savage; Tacitus provides details of many, although the bravery under torture of Epicharis stands out.[140] The mood in Rome was such that it was not difficult to find a reason for accusing almost anyone of complicity:

> *Line upon line of chained men were dragged along, and left lying at the gates of Nero's garden. As they pleaded their cases, services to the*

conspirators, and even chance conversations or encounters – at a party, for example – were taken as signs of guilt. These ferocious investigations were carried out not only by Nero and Tigellinus, but Faenius Rufus, too, who was hoping to divert suspicion from himself by the zeal with which he went about the interrogations.[141]

One of the prosecutors was the senator and epic poet, Silius Italicus, who thus prostituted his oratory in Nero's service and was rewarded with a consulship in AD 68.[142]

Those whose punishments are recorded include Seneca's brothers, Junius Gallio and Annaeus Mela, Publius Anteius Rufus, who was a friend of Agrippina's and probably related to Anteia, the wife of the younger Helvidius Priscus, Gaius Anicius Cerealis (consul in AD 65) and Gaius(?) Petronius, formerly Nero's adviser on matters of taste,[143] who was evidently framed by Tigellinus. Two suicides were ordered – those of Marcus Ostorius Scapula (consul in AD 59, and son of Publius Ostorius Scapula, a former governor of Britain); Scapula was a friend of Anteius and a man evidently feared by Nero. The other required suicide was that of Lucius Antistius Vetus, consul in AD 59 and, like Barea Soranus, a former proconsul of Asia; Antistius was the father-in-law of Rubellius Plautus. The frequency of connections with the province of Asia and Rubellius Plautus does seem to point to at least suspected disloyalty on the part of Corbulo that, as we have seen, had been hinted at by Tigellinus at the time of Rubellius Plautus' murder. A further possible connection emerges in the fact that Corbulo's daughter was married to Annius Vinicianus whose father had participated in two plots against Claudius and whose brother, Annius Pollio (who was exiled at this time for complicity in Piso's conspiracy), was the son-in-law of Barea Soranus, co-defendant with Thrasea Paetus in AD 66. A conspiracy, attributed to a Vinicianus, was detected at Beneventum (modern Benevento) in AD 66, although little is known beyond this.[144]

Corbulo himself was well-connected through his mother, Vistilia, and it is possible that the general was married to a daughter of the blind jurist, Gaius Cassius Longinus, a descendant of Julius Caesar's assassin. It is worth remembering that, at the time of Vindex's rebellion in AD 68, a coin, showing two daggers and the 'cap of freedom', that had been issued at the time of Caesar's assassination, was partially reissued in Spain (for Galba) as part of the anti-Nero propaganda.[145] The original coin had had the legend EID

MAR (The Ides of March), whilst the reissue bore the words, LIBERTAS P R RESTITVTA (The Liberty of the Roman People Restored). Thus, just as the poet, Lucan, had recalled the part played by the civil war between Caesar and Pompey in eventually bringing Nero to power, so now Nero's death was clearly linked in the political consciousness with the death of the 'tyrant' a century earlier.[146] At any rate, Cassius Longinus was one of those punished by Nero after the conspiracy; he was exiled, along with his wife's nephew, Lucius Junius Silanus Torquatus, who, as we have seen, may have been a rival figurehead to Gaius Piso in the conspiracy.

Thus, although there were no clear connections between the Stoic group and those involved in Piso's conspiracy, Barea Soranus, at least, can be shown to have had links with men of prominent family, some of whom were not totally above suspicion of dissidence. There may, indeed, have been further connections – for example, with the Scribonius brothers, legates in the German military districts, whose deaths by suicide were required by Nero in AD 67, and whose associates, Quintus Sulpicius Camerinus (consul in AD 46)[147] and Marcus Licinius Crassus Frugi (consul in AD 64) also perished at this time. It remains unclear whether these were thought guilty of involvement in the conspiracy or were feared as potential future figureheads.

We may, therefore, be able to see how Nero could view Barea Soranus as a dissident. Thrasea Paetus may have been attacked by association rather than as a result of any direct evidence of conspiratorial involvement. However, whilst Thrasea was no conspirator, he was a man who stood for old-fashioned principles of conduct and deportment, which were very different from current fashions, and whose dignity was impressive. Such adherence to tradition may have been enough, in Nero's eyes, to associate him with some whose connections and beliefs made them more dangerous than Thrasea himself.

Ultimately, therefore, despite the virulence of the attack on him orchestrated by Nero, Thrasea Paetus was not a revolutionary, although he did by his conduct reinforce the appearance of a connection between Stoicism and republicanism. In reality, however, he did little more than to press, like Seneca, for an improvement in the current situation. It was, then, both ironic and inevitable that he should himself become, like Cato, a luminary for future generations; for the increasingly extreme stance of the philosophical opposition under the Flavians readily added Thrasea Paetus to the list of martyrs. In their different ways, however, both Seneca and Thrasea Paetus demonstrated by their actions that there was no inherent inconsistency between Stoicism and the Principate. It was, however, Nero's action, in his 'assault on Virtue itself' in AD 66, that ensured that the political descendants of Caesar and Cato were now set on a collision course.

In the aftermath of the Pisonian conspiracy,[148] Nero evidently came to believe that his escape had been due to divine intervention: *Sol Invictus* (the Unconquerable Sun) had shed the light which revealed the plot. It was, then, little wonder that the crowning glory of Nero's new palace was the *Colossus* – the huge column on which stood the figure of *Nero-Helios*[149] (or *Nero-Apollo*), the Emperor of Rome at one with the Sun-god. Special thanks and gifts were offered to *Sol* for his part in unmasking the conspiracy,[150] and Anicius Cerealis, who was to die by suicide in the following year,[151] even proposed that a temple be built in Rome to 'the Deified Nero'; the Emperor, significantly perhaps, vetoed this on the ground that it would constitute a bad omen, as only dead Emperors were deified.[152] As we have seen, the Parthian, Tiridates, in Rome in AD 66, saluted Nero as Mithras, the vice-gerent of *Sol*. The dagger that was to have killed Nero in the plot of AD 65 was dedicated to *Jupiter Vindex* (Jupiter the Avenger)[153] who sanctioned Nero's revenge on those who, by conspiring, had shown their lack of gratitude. As we have seen, the contemporary coinage displayed the Emperor as under the guardianship of Jupiter,[154] whilst other issues concentrate on harmony and victory.[155]

One interesting coin of this period is that which shows an Emperor and Empress, the former of whom wears the radiate crown of the Sun, within the legend AVGVSTVS AVGVSTA.[156] Presumably, this represents Augustus and Livia, with a suggestion of Nero and Poppaea. Nero also ordered that a large donative should be given to the soldiers for their loyalty, whilst triumphal insignia were granted to Petronius Turpilianus, Nerva (the future Emperor) and Tigellinus; the latter two were further honoured with statues in the Forum and on the Palatine Hill.[157] Faenius Rufus' place as Praetorian Prefect was taken by Gaius Nymphidius Sabinus,[158] a man of shadowy credentials, who was to play a dubious part in the latter days of Nero's reign. The predictable sycophantic decrees were passed in the Senate, one of which was to rename the month of April, *Neroneus*, after the Emperor.

Some time after the conspiracy, Poppaea Sabina died, after being kicked during pregnancy by Nero.[159] Her distraught husband had her deified, and immediately sought to replace her. After failing to persuade Antonia, Claudius' surviving daughter and widow of Faustus Sulla, to become his wife, he married his mistress, Statilia Messalina,[160] a great-great-granddaughter of Augustus' prominent general, Statilius Taurus, and previously married to Nero's one-time friend, Vestinus Atticus (consul in AD 65). Statilia, like Poppaea, was older than Nero. He also had the young freedman, Sporus, castrated, and went through a form of marriage with him; in Nero's eyes, however, Sporus, whom he insisted on calling Sabina, was the true replacement for Poppaea; as Champlin says, it was as if the 'play' of Nero's grief was being acted out, with Sporus playing the part of Poppaea.[161]

Apart from some officers of the Praetorian Guard, there is no indication that significant elements of the army had so far been involved in conspiracy against Nero. However, the fact that, in AD 66 or AD 67 (whilst he was in Greece), Nero summoned to him the two Scribonius brothers and Domitius Corbulo, and ordered them to take their own lives, suggests that the Emperor continued to fear military disloyalty, and even perhaps was in possession of intelligence to that effect. It is, of course, perfectly possible that the reign of terror that had followed the Pisonian conspiracy had actually generated real disquiet amongst some army-leaders. A possible context is provided by Suetonius' reference[162] to the conspiracy of Vinicianus that had been uncovered at Beneventum in AD 66. As we have seen, nothing is known of this, apart from the fact that Annius Vinicianus was Corbulo's son-in-law, which suggests that this plot may have aimed at replacing Nero by Corbulo. The fact that Corbulo was summoned to the Emperor in Greece during AD 67 suggests a connection with the plot of the previous year.

Late in AD 66, Nero left for Greece, in the company of a court that included Calvia Crispinilla (his wardrobe-mistress) and Sporus, after what can only be described as three very bad years for him, during which time his government had slipped from apparent smooth working to a point where Nero had lost faith in virtually all sections of the community, and they in him. It will have seemed as if all of his earlier generosity and reasonableness had, in the end, brought him a very small dividend of gratitude. In Greece, he expected to find a more welcoming audience and, to them, as we have seen, his response was typically big-hearted – 'The Liberation of Hellas'. His freedman, Helius, was left in charge in Italy but, in view of all that had happened, it was clearly a very inopportune time to be leaving the Empire's heart to its own devices. The Emperor's absence gave surviving dissidents a new opportunity to marshal their forces and supporters in a final effort to bring down the last of the Julio-Claudians.

Chapter Nine

Rebellion and the fall of Nero

On 9 June, AD 68,[1] realising that his cause was lost, after drafting an appeal to the Roman people, Nero, with the help of his scribe, Epaphroditus, committed suicide.[2] Before his death, he had supervised the digging of a grave and the collection of random pieces of marble with which to adorn it. It was on this occasion that he is said to have uttered the famous words, *qualis artifex pereo*,[3] these have traditionally been translated as 'What an artist dies in me!'. Champlin has cogently suggested[4] that this is not the voice of the egotistical Nero but, referring to the mean nature of his final resting-place, the Emperor was reflecting on his fall from power; he was now the 'artisan', no longer the 'artist'.

The surviving accounts of his end are so similar as to suggest that, as Champlin argues, they derive from a common source; this, he has proposed, must have been the consular historian, Cluvius Rufus.[5] Cluvius was in Spain at the time but, judging from the richness of Neronian quotations in the various accounts, he must have subsequently interviewed eye-witnesses. Those present at the time included Nero's freedmen, Epaphroditus and Phaon, Sporus, the eunuch whom the Emperor had so disgracefully abused following the death of Poppaea,[6] together with his nurses, Ecloge and Alexandria, and his still-faithful mistress, Acte. It was the latter who ensured Nero a decent burial in the family-tomb of the Domitii on the Pincian Hill in Rome. Galba's freedman, Icelus, who seems to have been present, guaranteed that the body would not be mutilated, and evidently kept his word. Nero, however, was still alive when Icelus left to join Galba in Spain.[7]

So how had Nero fallen so low in so short a time? The run of events that had brought him to this had its origin not just in the increasing fear and hatred in which Nero was held in many quarters, but also in factors that were inherent in the system of government that had been established by Augustus after Actium. Nero's death did not bring an end to the military convulsions that had started with the rebellion of Gaius Julius Vindex in the spring of AD 68; they continued for another eighteen months, and saw the murders of two further emperors (Galba and Vitellius) and the suicide of another (Nero's friend, Otho), until, in the last days of AD 69, Vespasian established himself in power and inaugurated a new ruling dynasty – the Flavian.[8]

What, then, led to this protracted blood-letting that, according to the historian, Tacitus,[9] spread across the whole Empire after the manner of a contagion? The immediate cause was firmly rooted in the performance and conduct of Nero himself. The matricide, the murders of other members of his family, his treatment, particularly in the later years, of the Senatorial Order and the vicious attacks on some of its members, his undignified participation in performances in the arena, fear inspired by his unpredictability: all these were factors which led people to question his continued fitness to reign.

Discontent had been growing for some time, as is shown by the conspiracies launched by Gaius Calpurnius Piso (in AD 65) and the poorly-understood sequel, the conspiracy of AD 66 that has gone down in history under the name of Annius Vinicianus.[10] Whilst the conspiracy of Piso appears to have been an unimpressive and ill-organised affair, that of Vinicianus may have been more serious if, as appears likely, it involved elements of the military. After all, the destabilising of government through the conjunction of senators and elements of the Roman army represented the re-emergence of the 'vicious nexus' that had brought the Old Republic to its knees; it was this threat that Augustus had appeared to have removed. Nero's growing fear of senior members of the nobility and the dangerous effects of their liaisons with the army may have caused him to look increasingly for his army commanders to men whose pedigrees were less impressive.[11] It was probably this that led the Emperor to bestow commands upon men such as Lucius Verginius Rufus (commander in Upper Germany) and the future

Emperor, Titus Flavius Vespasianus (Governor of the province of Judaea).[12] Whilst such men may not have been wanting in energy, their inferior social status might, Nero hoped, leave them less open to the temptation to set themselves up as his potential rivals. In the event, they may also have lacked the *auctoritas* to enable them to maintain discipline in difficult times. At any rate, Nero obviously hoped that, without dangerous initiatives from their commanders, the armies would remain *politically* docile.

Nero's decision late in AD 66[13] to leave Italy for a tour of Greece and to take the opportunity to participate in a number of the great Greek literary and athletic festivals has all the appearance of escapism – the chance to leave his unpopularity behind and bask in the adulation of his Greek subjects. Predictably, as so often in the past, he reacted with pleasure and generosity to expressed signs of his own popularity. However, the Emperor's distraction provided an opportunity for men of Rome's governing class to take stock of the state of the nation: it is evident that letters were sent by at least one provincial governor, Gaius Julius Vindex of Gallia Lugdunensis, himself a Romanised Gaul, as a means of discovering how far his colleagues in the provinces would be prepared to go in joining him in a crusade to remove the wayward *princeps*.[14] In his abridgement of Dio, John of Antioch, although not to be regarded as the most reliable of writers, adds that approaches were also made to exiled senators.[15] Such approaches might together provide an explanation for Nero's threat to massacre all provincial commanders and exiles.[16]

Few details are known of the responses to Vindex's approaches, although it appears that, whilst some may have been sympathetic, others reported Vindex's 'treason' to the Emperor; yet others appear to have said and done nothing. Galba, for example, was evidently amongst those who failed to report to Nero regarding Vindex's approach. This failure on Galba's part may explain the instruction for his death that he is said to have intercepted, and that finally seems to have drawn him to join Vindex.[17] In assessing these responses or their absence, we should bear in mind how intimidating to the Senate and to individual senators Nero's behaviour had been in recent years.

Evidence of possible trouble appears to have led Helius, the freedman whom Nero had left in charge of Italy during his absence in Greece, to send urgent messages to the Emperor that he should return;[18] this Nero did late in AD 67, although it does not appear that he set in train any specific counter-measures; indeed, almost straightaway on his return, he went to Naples on holiday. This need not surprise us unduly: after all, Nero had no reason at that stage to suspect widespread disaffection in the army; further, Vindex was not from the highest echelon of the imperial service, and was, as an ex-praetor, governor of a province that was essentially unarmed. The Emperor, indeed, had no reason to doubt that, if Vindex did launch a serious attempt against him, nearby armies would be more than a match for him – in the two German military districts commanded by Gaius Fonteius Capito (Lower Germany) and Lucius Verginius Rufus (Upper Germany), and Hispania Tarraconensis that was governed by Servius Sulpicius Galba (Figure 9.1).

Figure 9.1 Map of Spain, the Gallic Provinces and the German Military Districts. Author's own.

It has been mistakenly suggested in the past that, as a Romanised Gaul, Vindex may have had a hidden agenda of raising a nationalist rebellion under the cloak of a movement against Nero.[19] This has, for some, appeared to gain in plausibility because of the outbreak in AD 69, in northern Gaul, of a rising under a Romanised Batavian, Gaius Julius Civilis. Although Civilis was encouraged in his venture by local Roman commanders, who supported the cause of Vespasian, seeking to prevent elements of the Rhine army from marching to Italy in support of the Emperor, Vitellius, the movement rapidly took on a full anti-Roman objective and led to the Gallo-German War, that was not extinguished until AD 70. However, despite certain superficial similarities with this, Vindex's aims are firmly characterised by our surviving sources as directed against Nero with the purpose of replacing him with a more acceptable Emperor. Not only this, but Vindex's propaganda, that survives in written sources[20] and in the legends of contemporary coinage issued in Gaul and Spain,[21] indicates clearly that he was operating within a totally Roman and anti-Neronian context. His propaganda was plainly intended to impact upon Romanised populations, and his choice of Galba as a successor to Nero was made as a means of reviving the traditional standards of Rome's governing élite – what, in a different context, has been dubbed 'back to basics'.

Inconsistencies of detail in our sources make it difficult to reconstruct, with any certainty, the precise sequence of events that led to Nero's downfall.[22] It seems, however, that Vindex, justifying his rebellion and the inauguration of the *bellum Neronis* (war against Nero)[23] on the grounds of Nero's murder of his mother and of his generally-unbecoming conduct,[24] may have raised the standard of revolt on or about the Ides (15th) of March, AD 68, accompanying this with the issuing of edicts criticising Nero. The anniversary of the removal of the 'tyrant', Julius Caesar, will have seemed a particularly auspicious moment at which to move against this latest Caesar. Further, the contemporary coinage included the re-issue of a *denarius* that had first been issued in 44 BC by Marcus Brutus in the wake of Caesar's assassination.[25] This date was also suitably close to the more recent anniversary of Nero's murder of his mother (19 March), during the festival of *Quinquatria*, that Nero generally spent on the Bay of Naples, where he was when he received the news of Vindex's rebellion.

There is no question of Vindex aiming to become Emperor himself; his social credentials would have made that an impossible ambition. Rather, his choice as figurehead for the rebellion and thus, potentially, Nero's successor was Servius Galba, a member of a highly-respected senatorial family, that had, over the generations, performed distinguished service for Rome.[26] Indeed, Galba himself had enjoyed a meritorious career:[27] he had commanded armies, had at one time been a confidant of Augustus' wife, Livia,[28] and had been thought of, following the death of Nero's father, as a possible new husband for the Younger Agrippina.[29] One advantage that Galba held for Vindex was that his province of Hispania Tarraconensis, of which he had been governor for eight years, was close to Vindex's and was guarded by a legion (VI *Victrix*), soon to be supplemented by another that Galba was to raise himself (VII *Galbiana*[30]). However, although a man with the reputation of being a disciplinary martinet, Galba was now elderly and reaching the end of his career. Events were to show that he had neither the energy nor the sharpness and flexibility of judgement to succeed in the confused and dangerous situations precipitated by civil war, and where he was subjected to the pressures brought by unscrupulous courtiers. Nymphidius Sabinus, for example, one of the Praetorian Prefects, who persuaded the Praetorian Guard to declare for Galba, did so in order purely to take personal advantage of such a situation.[31]

The breadth and depth of Vindex's support is hard to assess, although it seems clear that he was backed by a number of Gallic tribes – the Arverni (of his native Aquitania), the Aedui (of Lugdunensis) and the Sequani (of Belgica).[32] The Gallic city of Vienna (Vienne) joined him, although the main city of Vindex's province, Lugdunum (Lyon) remained loyal to Nero. The position of the province of Aquitania as a whole is more equivocal: its governor is reported to have asked Galba for help – whether against or in support of Vindex is left unclear. It is worth noting, however, that Galba is said[33] later to have put to death Betuus Cilo in Gaul; this man is otherwise unknown, but it is conceivable that he may have been that governor of Aquitania. Further, the fact that Fonteius Capito, the governor of Lower Germany, put one leading Batavian (Claudius Paulus) to death and sent another, Julius Civilis, to Rome in chains suggests support for Vindex in the north. That may offer a clue to what lay behind the boast made later by a group of Batavian auxiliaries that they had 'robbed Nero of Italy'.[34] In addition, Vindex may have had the support of leading Gallo-Romans, including the energetic, if unscrupulous, Antonius Primus from Tolosa (Toulouse).[35]

Support for Vindex in Italy is harder to assess: although, as we have seen, Galba had the services of at least one, and possibly both, of the Praetorian Prefects, there is on the other hand, a dedication to Jupiter, associating Verginius Rufus with vows for imperial safety and victory.[36] Syme suggested[37] that the vigorous Cornelius Fuscus turned his *colonia* in Galba's favour; this will have been particularly significant if the *colonia* in question was Aquileia, which will have been in a good position to exercise control of the route into Italy from the Danube provinces.

Thus, until Vindex was able to be sure of the support of Galba, his military resources will have been notably thin; we may be reasonably certain that Galba will have heard by 20 March that the rebellion had started – a little before Nero, but later than Verginius Rufus, the governor of Upper Germany, who was at the double-fortress of legions IV *Macedonica* and XXII *Primigenia* at Moguntiacum (Mainz). Calculating back from Dio's statement about the length of Galba's reign,[38] it would appear that Galba came to his decision to support Vindex on 2 or 3 April, although even then he remained circumspect, not allowing himself to be saluted as 'Emperor', but choosing instead the title of 'Legate of the Senate and People of Rome'.[39] This implied that it was his view that, ultimately, the choice of a new Emperor should rest with the Senate and people, not with armed insurgents – however sound their motives may have been.

In accepting Vindex's call, Galba was supported by his neighbour in Lusitania, Nero's former friend, Marcus Salvius Otho, and by Titus Vinius, commander (*legatus*) of legion VI *Victrix*, together with Aulus Caecina Alienus, who had been *quaestor* in the Spanish province of Baetica,[40] and whom Galba was to reward with the command of legion IV *Macedonica* in Upper Germany. Another significant adherent of Galba was Fabius Valens, commander of legion I *Germanica* at Bonna (Bonn); Valens will have kept Galba up-to-date with developments in the German military districts.[41]

For Vindex, however, despite the now-open adherence of Galba, there were still a number of complications on the horizon: as we have seen, one of these may have been the governor of his neighbouring province in south-west Gaul (Aquitania), who himself had appealed to Galba. Another was Fonteius Capito, the commander of the more distant German military district (Lower Germany), who showed his hostility to supporters of Vindex.[42] There was yet a further difficulty in north Africa: at some stage, after news of Galba's adherence to Vindex's rebellion had broken, intelligence arrived of another uprising that may have caused Vindex as much alarm as it will have Nero.[43] This was the rebellion of Lucius Clodius Macer, commander of legion III *Augusta*, in the province of Africa. Macer's purpose remains unclear, as does that of Nero's wardrobe-mistress and minder of Sporus, Calvia Crispinilla, who had accompanied Nero to Greece in the previous year. We cannot be sure from the available evidence whether her journey to Africa was intended to help or to undermine Nero; the latter is perhaps more likely, in view of the advantage that she had taken of her position with Nero to commit theft.[44]

It does not appear that Macer was in any sense attached to Vindex, and it is probably best to see his agenda as individual. In view of the fact that he appears to have been supported by north African landowners,[45] it is possible that Macer was utilising a local power-base, perhaps disgruntled over the tax-system, simply to make mischief. His coinage proclaimed him as the 'champion of liberty',[46] and he had a powerful weapon to deploy in the form of threats to disrupt Rome's grain-supply at what appears to have been a sensitive time.[47] He also set about raising extra troops. He may, therefore, have been intending to win concessions in a dispute primarily relevant to Africa, by aggravating Nero's unpopularity over a grain-shortage for which he (Nero) appears to have been responsible. It would also suit the known character of Calvia Crispinilla for her involvement to have been due to little more than opportunism.

However, the greatest anxiety for Vindex was without doubt due to the attitudes of the legions of Upper Germany and their commander, Lucius Verginius Rufus. These troops, that Nero will have seen as his principal line of defence against Vindex, were alarmingly close to Vindex's base in his province of Lugdunensis. Further, despite waverers amongst the senior officers in the western provinces, there is no evidence that Nero had, at this early stage, to fear defection amongst the legions of Germany; these, after all, had a long history of ties with the family of Nero's maternal grandfather, Germanicus Caesar.

Although Galba openly declared his adherence to Vindex's cause in the first days of April, it is unlikely, even then, that Vindex would have risked taking on the legions of Upper Germany with only Galba's legion for support. Further, as we have seen, Nero does not appear to have been unduly alarmed at the prospect of a rebellion mounted by Vindex alone: he had left for Naples almost immediately on his return from Greece, although he returned to Rome briefly, where he discussed the Gallic situation with political leaders, before turning to the subject of his new hydraulic organ.[48] However, the Emperor does appear to have seen Galba's entry into the fray as giving it a more serious character; we are told that, after throwing a tantrum at this latest manifestation of his subjects' lack of gratitude, he proceeded, in a more positive vein, to make military preparations.[49] He already had in Italy a new legion (I *Italica*), that he had raised in AD 66 or AD 67 for his projected expedition to the Caspian Gates, and set about raising another (I *Adiutrix*) from the fleet at Misenum.[50] In addition, he recalled from the Danubian provinces troops who had been gathering for the Caspian Gates expedition,[51] and who included XIV *Gemina Martia Victrix*; this legion had been transferred from Britain for the projected expedition and had been outstandingly loyal to Nero in the past.[52]

Nero's aim at this point was evidently to reduce the movement-options of Vindex and Galba by putting in place a line of defence in northern Italy, based on the river Po – thus anticipating a strategy that would become familiar in AD 69. In charge of these troops he placed Rubrius Gallus and Publius Petronius Turpilianus, a former governor of Britain, who had evidently performed some kind of service for Nero in the wake of the Pisonian Conspiracy.[53] It appears that Rubrius Gallus probably did not remain loyal to Nero for long, and it has been suggested that the Vestal Virgin, Rubria, whom Nero had violated, may have been a relative.[54] At any rate, Rubrius Gallus' subsequent favour with the Flavians[55] suggests that he did not have prolonged loyalty to Nero on his conscience. Petronius' loyalty, on the other hand, despite Dio's suggestion to the contrary,[56] is probably not in question, judging from the fact that Galba later had him put to death.[57] In particular, there seems to have been some confusion and dissension amongst the troops that Nero was assembling in Italy. Although it is not possible to identify any specific action on their part that might have merited such a claim, it is possible, as we have seen, that there was some form of collusion between the Batavians (attached to legion XIV) and the Gauls who were supporting Vindex. This, and the treachery of Rubrius Gallus, may have helped to convince Nero in the early summer of AD 68 that some, at least, of his troops in northern Italy had deserted.

Undoubtedly, then, Vindex's most pressing concern in late-March/early-April will have been with the legions of Upper Germany and their commander, Verginius Rufus;[58] these legions were plainly more than a match for any troops that Vindex could put into the field. Although our main sources of information are far from clear or consistent in their accounts of events, it appears that Vindex may already have been engaged in secret talks with Verginius Rufus, who does not personally appear to have entertained any great affection for his Emperor. Syme suggests that, although Verginius' attitude was 'ambiguous', he was not yet an 'open enemy of Nero'.[59] It seems reasonable to suppose that Vindex and Verginius must have placed their hopes in coming to an agreement that would have prevented bloodshed. Although Verginius Rufus mobilised his legions late in March,[60] perhaps to mislead them into thinking that they were about to do their duty by defeating their Emperor's enemies, it seems that he may in fact have intended it as part of a manoeuvre by the two commanders to allow them to approach closer to each other in order to continue their negotiations, without arousing the suspicions of the German legions.

Dio[61] certainly confirms a conference between Vindex and Verginius, although it is unlikely, as John of Antioch alleges,[62] that the purpose of this was to work out a detailed agreed strategy. This would appear to support an assessment that, although Verginius and his men were not, in fact, in total accord regarding their attitudes to Nero, Verginius' men were not yet aware of their commander's equivocation. Up to this point, therefore, Verginius would seem to have acted as if he were leading his men to deal with Vindex. It is highly unlikely that, given their attitude to Vindex's Gauls, the German legions would have tolerated anything that smacked of temporising.

Vindex opened his campaign by blockading Lugdunum (Lyon), a city that was not only proud of its Roman foundation and, therefore, somewhat aloof from native towns, such as neighbouring Vienna (Vienne), but that was also steadfast in its allegiance to Nero in return for benefits that it had received from him.[63] The siege of Lugdunum would thus have appeared natural and would have tied up pro-Neronian activists, and it would also have bought time for Vindex whilst Galba set about recruiting extra support in Spain.[64] Verginius, in the meantime, reached and proceeded to lay siege to Vesontio (Besançon), which Dio[65] viewed as a pretext – presumably for continuing discussions with Vindex. Certainly, Vindex appears to have lifted the siege of Lugdunum, and advanced[66] to Vesontio – at which point the 'alleged conference' presumably took place. It was probably late in April or early in May that Vindex made his last fateful move towards Vesontio.

We remain uncertain as to what really happened next, as the only certain outcome of this episode was a battle at Vesontio, presumably in the first half of May, between the German legions and Vindex's rather motley army. It does appear, however, that the battle was precipitated by the German legionaries acting without orders,[67] presumably partly because of their contempt for the Gauls who opposed them, but partly also because of impatience at the lack of action. The Gauls, who were no match for the legions, unsurprisingly were routed. Vindex, for his part, appears to have committed suicide when he saw the outcome, whilst Verginius Rufus is said by one source (John of Antioch) to have retired to his tent speechless and in despair; this suggests strongly that Vindex and Verginius had been negotiating a deal to cooperate against Nero. Certainly, it would seem likely that, if Verginius had acted positively *against* Vindex, Galba's subsequent treatment of him would have been less 'lenient'.

However, decisive as the battle's result had been, it did little to enhance the clarity of the political situation in western Europe. No sooner was the battle over than the German legionaries offered[68] the throne to their commander, Verginius Rufus, saying that, if he refused, they would resume their allegiance to Nero. He did refuse, arguing that only the Senate should make an Emperor. Verginius later tried to make out[69] that his refusal of the legions' offer had been due to his sense of patriotism and constitutionalism; it is far more likely, however, that it was due to a determination on his part not to become embroiled any further in the turbulent and traumatic politics of civil war – an assessment that received confirmation from his negative behaviour following the suicide of Otho in the following year.[70]

Xiphilinus,[71] in his abridgement of Dio, says simply that Verginius mourned the death of Vindex, but goes on to express doubt as to whether Verginius' refusal of the throne was due to a sense of constitutional propriety or to a personal lack of ambition. This is, indeed, likely to have represented the essence of the disagreement of interpretation that, as Pliny reports, exercised the historian, Cluvius Rufus, who asked for Verginius' indulgence if he should read anything in his (Cluvius') account that offended him. More than this, the wording of Verginius' epitaph, as quoted by Pliny, seems to indicate that Verginius may, during his thirty-year 'retirement' that followed these events, have been trying to associate himself with the vocabulary of the anti-Nero movement in AD 68 and, by so doing, absolve himself from the charge of having come close to wrecking that movement.

In other words, Verginius' epitaph was designed to place him 'on the side of the angels'.

After the disaster at Vesontio, Galba is said to have written[72] in desperation to Verginius Rufus, suggesting that they should combine their efforts to restore stability and bring peace to the Roman people. The time had clearly passed for this, and, when no response came from Verginius, Galba retired to Clunia in the interior of his province, presumably to await the imperial missive that was to be expected by a failed conspirator.

Yet, Nero's situation, that logically should have been strengthened by the outcome of the battle at Vesontio, seems to have been no less parlous than was the case with those who had opposed him. Indeed, we are told by Tacitus[73] that Nero was driven from his throne more by rumours than by force of arms; it would appear that Nero's understandable relief at the news from Vesontio must have been tempered by the further news of the German army's offer of power to Verginius Rufus. Nero, it seems, must, mistakenly as it happened, have taken this to mean that he had lost the support of the German legions, and perhaps also of his troops[74] on the line of the river Po. Evidently, the Praetorian Guard, encouraged by the bribes offered to it in Galba's name by one of its Prefects, Nymphidius Sabinus, did withdraw its allegiance. It is clear, too, that Tigellinus, who was later required by Otho to commit suicide,[75] had also deserted Nero, although the circumstances of this remain unclear. On 8 June, the Senate declared Nero an enemy of the state (*hostis*); Nero left Rome, and on the following day, as we have seen, with the help of his freedman, Epaphroditus, the last of the Julio-Claudians took his own life. On 9 June, Galba was declared Emperor by the Senate, an offer that he formally accepted early in July when he met a senatorial deputation in Narbo (Narbonne).[76]

Throughout the duration of this episode, Nero's military intelligence had been poor – or ignored by him: as it happened, he had not lost Petronius Turpilianus and the bulk of his northern Italian army; he had not lost the army of Upper Germany, nor – to judge from Galba's treatment of Fonteius Capito – had the Lower German army and its commander withdrawn their allegiance either.[77] Rumour, that Nero evidently believed, suggested that these armies had deserted; as Galba's short-lived heir, Piso Licinianus, was to put it when addressing the Praetorian Guard in the following January: 'It was Nero who deserted you, not you Nero'.[78]

Thus, the news that Galba received at Clunia about a week after Nero's death was not the death-sentence that he had been expecting, but an invitation to become Rome's sixth *princeps* and the first not to have been descended from the Julii or the Claudii. However, Nero's death and the accession of a new Emperor by no means brought a return to peace and stability. In the first place, the German legions, not unreasonably, thought that they had snuffed out Galba's cause at Vesontio and were in no mood now to take an oath of allegiance to him. We are told that they did so only as a result of the strenuous efforts of Galba's two allies in the German army, Fabius Valens and Caecina Alienus – a considerable service for which they expected a suitable reward from Galba. Tacitus describes Galba's progress from Spain to Italy as a 'blood-stained march', referring to the executions of, amongst others, Fonteius Capito and Petronius Turpilianus. Verginius Rufus, on the other hand, was simply sacked, presumably because Galba saw his as being sins of omission rather than of commission. Fatally, the two vacant German commands were given to men who were totally unsuitable: Hordeonius Flaccus was sent to replace Verginius Rufus in Upper Germany; according to Tacitus, his only distinguishing feature was gout.[79] The command of Lower Germany was given to the future Emperor, the dissolute and corrupt Aulus Vitellius; again, according to Tacitus, the fact that Vitellius had a distinguished father – Claudius' courtier, Lucius Vitellius – evidently seemed qualification enough in Galba's eyes. Such men were totally unsuitable to be put in command of armies that, to say the least, were volatile due to their unhappiness with the current political situation.

Although the civil war had had its roots in a sense of dissatisfaction, particularly amongst members of the senatorial order, with the quality of Nero's reign, its consequences extended over a broader canvas. First, as we have seen, the relationship between the army and its commanders had once again cast a dark shadow over the Roman political scene. As had been the case during the later years of the Old Republic, this was not due to any particular complaints on the part of the rank and file of the army itself, rather, the army once again became a tool in the acting out of the political agendas of its commanders. It had seemed that Augustus' reforms of the army and its command-structure had greatly reduced, if not removed, this kind of threat to political stability; the events of the first half of AD 68 demonstrated that this, in fact, was not the case. As Tacitus put it most succinctly, 'the secret of Empire was out, that an Emperor could be created elsewhere than at Rome'.[80] Nero had perhaps seen the possibility of this when he had initiated his policy of granting military commands to men whose social position did not encourage them to entertain thoughts above their station; perhaps Verginius' hesitancy had in part been due to such a consideration.

However, events were soon to show that a factor rather more insidious than the ambitions of individuals was at play: since the time of Augustus, the Roman legions had enjoyed permanent bases in the provinces. One effect of this had been the appearance of an attitude of superiority with regard to local populations; this, together with the sense of identity derived from long familiarity with a particular posting and, perhaps also, because of local recruiting, led to the emergence of an *esprit de corps* that went beyond the traditional pride in one's own legion. This creation of army groups with a sense of regional identity had been seen before, during the mutinous outbreaks on the Rhine and the Danube in AD 14. But it became much more potent in the events of AD 68–9: army groups committed themselves to their own candidates for power and, just as vigorously, opposed choices made by other army groups. This, together with the rivalry that existed between the legionary army and the Praetorian Guard in Rome, which was seen as effete, over-privileged and overpaid, provided a new edge and incentive to those fighting in the civil war. It also made post-war reconciliation difficult, if not impossible, as can be seen in the events which followed Otho's victory over Galba in January of AD 69 and Vitellius' over Otho three months later, in April.

Army-group rivalry, therefore, although not a new phenomenon, played a major rôle, particularly in the events which followed Nero's death, and had to be curtailed, at least in part, by the eventual victor, Vespasian. Thus, Augustus' solution to the military anarchy of the late Republic was shown to have been found wanting in the events which brought his dynasty to an end in AD 68. Nor should it be overlooked that one of the effects of this rivalry had been to bring instability to the provinces for which the legions were responsible; the rebellion of Venutius in northern Britain in AD 69 and the Gallo-German war of AD 69–70 provide two major examples of this.[81]

However, there were problems with the Augustan political settlement, too. Pointedly, in his account of the closing days of the reign of Galba, and the Emperor's search for a successor, Tacitus, as we have seen, put into Galba's mouth an oration that has since been called a 'manual of statecraft'.[82] The oration takes the form of an address of advice given by Galba to his chosen successor, Piso Licinianus – the first occasion on which an Emperor had sought to transmit power to a man to whom he was not related either by blood or marriage. Central to the oration is the relationship between a dynastic succession-policy and the concept of *libertas*, as understood during the Roman Republic. Although *libertas* had many shades of meaning in Latin, an important one of these was the ability of qualified men to compete for power, whether that be through a process of election or through the judgement of their peers. Tacitus, who, in his own lifetime, saw the *choosing* of Emperors become a reality, writes on another occasion that, through most of the first century AD, Principate and *libertas* were regarded as irreconcilable; the cause of this was the insistence on a dynastic succession-policy.

So long as there was, in effect, a dynastic qualification for the position of Emperor, it was not open to all qualified men; as Galba remarked, under Augustus and his successors Rome became the 'heirloom' of a single family.[83] For others, this amounted to domination (*dominatio*) by the Emperor and his family, and the consequent reduction of his subjects to what was seen as servile status. Galba also noticed a practical problem with dynasticism: a birth-connection with a past Emperor did not guarantee a fitness to rule. The Roman world had, after all, just witnessed and paid the price for the truth of that in its experiences under Nero:

> *Think of Nero, swollen with the pride of his long line of royal ancestry. It was not Vindex with a powerless province at his back, nor I with a single legion, that freed Rome's shoulders of that burden: it was his own barbarity and profligacy.*[84]

In Galba's view, the adoption of the best available man through an exercise of judgement on the parts of his predecessor and peers would be a guarantee of an improvement in the status and fortunes of all. This would create a political climate in which rulers and ruled would be able to cooperate openly and frankly, and in which all men would recognise their rôle in the system. The banal and cancerous flattery that had characterised the reigns of most of the Julio-Claudian Emperors would be a thing of the past. It was incumbent on the Emperor to set the standard; addressing Piso, Galba ended his oration with the observation: 'Evil men will always miss Nero: you and I must ensure that good citizens do not miss him too.'[85]

These were brave words that perhaps came somewhere near to fruition with the accession of Trajan in AD 98; in the immediate future, however, Galba was murdered by the Praetorian Guard at the instigation of his and Nero's former friend, Otho. Otho did not think that he had been sufficiently rewarded by Galba for his services in AD 68. Thereafter, the army installed two more Emperors, Vitellius and Vespasian, and, despite Galba's reservations on the subject, Vespasian established a new dynasty, passing power in turn to his two sons, Titus (AD 79–81) and Domitian (AD 81–96). The Flavian dynasty ended no more auspiciously than that of the Julio-Claudians; indeed, the fact that people named Domitian 'the bald Nero' indicates that, whether fairly or not, for some, the last of the Flavians depressingly recalled the last of the Julio-Claudians.[86]

Epilogue

❧❧❧❧❧❧❧

Nero's impact on Rome and the Empire, unsurprisingly, was considerable, although the Flavian general, Quintus Petillius Cerialis, is reported to have told the leaders of the Treveri during the Gallo-German war of AD 69–70 that bad Emperors had their most damaging effect on those close-at-hand to them.[1] In the oration composed for him by Tacitus,[2] the Emperor, Galba, warned that, whilst Nero would always be missed by the 'dregs' of Roman society, it was crucial that confidence in the Principate as a system of government should be rebuilt in order to prevent the 'better men' also coming to miss Nero. Whilst Galba laid most of the blame for what had happened personally at Nero's door, he also censured the sycophancy of some members of the governing class.

Galba's chief criticism, however, was reserved for the dynastic system of imperial succession, that had brought Nero to power and had encouraged him to think of Rome and its Empire as his personal inheritance. It was, therefore, essential to build a more positive, constructive and honest relationship between ruler and ruled,[3] together with a system of succession that brought forward, as a candidate for the position of *princeps*, the man who was endorsed by his peers – that is, in the Senate – as the best available. Tacitus evidently felt that this had been achieved under the Emperors, Nerva and Trajan, a period in which one could 'think what one wished, and say what one thought'.[4] This was much to be preferred to an absolute monarch who exercised clemency as and when he saw fit. Yet, somewhat disturbingly in his choice of wording, the Younger Pliny says of Trajan:[5] 'You bid us to be free; so free we shall be.' Liberty, therefore, was still not seen as a right protected by law, but remained a gift of imperial patronage.

Galba's advice had some merit; indeed, his successor, Nero's erstwhile friend, Marcus Otho, seems to a degree to have heeded it. Although Tacitus evidently took the view that a throne gained by murder could not be sustained by virtuous conduct, Otho did try to show his concern for the population *as a whole*. Despite the fact that he had himself deserted Nero during the crisis of AD 68, he appreciated the importance of Nero's memory in certain sections of the community. Thus, he did not encourage, but did not prevent, the paying of honour to Nero's statues.[6] Although, paying meticulous attention to constitutional proprieties, he did seek a senatorial decree for the restoration of statues of Poppaea Sabina;[7] he sought funds for the completion of the *Domus Aurea*;[8] and he allowed himself – for a time, at least – to be styled 'Nero Otho', even, according to the historian, Cluvius Rufus, on official documents.[9] Plutarch adds, however, that he gave up the practice because of the displeasure shown by 'men of the highest birth'.[10] Further, Otho's decision, in April of AD 69, to commit suicide – not as a route of personal escape, but as a way of preventing the continuing shedding of citizen-blood – was recognised by Tacitus as courageous.[11] Thus, we can see a conscious effort on Otho's part to capitalise on the popularity of his former friend.

At the same time, however, Otho attempted to do what Nero, at the beginning of his reign, had promised, but had failed, to do – namely to uphold the dignity and safety of members of the Senate. Tacitus records the occasion when Otho put himself in considerable personal danger to protect from the wrath of members of the Praetorian Guard senators and their wives who were dining with him.[12] He also tried to leave members of the Senate free to do their jobs, as is shown by his decision to leave control of the campaign in northern Italy against Vitellius to the established senatorial commanders at a point at which the troops themselves would plainly have preferred to have taken their orders directly from their Emperor. Indeed, it appears that, had Otho not been forced into fighting Vitellius, he might have established a Principate that demonstrated that lessons had been learnt from Nero's failings. Vitellius, too, attempted to capitalise on the memory of Nero, although in his case it was to pay tribute to Nero as a composer and performer.[13]

Not many later Roman Emperors appear to have set out deliberately to imitate or honour Nero, and his atrocious reputation was a matter of surviving memory;[14] a few instances are, however, worth recording: Elagabalus (AD 218–22), whose reign has been seen as an extended display of self-indulgent religious fanaticism, is said by his biographer – in what was perhaps an apocryphal story – to have driven a chariot drawn by four elephants around Nero's Circus at the foot of the Vatican Hill, destroying any of the tombs that were in his way.[15] Severus Alexander (AD 222–35) rebuilt and extended Nero's Baths into a new complex named after himself.[16] Finally, in the AD 390s, a 'medal' was issued commemorating Games put on by Nero in the *Circus Maximus*.[17]

The obscure circumstances of Nero's death and burial also contributed to a refusal by many to believe that Nero had really died in June of AD 68. Few had witnessed Nero's 'final performance', and those that had were unlikely to have been regarded as either reliable or credible. Dio Chrysostom of Prusa (in Asia Minor), writing at the turn of the first and second centuries AD, says[18] that there was no certainty that Nero was dead, and that most people both wished and believed that he was still alive. This disbelief afforded fertile ground for stories that he had escaped and remained alive, waiting to retake his throne. Indeed, the decades that followed Nero's death saw a number of appearances in the East of imposters (or 'false Neros').[19] Two reasons help to explain the fact that these appearances occurred in the East – Nero's popularity in Greece, where he was still remembered for the 'Liberation of Hellas' and for such projects as the Corinth Canal', and his continued high standing in Parthia and Armenia, following the settlement of AD 66.[20]

The first of these appearances occurred in AD 69 – perhaps in the spring, as the conflict between Otho and Vitellius was reaching its climax;[21] the perpetrator of the fraud is not named, but was evidently either a slave or a freedman, who bore a passing resemblance to Nero and who was an accomplished performer on the lyre. Unlike the two later frauds, there seems to have been no connection on this occasion with Parthia; rather the fraudster was probably capitalising on Nero's popularity in Greece, and utilising the contemporary turmoil in Italy as a distraction. In the short term, he gained supporters, but was eventually cornered and killed on the Aegean island of Cythnos by a former friend of Nero's, the senator, Lucius Nonius Calpurnius Asprenas. This man, despite having apparently had no significant military career, was much decorated, and may have been one of those who had lent their efforts to bringing the Pisonian conspirators to justice in AD 65 and AD 66.[22]

The other two frauds – in AD 79 and AD 88 – were connected with Rome's Eastern policies; in AD 79, a certain Terentius Maximus, who also resembled Nero and was a reasonable performer on the lyre, claimed to have escaped the soldiers searching for him in AD 68.[23] He sought help from the Parthians on the grounds that they owed him their support – at an opportune moment, it appears, as a Parthian pretender, Artabanus, was for reasons of his own contemplating attacking Roman imperial territory. Terentius was, however, recognised and put to death. Even less is known about the third 'false Nero' who appeared in AD 88/89,[24] again at a time when the Roman Empire was facing a number of difficult internal and external problems.[25] As in AD 79, however, this again appears to have been an attempt to capitalise on Nero's generosity to Parthia. An ironical feature that links these fraudulent attempts is that they were evidently based upon the reciprocation that the 'false Nero' expected for the generosity of the 'real Nero'. An indication that Nero's memory was not universally damned can be seen in the survival of his name in a variety of contexts into the third and fourth centuries – as a city name in Cilicia, as the name of a month in Pontus; most interestingly, the name, *stagnum Neronis*, survived at Baiae into the fourth century.[26]

No further appearances of 'false Neros' are recorded, although there survives a body of mostly non-Christian apocalyptic literature, known as the *Sibylline Oracles*,[27] predicting destruction that will be visited upon Rome and the Empire through the return of a figure who is frequently easily recognisable as Nero – a new agenda, perhaps, for 'false Neros'. The most striking of this apocalyptic material, however, is that which appears in early-Christian literature, starting with *The Revelation of St John the Divine*, where[28] the 'number of the beast' is given as '666', that is the sum of the numerical equivalents of the Hebrew letters that make the words 'Neron Caesar'. Nero had perpetrated such evil upon the early Christian community in Rome that, for many early Christians, he became the 'Antichrist' who would return in evil and destruction at the end of the world.[29]

The venomous hatred that lay behind this belief is clearly apparent in *On the Deaths of the Persecutors*, written in *c.* AD 313–6 by Lucius Caecilius Firmianus Lactantius, the tutor in rhetoric to Constantine's son, Crispus.[30] Whilst Lactantius was principally concerned with the last great persecution of the Emperors, Diocletian and Galerius, he prefaced this with accounts of earlier persecutions of Christians, and the often-terrible fates that befell their perpetrators; unsurprisingly, Nero figures prominently amongst these. After writing about St Peter's successful ministry in Rome, and Nero's violent reaction to it, Lactantius goes on:

Nero, being the abominable and criminal tyrant that he was, rushed into trying to overturn the heavenly temple and to abolish righteousness, and, the first persecutor of the servants of God, he nailed Peter to the cross and killed Paul. For this he did not go unpunished; God took note of the way in which his people were troubled. Cast down from the pinnacle of power and hurtled from the heights, the tyrant suddenly disappeared; not even a place of burial was to be seen on the earth for so evil a beast. Hence, some crazed men believe that he has been borne away and kept alive, since the Sibyl declares that 'the matricide, though exiled from the earth, will come back', so that just as he was the first persecutor, so he may also be the last, and herald the arrival of the Antichrist; and, although it is not right to believe this, yet, just as certain holy men maintain that two prophets have been borne away until the last days before the holy and eternal rule of Christ, so these men think that Nero, too, will come as the forerunner and herald of the devil when he comes to lay waste the earth and overturn the human race.[31]

A similar theme is taken up a century later by Augustine:

Some suppose that Nero will rise again as Antichrist. Others think that he is not dead, but was concealed, so that he might be supposed to have been killed, and that he still lives on as a legendary figure, of the same age as that at which he died, and will be restored to his kingdom.[32]

The legend lived on into the Middle Ages; Michael Grant cites[33] the story of Pope Paschal II (1099–1118) who used to listen to crows cawing in a walnut tree near to the tomb of the Domitii on the Pincian Hill in Rome. After dreaming that the crows were demons serving Nero, the Pope destroyed the tomb and erected on the site a chapel, that became the Church of Santa Maria del Popolo. Although the crows went away, the belief persisted that they were still serving Nero's wandering spirit.

Whilst the demonisation of Nero has been left behind in the past, and fear of him, alive or dead, no longer haunts the living, he remains into the modern age a figure, sometimes of revulsion, always of fascination. Nero was a man of contrasts: we may ask, as did many of his contemporaries, how a man could sink to the depths of murdering his mother and his wife, but then we look again, and we find a man of clemency and generosity. These different sides of Nero were, however, plainly the products of the same character; nor is that character to be explained away by madness. There is, indeed, no sign of madness; his reactions to both his good and bad deeds, although totally self-centred, are thoroughly intelligible.

That he was not the right man for his job is clear; that he possessed talent is clear, also; but he was too immature and, in that immaturity, too reliant on others in a way that he often resented, to make a sound and trustworthy *princeps*: as Galba was to say six months after Nero's death, the accession to imperial power of a man like Nero simply highlighted the fatal flaw of a dynastic succession-system. Nero showed himself to be content in his job just so long as he could, through the exercise of its powers and privileges, win popularity. Whether it was a matter of conciliating the Senate, reaching good decisions when sitting in judgement, attacking corrupt provincial governors, performing in public, organising relief-work after the Fire, or planning and building his 'People's Palace', his motive, albeit utterly self-indulgent, was always the winning of gratitude and popularity. Like a spoiled child, when he succeeded in this aim, his response would be characteristically warm-hearted, as he showed in his 'Liberation of Hellas'; but when he did not succeed, then his reaction would consist of tantrums and lashing out, often with great cruelty, against those who, in his view, had let him down.

In recent years, there have been not only many books on Nero, but also representations of him on film and television – some of these memorable, and none more so than that of the then-youthful Peter Ustinov in *Quo Vadis?* However, those representations fail if they lean too far in the direction of insanity; in the disturbed societies of the western world in the twenty-first century, we can readily recognise in Nero the unfulfilled young man with 'acute behavioural problems', who wanted constantly to occupy the centre of attention. As Servius Galba strongly hinted[34] in his review of the immediately post-Neronian Roman state, in Nero Caesar Augustus, the last of the Julio-Claudians, Rome effectively had had the Emperor it deserved.

Appendix 1: Principal Dates relating to the Life and Reign of Nero

AD 4	Adoption of Germanicus Caesar as son (and intended successor) of Tiberius
10–16	Germanicus and his family on the Rhine
14	Death of Augustus and accession of Tiberius
15	Birth of Agrippina (mother of Nero)
17–19	Germanicus in the eastern provinces, particularly to establish a new king (Zeno/Artaxias) in Armenia
19	Death of Germanicus (probably from natural causes)
c. 24–31	Sejanus' attacks on the Elder Agrippina and her family
28	Marriage of the Younger Agrippina to Cnaeus Domitius Ahenobarbus
29	Death of Augustus' widow, Livia; judicial proceedings for treason brought against the Elder Agrippina and her elder sons, Nero and Drusus
31	Caligula and his sisters transferred to Tiberius' care on Capri; Nero Caesar dies in prison (AD 30); execution of Sejanus (18 October)
33	Deaths in prison of the Elder Agrippina and her second son, Drusus; marriages arranged for the Younger Agrippina's sisters
37	Death of Tiberius and accession of Caligula (Nero's uncle); birth of Nero (15 December)
39–41	Agrippina in exile; Nero left in the care of his aunt, Domitia Lepida, the mother of Messalina
40	Death of Nero's father, Cnaeus Domitius Ahenobarbus

41	Assassination of Caligula and accession of Claudius; return of Agrippina from exile; Agrippina's marriage to Gaius Sallustius Passienus Crispus
48	Messalina's bigamous 'marriage' to Gaius Silius, leading to their deaths
49	Agrippina's marriage to Claudius; Octavia's engagement to Lucius Junius Silanus annulled; Nero adopted by Claudius as his son, and engaged to marry Octavia; Seneca chosen as Nero's tutor
51	Nero's assumption of the 'toga of manhood'; Sextus Afranius Burrus becomes sole Prefect of the Praetorian Guard
51–53	Nero delivers petitions to the Senate on behalf of various cities
52	Nero's marriage to Octavia
54	Death of Claudius (October) and accession of Nero; Corbulo appointed as Eastern commander
54–66	War in the East
55	Death of Britannicus; removal of Pallas; Seneca publishes his treatise, *On Clemency*, beginning of Nero's relationship with Acte
57	Nero builds a new amphitheatre; makes a large gift (*congiarium*) to the people of Rome
58	Possible beginning of Nero's affair with Poppaea Sabina
59	Murder of Agrippina; inauguration of the *Juvenalia* games
60	Inauguration of the *Neronia* games; Faustus Sulla and Rubellius Plautus exiled
60–61	Rebellion of Boudica in Britain
62	Death of Burrus; two Praetorian Prefects (Ofonius Tigellinus and Faenius Rufus) appointed to replace him; retirement of Seneca; reintroduction of treason (*maiestas*) trials; murders of Octavia, Faustus Sulla and Rubellius Plautus; Nero's marriage to Poppaea Sabina; inauguration of Nero's baths and gymnasium
63	Birth (and death) of Nero's daughter, Claudia Antonia
64	Nero performs in public in Naples; Fire of Rome; punishment of Christians in Rome; rebuilding of the city begins; work commences on the *Domus Aurea*; reform of the coinage
65	Conspiracy of Gaius Piso; enforced suicide of Seneca; Nymphidius Sabinus replaces Faenius Rufus as Praetorian Prefect; death of Poppaea Sabina, whilst pregnant; corn-fleet wrecked by storm;

	work begins on canal from Lake Avernus to Ostia; second celebration of the *Neronia* games
66	Tiridates crowned in Rome as king of Armenia; trials for treason of Thrasea Paetus and Barea Soranus; Nero marries Statilia Messalina; Conspiracy of Vinicianus (?); beginning of Jewish revolt; Nero departs for Greece
67	Enforced suicides of Scribonius Proculus, Scribonius Rufus and Domitius Corbulo; Nero participates in the Panhellenic Games and wins 1,808 first prizes; 'liberation of Hellas'; work begins on the Corinth canal; planned expeditions to Ethiopia and the Black Sea; Vespasian given the Jewish command; Julius Vindex contacts provincial governors regarding a possible coup d'état against Nero
67–73	Jewish War (sack of Jerusalem in AD 70; sack of Masada in AD 73)
68	Nero returns to Italy (Naples) from Greece; Vindex launches his rebellion (March); Galba hailed as Emperor (although initially declining the actual title: April); battle at Vesontio (Besançon; May); death of Nero (9 June or soon after); Senate proclaims Galba Emperor (9 July)

Appendix 2: The Distribution of Roman Legions in the Mid-First Century AD

꧁꧂꧁꧂꧁꧂

a) The Reign of Claudius (*c.* AD 46): 27 Legions

Spain (Tarraconensis)	2	VI *Victrix*; X *Gemina*
Britain	4	II *Augusta*; IX *Hispana*; XIV *Gemina Martia Victrix*; XX (see above on p. 218)
Upper Germany	3	IV *Macedonica*; XXI *Rapax*; XXII *Primigenia*
Lower Germany	4	I *Germanica*; V *Alaudae*; XV *Primigenia*; XVI *Gallica*
Dalmatia	2	VII *Claudia Pia Fidelis*; XI *Claudia Pia Fidelis* (formerly respectively *Macedonica* and *Actiaca*)
Pannonia	2	XIII *Gemina*; XV *Apollinaris*
Moesia	3	IV *Scythica*; V *Macedonica*; VIII *Augusta*
Syria	4	III *Gallica*; VI *Ferrata*; X *Fretensis*; XII *Fulminata*
Egypt	2	III *Cyrenaica*; XXII *Deiotariana*
Africa	1	III *Augusta*

b) The Reign of Nero (*c.* AD 65): 27 Legions

Spain (Tarraconensis)	1	VI *Victrix*
Britain	4	II *Augusta*; IX *Hispana*; XIV *Gemina Martia Victrix*; XX *Valeria Victrix*
Upper Germany	3	IV *Macedonica*; XXI *Rapax*; XXII *Primigenia*

1 Denarius of Claudius, showing Agrippina (obverse) and Nero (reverse)

2 Cistophorus of Claudius' reign from Ephesus, showing Claudius and Agrippina together

3 Aureus *of Nero, showing (obverse) Nero and Agrippina facing each other*

4 Denarius *of Nero, showing (obverse) jugate busts of Nero and Agrippina*

5 Aureus *of Nero, showing (reverse) oak-leaf crown*

6 Denarius *of Nero, showing (reverse)*
Nero and Poppaea

7 Denarius *of Nero, showing (reverse)*
Nero radiate

8 Denarius *of Nero, showing (reverse)* *Jupiter the Guardian*

9 Denarius *of Nero, showing (reverse)* *the Temple of Vesta*

10 Sestertius *of Nero, showing (reverse)* *Ceres*

11 Sestertius *of Nero, showing (reverse)* *Triumphal Arch*

12 Sestertius *of Nero, showing (reverse)*
Harbour at Ostia

13 Dupondius *of Nero, showing*
(reverse) Nero's Market-Building

14 Dupondius *of Nero, showing (reverse) the Temple of Janus*

15 As *of Nero, showing (reverse) Apollo Citharoedus*

16 Tetradrachm *from Alexandria, showing Nero (observe) and Poppaea (reverse)*

17 Denarius *of the Civil War, showing (obverse) the 'Health of the Human Race'*

18 Denarius *of the Civil War, showing (obverse) the Deified Augustus*

19 Denarius *of Galba, showing (reverse) the Rebirth of Rome*

Lower Germany	4	I *Germanica*; V *Alaudae*; XV *Primigenia*; XVI *Gallica*
Dalmatia	1	XI *Claudia Pia Fidelis*
Pannonia	2	X *Gemina*; XIII *Gemina*
Moesia	2	VII *Claudia Pia Fidelis*; VIII *Augusta*
Syria/Armenia	7	III *Gallica*; IV *Scythica*; V *Macedonica*; VI *Ferrata*; X *Fretensis*; XII *Fulminata*; XV *Apollinaris*
Egypt	2	III *Cyrenaica*; XXII *Deiotariana*
Africa	1	III *Augusta*

c) The Civil Wars (AD 68): 31 Legions

(* indicates a newly-raised legion; see Parker 1928 and Keppie 1984, p. 213)

Spain (Tarraconensis)	2	VI *Victrix*; X *Gemina*
Britain	3	II *Augusta*; IX *Hispana*; XX *Valeria Victrix*
Upper Germany	3	IV *Macedonica*; XXI *Rapax*; XXII *Primigenia*
Lower Germany	4	I *Germanica*; V *Alaudae*; XV *Primigenia*; XVI *Gallica*
Gaul (Lugdunensis)	1	I *Italica**
Rome	1	I *Adiutrix**
Dalmatia	2	*XI Claudia Pia Fidelis*; XIV *Gemina Martia Victrix*
Pannonia	2	VII *Gemina* (*Galbiana*)*; XIII *Gemina*
Moesia	3	III *Gallica*; VII *Claudia Pia Fidelis*; VIII *Augusta*
Syria	3	IV *Scythica*; X *Ferrata*; XII *Fulminata*
Judaea	3	V *Macedonica*; X *Fretensis*; XV *Apollinaris*
Egypt	2	III *Cyrenaica*; XXII *Deiotariana*
Africa	2	III *Augusta*; I *Macriana**

d) Following Vespasian's Reorganisation (AD 71): 29 Legions

| Spain (Tarraconensis) | 1 | VII *Gemina* |
| Britain | 3 | II *Augusta*; IX *Hispana*; XX *Valeria Victrix* |

Upper Germany	4	I *Adiutrix*; VIII *Augusta*; XI *Claudia Pia Fidelis*; XIV *Gemina Martia Victrix*
Lower Germany	4	II *Adiutrix**; VI *Victrix*; X *Gemina*; XXI *Rapax*
Pannonia	3	XIII *Gemina*; XV *Apollinaris*; XXII *Primigenia*
Moesia	5	I *Italica*; IV *Flavia Felix**; V *Alaudae*; V *Macedonica*; VII *Claudia Pia Fidelis*
Syria	3	III *Gallica*; IV *Scythica*; VI *Ferrata*
Cappadocia	2	XII *Fulminata*; XVI *Flavia Firma**
Judaea	1	X *Fretensis*
Egypt	2	III *Cyrenaica*; XXII *Deiotariana*
Africa	1	III *Augusta*

Area-Distribution of the Legions

AD	14	46	65	68	71
Britain	–	4	4	3	3
Italy	–	–	–	1	–
Germany/The West	11	9	8	10	9
Central/Eastern Europe	7	7	5	7	8
The East	4	4	7	6	6
North Africa	3	3	3	4	3
TOTALS	25	27	27	31	29

Appendix 3: Glossary of Latin Terms

Auctoritas: This concept, that was central to the Augustan Principate (as it had been to the nobility of the Old Republic) is hard to render precisely in an English translation; it means 'influence' and 'prestige', and embraces the idea of being in possession of these through a combination of heredity, wealth, personality and achievement. The consequence of having it was the ability to prevail by patronage on a large scale. Whilst members of aristocratic families were assumed to possess it, an outsider, such as Vespasian, had to devise the means to acquire it.

Auxilia: Under Augustus' reform of the Roman army, the auxiliary units were recruited from men from the provinces who were not Roman citizens; the *auxilia* were organised into units of 500 (quingenary) or 1,000 (milliary) men, made up of infantry alone (*cohortes peditatae*), mixed infantry and cavalry (*cohortes equitatae*) or cavalry alone (*alae*). Auxiliary units were associated with the legions and often served alongside them; in Britain, the garrisoning of Hadrian's Wall was made up almost entirely of such units. They served for twenty-five years, and could win Roman citizenship for valour in battle; however, all those auxiliaries who were not Roman citizens by the time of their retirement then received it as part of their discharge-gratuity.

Clementia: This means clemency, and acting in a sparing fashion to political adversaries. Julius Caesar, for example, prided himself on it, as he tried to draw his opponents into his confidence. However, whilst a display of this virtue might on particular occasions be welcome in its effects, in principle it related to men of overwhelming (and thus, frequently, unwelcome) power, and could be denied as capriciously as it was exercised. Despite Seneca's urging of it on the young Nero, it remained a characteristic of a *dominus* – or tyrant.

Colonia: A city founded deliberately with a hand-picked population of Roman citizens who, in the imperial period, were intended to act as a military reserve and as overseers of the neighbouring local population with a view to Romanising it. This duty (*munus*) was compensated for by the allowance of a certain degree of self-regulation of affairs. The planting of *coloniae* had a long history in the growth of Roman power in Italy and beyond, and was used in the provinces during the Principate as a way of settling legionary veterans in sensitive areas. Under the Principate it was also used in some cases in Italy to revive towns that were in decline or occasionally as a mark of honour. The *colonia* differed from a *municipium*, which was a status involving the granting of citizen-rights to an *existing* population.

Consul: During the Old Republic, the *consuls* were the head of the executive branch of the government; two were elected each year, and were accountable to the electorate for their conduct during their tenure of the office. They presided over meetings of the Senate and the assemblies of the whole people (*populus*), and regularly commanded the armies in battle, until the late-third century BC, when this function was increasingly taken over by promagistrates (*proconsul, propraetor*). Under the Principate, whilst prestige still attached to the office, its significance came to relate more to the provincial and army commands, for which it effectively represented a qualification. Also, under the Principate, it became normal for the consuls who took office on 1 January (*ordinarii*), and who gave their names to the year, to resign midway through the year in favour of replacements (*consules suffecti*). This was a method of increasing the numbers of men qualified for senior commands.

Cursus Honorum: The ladder of offices climbed during the time of the Old Republic by senators in their quest for the consulship. It was subject at that time to a number of organising laws (e.g. the *Lex Villia* of 180 BC, and a *Lex Cornelia* of Sulla), that established intervals between offices as well as the proper order in which they had to be held. Under the Principate, the *cursus* remained in place, although a man's progress along it was affected by imperial favour (or the absence of it), and by the number of his legitimate children. The chief offices under the Principate (and normal ages of tenure) were:

Vigintivirate ('Board of Twenty')	18
Military Tribune	21–22
Quaestor	25
Tribune of the Plebeians (often omitted)	
Aedile (often omitted)	
Praetor	30–35
Legionary Commander (*Legatus Legionis*)	30+
Consul	37+
Proconsul (or *Legatus Augusti*)	38+

Dignitas: this dignity referred specifically to the holding of offices of the *cursus honorum*, and was taken very seriously by senators as it provided the proof that they were acting in a manner that was worthy of their ancestors. The Emperor, Tiberius, for example, took it as an affront to his *dignitas* when, in 6 BC, he thought that he was being given a grant of *tribunicia potestas* by Augustus simply to annoy Gaius and Lucius Caesar.

Dominatio: The state of being a master (*dominus*); the word originally and properly referred to the state of being a master of slaves, but it was increasingly used to describe the behaviour of Julius Caesar, Augustus and their successors because of their perceived undermining of liberty (*libertas*). *Dominus Noster* (Our Lord) became a regular title of Emperors in the fourth century AD, and a few Emperors, such as Domitian (AD 81–96), used it at an earlier stage.

Equites: Members of the equestrian order during the Principate constituted Rome's second social class. Originally rather a disparate body, the order acquired coherence through its commercial activities following the expansion of the Roman Empire from the second century BC. Companies formed within the order (*societates*) undertook for profit many tasks during the period of the Old Republic that, in the context of a modern state, would be undertaken by a civil service. Augustus reorganised the order so that it had a career-structure similar in nature to that of senators, and in which it carried out tasks for salaries rather than for profits. These posts included, for example, the command of auxiliary units of the Roman army and the great Prefectures of the Praetorian Guard and of Egypt.

Imperium: The executive power bestowed upon consuls and praetors during the Old Republic, through which they exercised effective control of the government. Under the Principate, *imperium* was tenable as it was defined – consular or proconsular; Augustus, under the First Settlement of the Principate (27 BC), controlled the provinces of Gaul, Spain and Syria (and the armies which they contained) by means of a proconsular *imperium*, that was enhanced to superiority over others (*maius*) under the Second Settlement (23 BC). He had a permanent residual *imperium* that could be temporarily redefined to enable him to undertake other tasks, such as censorial duties, which included the regulation of the Senate's membership.

Imperator: The word means General, and was used during the Old Republic. Generals who received an imperial salutation could use the title, *imperator* (abbreviated to *IMP*), after their names. It was used in the titulature of Emperors to indicate their tenure of *imperium* and their overarching Generalship. It was abbreviated to *IMP* on inscriptions and on the coinage and, by Nero's time, was placed before the Emperor's name as a *praenomen*.

Legatus: Originally a man to whom authority had been delegated to act as an assistant to a man of superior rank. Pompey, for example, conducted his eastern campaigns in the 60s BC with a number of *legati* in attendance. Under the Principate, a man became a *legatus* of a legion after the praetorship, although there are a few examples of men who were allowed to jump the praetorship in order to speed their passage to military commands. The term was, however, principally employed of those to whom the Emperor delegated *de facto* control of his – the so-called imperial – provinces. The full title of such men was *Legatus Augusti Pro Praetore*, where the term *pro praetore* was used of ex-consuls in order visibly to subordinate them to the Emperor's proconsular *imperium*.

Lex: A law that had been passed either by one of the assemblies (*comitia*) of the whole people (*populus*), or by the assembly of the plebeians (*concilium plebis*). Under the Principate, the participation of these bodies became a mere formality, as is shown by the *Lex de Imperio*, by which Vespasian received his powers.

Libertas: Freedom had a wide variety of connotations at Rome, although that most frequently mentioned was the traditional *freedom* of the nobility to progress along the *cursus honorum* without undue interference from others. It was this *libertas* that was seen as being in conflict with the Principate, particularly in the context of a hereditary system of succession to supreme power.

Maiestas: Maiestas Minuta, or the 'diminishing of the majesty of the Roman state' was the Roman form of treason, embodied in a number of laws from the latter years of the Old Republic to the time of Augustus. At times, as in the reign of Tiberius and in Nero's later years, the operation of this law became an instrument of tyranny. This was principally because Rome lacked a public prosecutor, and prosecutions were initiated by informers (*delatores*), who received as their reward a proportion – usually one quarter – of the value of the property of a convicted man; hence ruining rich people became a profitable enterprise.

Municipium: See above, under *colonia*.

Nobilis: Literally, one who was 'known'; the *nobiles* (aristocracy) defined themselves as deriving from families whose members had reached the consulship in earlier generations, and who regarded the office as virtually their birthright.

Pater Patriae: An honorific title, Father of the Country, that was awarded for outstanding service to the state; Cicero, for example, received it in 63 BC for his defeat of the Catilinarian conspiracy. It was awarded to the Emperor, Augustus, in 2 BC, and subsequently became part of the imperial titulature, **P P** appearing on inscriptions and on the coinage. At the opening of his reign, Nero refused it on the ground that he had not yet done anything to merit it; he had changed his mind, however, within the first two years.

Patrician: In the early history of Rome, society was divided into two groups – the **Patricians**, who constituted the aristocratic element, and the **Plebeians** who were the remainder of the citizen body; the origins of these two groups was unclear, although it may be that the **Patricians** were the king's advisers, the heads of households (*patres*), who constituted the early Senate. The **Patricians** at first maintained a stranglehold over the political, military, legal and religious machinery of the state. The 'struggle of the orders' (traditionally 509–287 BC) gave more say to *wealthy* plebeians, so that the real effectiveness of the distinction between the classes was eroded; the real force in the government of the Old Republic thus became the **nobility**, an aristocracy consisting of both patricians and plebeians. Augustus tried to revive the patriciate as the central core of his patronised aristocracy. Patricians were debarred from holding plebeian offices, such as the tribunate of the plebeians and the plebeian aedileship.

Pietas: The sense of duty to gods, state and family that represented the traditional focal points of loyalty for the Roman *nobilis*, and which Augustus tried to exemplify and revitalise.

Praefectus: Under the Principate, the term was applied to various grades within the reformed equestrian order, from commands of auxiliary units within the army to some of the most senior officers within the order – for example, the *Praefecti* of the Praetorian Guard and of Egypt.

Praetor: This office was second in importance to the consulship, although in Rome's very early days the *praetors* may have been the chief officers of the state – *prae-itor* meaning 'one who goes in front'. From the time of Sulla in the Old Republic, they had an increasing significance as presiding officers in the courts (*quaestiones*), a rôle that they retained under the Principate. The post led directly on to legionary commands and/or governorships of second-rank provinces.

Princeps: The term, chief man (or 'first among equals', as it is sometimes rendered) was favoured by Augustus as a form of address; it did not imply the holding of a particular office but, through the period of the Old Republic and into the Principate, had been applied to those who, in or out of office, were deemed to be prestigious, influential and, therefore, dispensers of patronage. The nature of the *Lex de Imperio* passed for Vespasian shows that, by AD 70 at least, the position of *princeps* had come to be regarded as an office. The honorific title, *princeps iuventutis* ('leader of youth') was sometimes bestowed on young members of the imperial family, such as on Gaius and Lucius Caesar (by Augustus) and on Nero himself in AD 50 (by Claudius).

Princeps Senatus: A term deriving from the Old Republic that was applied to the man who, in terms of seniority (however conceived), was placed at the head of the list of senators, as happened to Augustus following the senatorial revision that was carried out by Marcus Agrippa and himself in 28 BC.

Proconsul: The term was originally applied to a consul whose *imperium* had been extended beyond his term of office as consul to enable him to continue command of an army; by the second century BC, it was regularly used of those who commanded provinces after their year of office in Rome. During the Principate, it was used of the governors – whether ex-consuls or ex-praetors – of the public provinces. The Emperor was strictly the *proconsul* of the imperial provinces, although he rarely made direct use of the title – for example, on inscriptions – unless he was outside Italy.

Procurator: This term was used of various grades of equestrian officials in the Emperor's financial service – from the chief agents in the provinces (*Procuratores Augusti*) down to quite minor officials in their departments. These were officially distinguished by an adjective describing their different salary levels (e.g. *procuratores ducenarii*).

Respublica: This word, that, of course, provides the origin of our word, Republic, meant simply 'the public concern'. It was often used emotively to describe the nature of the state that Augustus supplanted after the battle of Actium in 31 BC. We have used the term Old Republic to describe this pre-Augustan state, because Roman writers often continued to refer to Rome as *respublica*. By definition, however, the *respublica* would be negated by anyone with overwhelming and capriciously exercised powers (*dominatio*).

Senatus consultum: The decree issued at the close of a senatorial debate, that was not *legally* binding, but rather an advisory statement passing on the view of senators to those popular bodies that were responsible for making the final decisions and passing laws. Because the Senate had a notional involvement in the production of the bronze and copper coinage, the letters **S C** (*Senatus consulto*) appear on the reverse of those coins until the third century AD.

Tribune of the Plebeians: According to tradition, these officers were originally appointed in 494 BC, charged with defending their fellow plebeians against injustice and injuries perpetrated by the Patricians. The decisive elements in their armoury were the veto, by which they could bring political business to a halt, and the sacrosanctity of their persons, by which all plebeians were under oath to defend an injured or wronged tribune. Gradually, during the period of the Old Republic, the tribunes were drawn into the regular business of government and office-holding, where their special privileges made them a powerful and potentially disruptive force. Under the Principate, their old powers remained, but were of little practical use, dwarfed as they were by the Emperor's tribunician power (*tribunicia potestas*). Augustus, because he was by adoption a patrician, was unable to hold the *office* of tribune, although between 36 and 23 BC he acquired most of the elements of the office, and outwardly used them as the basis of his conduct of the government in Rome. The *tribunicia potestas* served to stress the Emperors' patronage and protection of all plebeians; in fact, Emperor's counted their 'regnal years' by their tenure of the tribunician power. There are a few instances recorded of plebeian tribunes, during the Principate, attempting to utilise the powers of their office, vestigial though these were: for example, in Nero's reign, during the trial of the Stoics in AD 66, one of the tribunes, Arulenus Rusticus, offered to put his veto at the disposal of the defendants.

Appendix 4: Further Sources of Information for Nero's Reign

✦✦✦✦✦

In the Introduction, we looked at the three principal surviving sources of information for Nero's life and reign – the historians, Tacitus and Dio Cassius, and the biographer, Suetonius. There are, however, many other Classical writers of various types and periods who, in various contexts, have left us information about Nero; it is the purpose of the present Appendix to provide a brief review of these. The opportunity will also be taken to provide an assessment of the contribution made to our understanding of the Emperor and his ambitions by a study of his coinage.

Literary Sources

Principal amongst the writers contemporary with Nero is his adviser and one-time tutor, the Stoic philosopher, Lucius Annaeus Seneca.[1] He came under a considerable degree of criticism in antiquity both because of the wealth that he amassed in the Emperor's service, and because of inconsistencies that were perceived between his professed beliefs and his actions. Perhaps the most significant of Seneca's works for our present purpose are his ethical treatises, especially that concerned with clemency (*De Clementia*), that was written for the young Nero to indicate to him the proper path for a ruler to follow, and presented to Nero on the occasion of his birthday in AD 55.[2] Such a work as this will have constituted an answer to Seneca's critics, showing that, if it was not possible to have a ruler who was a philosopher, the next best alternative was to have one who was instructed by a philosopher.

Although Seneca was clearly (and reasonably) trying to urge acceptable standards of conduct upon Nero, the trouble with clemency, as we have seen, is that it was subject to no kind of external control; it was outside of the law, as the Emperor, Tiberius, had shown very clearly when he trumpeted it as one of his principal virtues. In the context of Nero's reign, clemency appeared to sit very comfortably with the concept of a 'golden age', presided over by a young and outwardly attractive *Princeps*; it left unanswered, however, the extremely uncomfortable question of what would happen if (or when) Nero chose not to be clement. There is also a collection of *Moral Epistles*, that provide incidental information on issues of the day, and that are in reality short essays rather than true letters.[3]

In a completely different vein is the irreverent and abrasive satire on the deification of the Emperor, Claudius, entitled *Apocolocyntosis* (or 'Pumpkinification'),[4] that Seneca may have produced as a piece of entertainment for the festival of *Saturnalia* in Nero's first year of office. This may, in view of the character of that first celebration of the festival,[5] have been intended to weaken the position of Agrippina by undermining the memory of her late husband, and to contribute to the marginalisation of Britannicus.

A work that has often in the past been attributed to Seneca is the historical drama, *Octavia*;[6] it is the sole surviving example in Roman literature of such a fact-centred play. Although commonly bound into the *corpus* of Seneca's plays, it is now generally accepted that *Octavia* was, in fact, written shortly after Nero's death,[7] since it contains, in the form of a prophecy, a description of the death of the Emperor.[8] It may be, then, that it should be ascribed to the early-Flavian period, when anti-Neronian sentiments were at their height, and to an author who felt moved to recount the sufferings of Octavia, the wife who, as we have seen, lent legitimacy to Nero's claim to succeed Claudius, and who was treated first with disdain by Nero, and ultimately with exceptional cruelty in his desire to free himself from her in order to marry Poppaea Sabina. Whilst few would have failed to sympathise with Octavia, the play, in some of its details, goes beyond the facts in its hostility towards the tyrant.

We have mentioned the historical works of the Elder Pliny,[9] that were undoubtedly used by our chief sources; however, whilst these do not survive, his *Natural History* does.[10] This was published in the late-70s, shortly before the author's death during the eruption of Vesuvius in AD 79 when, as Prefect of the fleet based at Misenum (on the northern side of the Bay of

Naples), he was attempting to rescue victims of the eruption. The *Natural History* is an encyclopaedic work that fills in a great many factual gaps and topics that would not have been of primary interest to the Classical historians. In its references to Nero and his government, it is generally hostile – as one would expect of an author of the Flavian period.

Also writing during the Flavian period was the Jewish historian, Flavius Josephus;[11] he was initially involved on the Jewish side in the rebellion of AD 66, but was captured and became a favoured member of Vespasian's court. His *Jewish War* thus provides a near-contemporary account of those hostilities, coming as it does from the pen of a man who presumably had an understanding of the feelings on both sides of the quarrel. This was followed some years later by his *Jewish Antiquities.*

The surviving portion of the satire/novel, the *Satyricon*, by Nero's one-time friend, Petronius,[12] provides us with an insight into the lives of those lower elements in Roman society, with whom Nero seems particularly to have empathised. Petronius had been very close to Nero, who took the view that nothing was in good taste unless Petronius, his 'arbiter of elegance',[13] said that it was. Tacitus[14] provides a lengthy account of Petronius' fall in AD 66: Tigellinus was evidently jealous of Petronius' relationship with Nero, and so 'framed' him by making much to Nero about Petronius' alleged friendship with Scaevinus, one of those implicated in the Pisonian conspiracy. Petronius committed suicide, as he felt the loss of Nero's favour, but not before penning a document containing a narrative account of the Emperor's debauchery. This was once thought to have been a lost portion of the *Satyricon*, but this idea is now discounted.

A problematical work of the early-third century AD is the *Life of Apollonius of Tyana*, a controversial philosopher, sage and magician, who lived through Nero's reign.[15] The biography – or, perhaps more appropriately, novel – was written, probably in the AD 220s, by the Greek sophist, Philostratus, who came to Rome and was patronised by Julia Domna, the wife of the Emperor, Septimius Severus (AD 193–211). It is recorded[16] that, in AD 215, Domna and her elder son, the Emperor, Caracalla, visited Tyana (in the province of Cappadocia) to erect a shrine to Apollonius. It is clear, however, that very divergent views were taken of Apollonius in antiquity, and the tradition about him is generally regarded as unreliable. As a result, as Bowersock has said, each ostensibly factual statement has to be scrutinised with great care for its reliability.

This is clearly apparent in the account of the Cynic philosopher, Demetrius, given in Books 4 and 5 of the *Life*: we are told that Demetrius verbally attacked Nero's gymnasium in Rome (constructed in AD 60–2[17]), and that he was consequently exiled from Rome at the instigation of Tigellinus – although Tigellinus had not at that stage yet risen to the post of Prefect of the Praetorian Guard. Further, we are told that, in AD 66,[18] despite having been exiled four years previously, Demetrius was in Rome; yet, in the following year, we are informed, he was in Athens, *still in exile*. Similar inconsistencies and blunders are evident in references in Book 5 to the rebellion of Gaius Julius Vindex in AD 68.[19]

A few poets are also relevant to us: Seneca's nephew, Lucan,[20] wrote an epic on the civil war between Julius Caesar and Pompey in the mid-first century BC (*Pharsalia*); this work was not finished, but seems to hint at a growing disillusionment with Nero on Lucan's part. The poet was certainly at one time a leading figure amongst Nero's literary friends, and won first prize at the celebration of the *Neronia* in AD 60 with a poem in praise of the Emperor. At times, Lucan's flattery of Nero may seem gross, although some of it may have been written with 'tongue in cheek'. By AD 65, however, the friendship was obviously at an end: Lucan was involved in Piso's conspiracy of that year and, as a consequence, was required to commit suicide,[21] although he attempted to exculpate himself by blaming his mother for his involvement.

Another poet, contemporary with Nero, was Titus Calpurnius Siculus,[22] who was evidently, to judge from his gentile (family) name, a client of Gaius Calpurnius Piso who, before becoming the figurehead of the conspiracy of AD 65, had been a close friend of Nero. Whilst, on the face of things, Calpurnius Siculus composed his *Eclogues* as a mark of respect for the Augustan poet, Virgil,[23] their true purpose was plainly to flatter Nero – presumably on his patron's behalf, as well as his own. For Calpurnius Siculus, Nero was a handsome, youthful leader, whom he equated with Mars and Apollo, two divinities with whom others (including Nero himself) associated the Emperor. For this poet, the reign marked the opening of a new 'golden age', that had been predicted by a comet;[24] he also writes about splendid games in Nero's amphitheatre, and the speech that Nero made in support of the people of Ilium (Troy).[25]

Aulus Persius Flaccus[26] was a Stoic contemporary of Nero, who wrote satiric poems in a style that is stilted and difficult to read; most of these have a strong element of Stoic moralising, and are by implication, although not directly, critical of the moral standards that prevailed in Nero's reign. Persius died in AD 62, at the early age of twenty-eight years. His *Satires* lack the apparently-angry edge of those of Tacitus' contemporary, Juvenal,[27] who attacks the depths to which Roman society had, in his view, sunk by the late-first century AD; it needs, however, to be said that some of Juvenal's ferocity – for example, against Egyptians – probably derives more from his own bigotry than from real problems in society. Like Petronius, however, Juvenal allows us to see how closely Nero was probably in tune with the lower orders of society, thereby illuminating the origins of the imperatives and inspiration that appear to have driven the Emperor, particularly in his later years.

Thus, whilst Nero evidently had few supporters (for whatever reasons) amongst our surviving sources, it is not a valid course of action to reject those sources simply because they may not appear convincing. It may be attractive to contemplate an exculpation of Nero: the variety of information within the totality of our sources, however, may suggest that an explanation of the Emperor may not only be feasible, but also a great deal more valuable. For the modern reader, perhaps the most aggravating feature of the ancient literary sources lies in the degree of their 'Rome-orientation'; for many of them the conflict between the Emperor and the senatorial order was the principal theme of significance. Suetonius, for example, as we have seen,[28] fails even to mention events in Britain and the East during Nero's reign. Further, even when Tacitus does attempt to look to the wider Empire, his accounts are clouded by his own and others' vagueness over details of chronology and topography; nor is it likely, to judge from his accounts of other events, that a 'final polish' – if, indeed, this was missing in the case of the Neronian books of the *Annals* – would have significantly retrieved the situation.

The Coinage of Nero[29]

In terms of weight and metallic quality, Nero's coinage can be simply divided into two parts – before and after the reforms of AD 64,[30] that appear to have been precipitated principally by the need to pay the bills arising from the rebuilding of Rome after the Fire of AD 64 and from the Emperor's other extravagances. Both periods of the coinage, however, effectively hold up a mirror to the tensions evident in Nero's court – due principally to the aspirations of his advisers, and the Emperor's own changing preoccupations.

Between AD 54 and AD 62, coins were minted only in gold and silver; no *aes* was struck in Rome during this period.[31] The coins themselves provide a commentary of sorts on the reign's development. An immediate and obvious point for comment is the appearance for the first time of EX S C (by senatorial decree) on the early gold and silver – until, that is, AD 62. The letters, S C, had previously appeared on the *aes*-denominations, and seemed to confirm that, whereas the Emperor exercised personal control over the gold and silver coinage, much of which will have been used to pay his armies and officials, the Senate maintained some element of control over the 'small change' in the system. Griffin,[32] however, has suggested that the appearance of the formula on the gold and silver of Nero may not indicate the Senate as the sanctioning authority of that coinage, but rather of the powers and honours expressed on it. The standard reverse on these pre-reform coins consisted of Nero's titles (annually updated) and the oak-leaf crown (*corona civica*); by recalling a device found on the coinage of Augustus, Nero was emphasising his wish to be seen as the restorer of an Augustan Principate – presumably the chief aspiration of Seneca and Burrus.

The first issues (of AD 54) have facing portraits of Nero and his mother, Agrippina, on the obverse, whilst the reverses take up the theme of Nero's links with his two deified predecessors, Augustus and Claudius. In the former case, this is signified by the appearance of the *corona civica*, that had been awarded to Augustus for 'saving the state' and which a number of his successors used on their coinage to emphasise their links with the founder of the Principate. In Claudius' case, the Emperor's funeral-procession is the chosen device. The prominence afforded to Agrippina is striking, and may indicate the continuing influence at the mint of her ally, Claudius' freedman, Antonius Pallas. It is worth noting that Agrippina is displayed with similar prominence on local provincial coinages at this time.[33] The issues of AD 55, on the other hand, whilst retaining the emphases on Augustus and Claudius, show Nero's portrait taking precedence of position over that of his mother on the obverse, although she continued to be commemorated.

From the issues of AD 56, however, Nero's head appears alone, bare, on the obverse, usually with his titles and the *corona civica* on the reverse. In AD 56, too, the title of *Pater Patriae* (P P: 'Father of the Fatherland') appears for the first time, Nero having previously refused it as unmerited by him at this early stage of his life. In this way, he appears to have been emulating the modest conservatism of Tiberius in respect of his titulature.[34]

There is a 'victory-issue' in AD 56, that may have been intended to put some weight behind Nero's use of the title, *Imperator* (Commander), that at this stage appeared at the end of his name as a *cognomen*. This totally-constitutional pattern remained in place until AD 60; from then on, until AD 64, three types are used – the grain-goddess, *Ceres* (indicating Nero's responsibility for his people's food-supply), manly courage, *Virtus*, (emphasising traditional strength and uprightness, especially in the military sphere) and *Roma* (again with a military emphasis, but also embracing the important concept of ancestral custom). Apart from annual updating, the reverse legend remained the same, including EX S C, until AD 63–4;[35] the *corona civica*, however, disappeared from AD 61. Whilst these changes presumably mirror, outwardly at least, the continuing importance of the Augustan style of Principate, there is also a perceptible growth of independence on Nero's part. We should not overlook the fact that these years saw the deaths of his mother (AD 59) and his wife (AD 62), the death of Burrus and the retirement of Seneca (AD 62), as well as the rise to prominence of Poppaea and Tigellinus (AD 62). Nero's Principate was thus consciously moving into new territory.

The new coin-types from AD 65 show greater variety than before, as well as an Emperor who evidently felt freed from restraint.[36] The new obverse showed Nero looking more jowly and, for the first time, occasionally bearded – perhaps, as with his carefully managed hair-style, to enhance a perceived association with the god, Apollo. Further, on one reverse type, Nero is shown wearing the radiate crown of the Sun, again pointing to a connection with Apollo. However, before concluding that this was simply a way of hinting at his own divinity, we should remember Nero's own observation that 'the only deified Emperors were dead ones'.[37] This coin also splits Nero's titles between the obverse (NERO CAESAR) and reverse (AVGVSTVS GERMANICVS), perhaps with the aim of aligning the military successes of Nero's reign with those of Augustus and of Germanicus Caesar. The rendering of the title, *Augustus*, in full certainly points to a deliberate attempt by Nero to associate himself with Augustus, and looks forward to a similar usage – and for a similar purpose – by Hadrian.[38] In the situation of AD 64 and the years following, when Nero's popularity especially with the higher echelons of Roman society had reached a low ebb, reminders of happier and more positive connections probably provided a welcome distraction from current woes.

The legend, AVGVSTVS AVGVSTA, is obviously a celebration of Nero's marriage to Poppaea Sabina, and the veiled figure of the Empress is clearly intended to convey the idea of the demure purity of the Emperor's new wife, despite the atrocious treatment of Octavia, that had been instigated, in part at least, by Poppaea, and that had allowed the marriage to take place. The Emperor is shown on the reverse wearing the radiate crown, again suggestive of Apollo's protection, a god who was eminently suited to another interpretation of this coin – that the two figures on the reverse may also represent Augustus who, in his own lifetime, had set great store by Apollo's protection, and his wife, Livia. This allusion to the deified predecessor would also provide another explanation of the radiate crown that is commonly used on the coinage to indicate deification. It is also worth noting that the year of issue, AD 64, marked the fiftieth anniversary of Augustus' death and deification.[39] We may reasonably assume that another legend, CONCORDIA AVGVSTA, also refers, at one level at least, to Nero's marriage, although, on another, it was probably a claim for a more general concord that was fast disappearing: as frequently with the celebration of CONCORDIA on the coinage, the wish was probably 'father to the thought'.

Military success in the East lies behind two further issues – PACE P R TERRA MARIQ PARTA IANVM CLVSIT ('having won peace by land and sea for the Roman people, he closed the gates of the temple of Janus'); the gates of Janus' temple were closed only when the Roman world was completely at peace. From the point of view of minting, it is interesting that, on different issues, the gates were placed in different parts of the temple. The ROMA issue is definitely to be seen in the same context of the successful conclusion of war in the East, that was formally celebrated in Rome in AD 66. Of the issues of AD 64–5, one further coin should be mentioned – IVPPITER CVSTOS; the reference must surely be that Jupiter (the Guardian) had saved his vice-gerent on earth (Nero) from the peril of the Pisonian conspiracy.[40]

The AVGVSTVS AVGVSTA and IANVM CLVSIT issues were continued into AD 66, and joined by two new coins – SALVS (the *well-being* of Rome and its Emperor after recent disasters) and VESTA. The latter shows the circular temple of the goddess in the Roman Forum; Vesta was the goddess associated with hearth and home and, so long as her sacred flame continued to burn in her temple, Rome would be safe. The temple had been damaged in the Fire;[41] Nero repaired it, and it stood as a symbol of his new Rome rising from the ashes. In addition, however, the Emperor had recently experienced a trembling-spasm whilst in the temple,[42] that may have been an epileptic fit but which, to his superstitious mind, evidently called for apotropaic action.

Nero's *aes*-coinage commenced in AD 62: from this time, the Emperor's radiate head appears regularly on the obverse of the *dupondii*; this has some-times been assumed to have been a claim for divine status on Nero's part, but is more likely to have been principally a means of more easily distin-guishing the *dupondius* from the *as*, two coins that were of similar diameter and general appearance. That, in any case, seems to have been the signi-ficance of the device on the coinage of Nero's successors. One important change to the titulature of the Emperor was the introduction, in AD 66, of *Imperator* (IMP) as his *praenomen* (forename), evidently to coincide with the homage paid to Nero, the supreme commander in the Eastern settle-ment, by the Parthian, Tiridates.

On the *aes*-coinage, much attention is paid to Nero's relationships with various sections of the community and his benefactions, just as the early gold and silver issues had, by implication, stressed his relationship with the Senate as the responsible guardian of Roman tradition. On the *aes*, the Emperor is shown in close proximity to his armed forces (addressing the cohorts; 'taking the salute' at the equestrian 'ride-past'), caring for his people and their well-being (grain-supply; money hand-outs; games and shows), improving Rome's physical facilities (the market-building; the new harbour at Ostia), and resolute and successful in the defence of the Empire's military interests and territorial integrity (triumphal arch; temple of Janus; security; Roma; victory). Amongst the many finely and elaborately designed *aes*-issues of the reign, we may perhaps pick out those commemorating the opening of the new harbour at Ostia and the Emperor's on-going care for the corn-supply,[43] as exemplified by his grandiose, though sensible, plan for a ship-canal linking the Bay of Naples with Ostia and Rome.[44]

Nero's connection with Augustus is emphasised with an issue recalling the latter's Altar of Peace (*Ara Pacis Augustae*), that had had the purpose of stressing the Emperor's harmony with the senatorial order and with tra-dition; this will have become a particularly sensitive subject in Nero's later years. His populist image will also have been brought to the fore through the issues commemorating Apollo the Lyre-Player (*Apollo Citharoedus*) and

Genius. It is worth noting that the only mention of Nero's games on his coinage comes in AD 65 on half-*asses* (*semisses*), almost the smallest coin – and presumably the most in use by ordinary people – in the money-system.[45] Whilst, as we have seen, Nero did not evidently regard himself as a god upon earth, nonetheless, as Suetonius clearly appreciated,[46] the Apollo-coin carried Nero's principate a considerable distance from the Augustan conception of the institution.

As a whole, the *aes*-coinage shows us Nero projecting images of success (military and otherwise), stability, security, respect for tradition and for the gods, harmony with his troops and care for his subjects. All of this was, in effect, a manifestation of his boundless generosity that, to his mind, was shown by the events from AD 62 onwards as inadequately reciprocated. In short, the coinage indicates an Emperor who was sane, who knew what he wanted to achieve, but who ultimately found himself increasingly frustrated and angry because of the refusal or inability of others to recognise his aims.

The hostile views of Nero taken publicly (or, in some cases, privately) by senators are reflected in the profuse coinage that emanated from Gaul and Spain in the spring and early-summer of AD 68;[47] these coins were issued mainly in accordance with the standards in place after Nero's coinage-reforms of AD 64. If there were any lingering doubts regarding the true motivation that lay behind Vindex's rebellion, these coins should unequivocally lay them to rest. The issues are related closely to Rome and its welfare, with no hint of the Gallic nationalism of which Vindex has occasionally been accused. Nothing, indeed, highlights the aims of Vindex and Galba more sharply than the imitation of the 'Ides of March' coin that had been issued by Marcus Brutus a century previously to celebrate the murder of Julius Caesar;[48] in AD 68, it signalled the death of the tyrant and of the dynasty, founded by Caesar, of which that tyrant was a part.

Apart from the 'Augustus' and 'Divus Augustus' issues, these coins bear no imperial heads, but rather gods, goddesses and personifications of traditional virtues, including the very relevant *concordia* between Spain and Gaul; the absence of such heads echoes the reluctance of Galba and others explicitly to assume the imperial titulature prior to senatorial sanction.

The reverses provide a sight of what was, in effect, the true agenda of the rebellion – the rebirth of Rome (ROMA RENASCENS) and a renewed emphasis on traditional virtues, such as Liberty (and its restoration), Safety, Security, Revenge and Victory. Further, Rome's traditional gods are seen to have been in support of the programme – Jupiter (as Saviour, Guardian and Liberator), Mars and Vulcan (as Avengers). Hercules is also invoked: but this is a strong Hercules defending the Roman Republic, not the drunken and distraught figure that Nero had gained such satisfaction from playing on the stage. Emphasis is placed on the Senate and people, the armies that, importantly, belonged to the people, and a return to the Principate as Augustus had devised it. This latter aim is explicit and implicit in numerous coins that show the *corona civica* and in a series of re-issues of coins of Augustus and Divus Augustus. Such coins were surely intended to make very clear how far Nero had strayed from his initial agenda, that it was he who was the inheritor of the political mantle of Augustus Caesar.

Notes

❧❧❧❧

Preface

1 See below in the Introduction and in Appendix 4.
2 The Greek Stoic philosopher, Epictetus, who was a slave of Nero's freedman and scribe, Epaphroditus, saw Nero as spoiled, morally bad and unhappy (*Discourses* 2.16, 31; 3.22, 30; 4.5, 17; *Encheiridion* 4.5, 18).
3 Tacitus *Histories* 1.15–16; Galba's thoughts on Emperors and the Principate are contained in an oration of advice which he is purported to have made to his intended successor, Piso Licinianus, shortly before they were both murdered by troops supporting Marcus Otho; see Syme 1958, Vol. I, 206ff.

Introduction: The Quest for Nero: The Principal Sources

A Note on translations: For Tacitus' *Histories*, the most accessible is that by K. Wellesley in the *Penguin Classics* series (Harmondsworth, 1972); recommended for Tacitus' *Annals* are M. Grant, *Tacitus: The Annals of Imperial Rome*, in the *Penguin Classics* series (Harmondsworth, 1996) (although this lacks the normal division of the text into sections) and A. J. Woodman, *Tacitus: The Annals* (Indianapolis, IN, 2004). For the Neronian books of Dio Cassius' *Roman History*, the most accessible translation is that of E. Cary (Volume 8 in the *Loeb Classical Library* translation of Dio) (London, 1925); for Suetonius' *Lives of the Caesars*, see R. Graves, *Suetonius: The Twelve Caesars*, in the *Penguin Classics* series (Harmondsworth, 1957).

1 For the inscription giving the official version of Claudius' speech, see *ILS* 212; for Tacitus' version, see *Annals* 11.24, and for a comparison of the two, see Wellesley 1954, 13–33. It can be seen in this example that, whilst the historian broadly reflected Claudius' sentiments, he was very free in the way in which he expressed them.
2 See plate 26; Castrén and Lilius 1970, p. 121 (no. 3).

3 See below on pp. 189ff.

4 See, for example, Syme 1958; Stolte 1973; Martin 1981; Shotter 1991; Mellor 1993.

5 See Townend 1967; Wallace-Hadrill 1983.

6 Millar 1964.

7 For Tacitus' political career, see most recently Birley A. R. 2000.

8 See Ogilvie and Richmond 1967.

9 There is, however, a possibility that he may have originated in Hippo (Bône, in modern Algeria); see Townend 1961b.

10 Writers of the Augustan History, *Life of Hadrian* 11, 3; Syme 1958, Vol. II, pp. 779–80; Townend 1967, p. 80; Wallace-Hadrill 1983, p. 6.

11 Millar 1964, pp. 8–9.

12 Dio 75.8, 1–3; 77.17, 3–4.

13 A dismissive comment by Thucydides (1.22, 4) is thought to refer to Herodotus.

14 Collingwood 1946, pp. 17–40.

15 There is no evidence to suggest that these were the titles chosen by Tacitus himself.

16 Tacitus *Histories* 1.1, 4.

17 Juvenal *Satire* 1.9–21. For Juvenal, see Highet 1954.

18 It is worth noting in the letters that the Younger Pliny (nephew of the Elder Pliny, who was Prefect of the Fleet at Misenum, and who died in the eruption of Vesuvius in AD 79) wrote to Tacitus on the subject of that eruption, that Tacitus had specifically requested material that would allow him to recapture details of the events with this kind of immediacy (The Younger Pliny *Letters* 6.16 and 20).

19 See, for example, Tacitus' comments about his material in *Annals* 4. 32–3.

20 See Tacitus *Histories* 1.1, 1–3 and *Annals* 1.1, 4–5.

21 This does, for example, become a problem in using the Tiberian historian, Gaius Velleius Paterculus; see Woodman 1977, pp. 28ff.

22 Josephus *Jewish Antiquities* 20.8, 3.

23 On the Jewish war, see below on pp. 100ff.

24 Tacitus *Histories* 1.15–16.

25 Thucydides 1.22, 1.

26 For the origin and meaning of this term, see below on pp. 11ff.

27 For the likely structure of the *Annals*, see Syme 1958, Vol. I, pp. 253ff.

28 It has sometimes been suggested that the fact that *Annals* 16 breaks off in mid-sentence supports the proposition that it was left unfinished.

29 Griffin 1984, pp. 235–7.

30 Tacitus *Histories* 4.43, 1; *Annals* 13.20, 1 and 14.2, 1; see Townend 1964.

31 The Younger Pliny *Letters* 9.19, 5; see below on pp. 160ff.

32 Tacitus *Annals* 13.20, 2–3; 14.2, 3; 15.53, 4; 15.61, 6.

33 Tacitus *Annals* 4.53, 3 (Agrippina) and 15.16, 1 (Corbulo); see also The Elder Pliny *Natural History* 2.180.

34 See below on pp. 92ff. See the Elder Pliny *Natural History* 5.12 (Syme 1958, Vol. I, p. 297).
35 Tacitus *Annals* 5.4, 1 and 15.74, 3; for a possible example of their use, see *Annals* 13.31–3 (Syme 1958, Vol. I, p. 296).
36 For an example in Tiberius' reign, see Tacitus *Annals* 3.16, 1.
37 See below on p. 61.
38 See below on p. 120.
39 Millar 1964, p. 2.
40 See below on p. 162.
41 Dio 53.19, 6.
42 Griffin 1984, p. 235.
43 Dio 62.9, 3–4.
44 Dio 53.2–19.
45 Dio 55.14–22; Millar 1964, p. 78.
46 Millar 1964, p. 77.
47 Dio 55.10, 3.
48 The Younger Pliny *Letters* 1.24.
49 The Younger Pliny *Letters* 10.94, 1.
50 The Younger Pliny *Letters* 9.34 and 5.10.
51 Townend 1959, pp. 290ff.
52 For the *Life of Nero*, in particular, see Warmington 1977 and Bradley 1978a.
53 See *Life of Gaius Caligula* 8.
54 For example, *Life of Tiberius* 21.
55 See *Life of Nero* 52; Bradley 1978a, p. 116.
56 Gallivan 1974a.
57 Townend 1967, 84ff; Wardle 1992.
58 See *Life of Gaius Caligula* 22, 1.
59 See, for example, *Life of Tiberius* 61, 5, where a general point about Tiberius' reign appears to have been based solely upon what happened to the daughter of the Praetorian Prefect, Lucius Aelius Sejanus, when he fell from power in AD 31.
60 *Life of Tiberius* 43–5.
61 See Macé 1900, p. 243; Wallace-Hadrill 1983, p. 43. Compare, for example, the stated attitude of the Greek historian, Herodotus (7.152, 3), that it was his duty 'to report what he had heard, but not necessarily to believe it'.
62 See, for example, Pliny *Letters* 1.18.
63 Compare *Life of Gaius Caligula* 45, 1 with *Life of Galba* 6.2–3.

Chapter 1 The Political Background to the Reign of Nero

1 Gaius Julius Caesar Octavianus will have been the formal name of the former Gaius Octavius following his adoption by Julius Caesar; he was generally known

as Caesar until he received the name/title, Augustus, from the Senate and people in 27 BC.

2 Shotter 2005a, pp. 4–38.

3 For a brief account of the Republic and its strengths and weaknesses, see Beard and Crawford 1999; Lintott 2000; Shotter 2005b.

4 Polybius *Histories* 6.2–18; von Fritz 1954; Millar 2002, pp. 12ff.

5 *Nobiles* literally meant 'men who were known'. For the nobility of the Principate, see Gelzer 1969.

6 For the Republic's voting-assemblies, see Taylor 1966; Staveley 1972, pp. 121ff; for the rôle of patronage in the early Principate, see Saller 1982.

7 See particularly Gelzer 1968 (on Caesar) and Seager 1979 (on Pompey); for an account of the events leading up to civil war, see Syme 1939, pp. 10–77.

8 Earl 1967, pp. 11ff.

9 Horace *Odes* 3.1–6.

10 Cicero *In Defence of Milo* 10.

11 Because the Emperor's power was founded upon his military leadership, the term, *imperator* (IMP) came to carry the meaning of 'Emperor'.

12 For example, in his *On the Republic*, a work written in the late-50s BC, when he became a marginal figure in the power-politics of the Republic; see Stockton 1971, pp. 163–5.

13 See, for example, Cicero *Letters to His Friends* 5.7, 3 (written to Pompey in 62 BC).

14 Keaveney 1982.

15 Huzar 1978, pp. 93ff.

16 Tacitus *Annals* 1.2, 1.

17 See Barrett 2002, p. 6; Wiseman 1965, pp. 333–4.

18 For a general summary, see Rowell 1962; Earl 1967, pp. 59ff; Millar 1977.

19 See below in chapter 9.

20 Tacitus *Annals* 4.2, 1–3. For the Praetorian Guard, see Durry 1968.

21 Written in Augustus' account of his life (*Res Gestae Divi Augusti* 34, 3).

22 See Tacitus *Histories* 4.7–8.

23 Shotter 2004a; Suetonius *Life of the Deified Vespasian* 7, 2.

24 The surviving sections of the law passed when Vespasian became Emperor (*Lex de Imperio Vespasiani* – *ILS* 244) demonstrate how wide-ranging the imperial powers really were.

25 Wirszubski 1950; Talbot 1984.

26 Shotter 1966b.

27 For examples of this attitude on Claudius' part, see *ILS* 206 (Smallwood 1967, no. 368; 15 March, AD 46) for his response to tribes who had usurped Roman citizenship, and his letter to the Greeks and Jews of Alexandria (Smallwood 1967, no. 370; 10 November, AD 41).

28 Tacitus *Histories* 3.83, 1.

29 Suetonius *Life of the Deified Vespasian* 18.

30 *Res Gestae Divi Augusti* 20, 4 (edition of Brunt and Moore 1967).

31 In general, see Ogilvie 1969 (esp. pp. 112ff) and Ferguson 1970.

32 Cicero *On The Nature of the Gods* 3.87.

33 Tacitus *Annals* 1.9–10 (Shotter 1967c).

34 Syme 1986.

35 Tacitus *Histories* 1.15–16; see above on p. 5.

36 Tacitus *Annals* 1.2, 1 and 1.3, 7.

37 Tacitus *Annals* 1.4, 1–2.

38 See, for example, *Res Gestae Divi Augusti* 34.

39 *Res Gestae Divi Augusti* 14, 1; also Tacitus *Annals* 1.10, 5.

40 Tacitus *Annals* 1.7, 10.

41 Suetonius *Life of Tiberius* 24–29.

42 Dio 57.8, 2; also Suetonius *Life of Tiberius* 27. See Shotter 1988.

43 Shotter 1966a.

44 We might compare with this the easy charm of Trajan, as recounted by the Younger Pliny in his *Panegyric of Trajan* (69–71).

45 Tacitus *Histories* 1.15, 3–4.

46 See Tacitus *Annals* 4.1ff; Seager 2005, pp. 178ff; Birley, A. R. 2007. Tiberius referred to Sejanus as the 'partner of his labours' (*socius laborum*) – see Tacitus *Annals* 4.2, 4. See also Crook 1955.

47 Suetonius *Life of Tiberius* 67, 2; Tacitus *Annals* 6.6, 1.

48 Tacitus *Annals* 1.11, 1.

49 Barrett 1989, pp. 17ff.

50 See Tacitus *Annals* 6.20, 2 (the view of Passienus Crispus, later to be the husband of Nero's mother); 6.48, 4 (the view of the Tiberian senator, Lucius Arruntius, who committed suicide rather than carry on living under Caligula).

51 For Tiberius' views, see Tacitus *Annals* 6.46, 2–5; Suetonius *Life of Caligula* 11.

52 Balsdon 1934, p. 15.

53 Tacitus *Annals* 1.31–52; *Oxyrhynchus Papyrus* 2435 (Turner 1959, pp. 102ff).

54 Tacitus *Annals* 2.82.

55 Tacitus *Annals* 2.72, 1.

56 Tacitus *Annals* 4.52, 6.

57 Tacitus *Annals* 4.17, 4.

58 Tacitus *Annals* 3.65, 3–4.

59 Philo *Legation to Gaius* 56 (translation by F. H. Colson in the *Loeb Classical Library* series (Cambridge MA, 1962).

60 Tacitus *Annals* 13.17, 5.

61 The Emperor, Claudius, for example, in his edict (*ILS* 206; see above in note 24) regarding the status of three Alpine tribes, indicates that confusion over their status had arisen because Caligula had failed to ask the commissioner who had been sent to investigate the matter for a report.

62 Tacitus at one point (*Annals* 1.4, 4) refers to the royal family as *domus regnatrix*.

63 Balsdon 1934, pp. 157ff.

64 Tacitus, *Annals* 3.18, 6–7.

65 Tacitus *Annals* 11.35, 1; note a similar reaction on the part of the Britons at seeing, in the wake of Boudica's rebellion, complete Roman obedience to the dictates of the freedman, Polyclitus (see below on p. 94). Griffin (1984, p. 55) notes that Nero's freedmen were the most hated of his courtiers; see Weaver 1972.

66 Tacitus *Annals* 12.1, 1.

67 For her mother (the Elder Agrippina), see above on p. 22.

68 Tacitus *Annals* 12.3–4.

69 Levick 1999, p. 76.

70 *RIC* 1² (Claudius), 7 and 11; Sutherland 1951, p. 126.

71 Tacitus *Histories* 1.4, 2.

72 Nero's ex-slaves, such as Helius, Polyclitus, Petinus and Patrobius, were particular objects of hatred, and were put to death by Galba (Plutarch *Life of Galba* 17, 2; Griffin 1984, p. 55).

Chapter 2 Nero's Family

1 Levick 1975; Wiedemann 1989; Barrett 2002.

2 The story is told in the Epic, the *Aeneid*, composed in the Augustan period by the court-poet, Virgil (Publius Vergilius Maro).

3 Livy 2.16, 4–6.

4 Suetonius *Life of Tiberius* 1–2.

5 Everett 2001, pp. 108ff.

6 Gelzer 1968, p. 19.

7 Octavius (the future Augustus) was the son of Atia, the daughter of Marcus Atius Balbus and Julius Caesar's sister, Julia.

8 Suetonius *Life of the Deified Augustus* 1–2.

9 Suetonius *Life of the Deified Augustus* 3.

10 Tacitus *Histories* 1.16, 1.

11 Tacitus *Life of Agricola* 3, 1.

12 Shotter 1978.

13 See Hurley 2003.

14 Shotter 1968 (Germanicus); Shotter 2000 (Agrippina).

15 For a mini-biography of Germanicus, see Suetonius *Life of Gaius Caligula* 1–7; he inherited the name/title, Germanicus, from his father, but was born Nero Claudius Drusus (Warmington 1969, p. 13).

16 Velleius Paterculus 2.96, 1.

17 Tacitus *Annals* 1.12, 2–6; Dio 57.2, 5–7.

18 Suetonius *Life of Tiberius* 10–13.

19 *RIC* 1² (Augustus), no. 205.

20 Velleius Paterculus 2.100, 2–5.

21 Tacitus *Annals* 1.53.

22 Velleius Paterculus 2.102, 3; for Augustus' reaction, see *Res Gestae Divi Augusti* 14, 1 and Suetonius *Life of Tiberius* 23.

23 Tacitus *Annals* 1.10, 4.

24 Shotter 1974c; Barrett 2002, p. 318.

25 Dio 55.15–22.

26 Suetonius *Life of Tiberius* 15, 2; Shotter 1971a.

27 Tacitus *Annals* 1.31–52 and 64–9.

28 Dio 55.32 (Agrippa Postumus); Tacitus *Annals* 4.71, 6–7 (Julia).

29 The fact that Tacitus (*Annals* 1.5, 6) reports that Livia's bulletin concerning the succession referred to Tiberius as *Nero* (rather than using his adoptive name) indicates the dynastic significance that he (and presumably Livia) attached to Tiberius' accession.

30 Tacitus *Annals* 1.4, 3–4; 1.33, 5–6.

31 Tacitus *Annals* 1.6.

32 Tacitus *Annals* 1.7, 10.

33 Tacitus *Annals* 1.35, 6–7.

34 Tacitus *Annals* 2.59, 2–3; Tiberius' chief criticism of Germanicus on this occasion was, however, directed towards the latter's unauthorised entry into Egypt that was reserved as imperial property.

35 Tacitus *Annals* 4.52, 1–6; Suetonius *Life of Tiberius* 53.

36 Shotter 2000a; hence, Sejanus' reference to 'the party of Agrippina' (*partes Agrippinae*: Tacitus *Annals* 4.17, 4).

37 Tacitus *Annals* 4.52, 6.

38 Tacitus *Annals* 2.72, 1.

39 Shotter 1974a. Dealings between Germanicus and Piso in the East have been to some extent clarified by the discovery in Spain of a text of the senatorial decree passed by the Senate after Piso's trial, the *Senatus Consultum de Gn. Pisone Patre*; see Eck, Caballos and Fernandez 1996 and Griffin 1997.

40 Bauman 1992.

41 Boddington 1963.

42 Tacitus *Annals* 4.2, 4; Dio 58.4, 3.

43 Tacitus *Annals* 4.2, 1–3.

44 Tacitus *Annals* 4.8, 1.

45 Tacitus *Annals* 5.3.

46 Tacitus *Annals* 1.12, 2–6; Shotter 1971b.

47 Tacitus *Annals* 6.25.

48 Tacitus *Annals* 6.24; Shotter 1974b.

49 Tacitus *Annals* 4.41, 2; 4.57.

50 Blake 1959, pp. 16–17; Boethius and Ward-Perkins 1970, pp. 324–6.

51 Tacitus *Annals* 4.39–40.

52 Josephus *Jewish Antiquities* 18.181ff; Dio 65.14, 1–2.

53 Juvenal *Satires* 10, 71–2.

54 Suetonius *Life of Tiberius* 61, 1.

55 Tacitus *Annals* 6.3, 4.

56 Suetonius *Life of Tiberius* 73, 2.

57 Dio 59.8, 1.
58 Tacitus *Annals* 4.75; Ahenobarbus became consul in AD 32.
59 Suetonius *Life of Nero* 5.
60 The Elder Pliny *Natural History* 7.45; Holland 2000, p. 20.
61 Dio 61.2, 3.
62 Suetonius *Life of Nero* 1.
63 E.g. Crawford 1974, no. 519.
64 E.g. *RIC* 1² (Nero), plate 19, no. 110; Mac Dowell 1979, plate 6, no. 180. Nero is shown bearded on a graffito from the *Domus Tiberiana* in Rome (Correra 1894; Castrén and Lilius 1970, p. 121, no. 3); see also Hiesinger 1975.
65 Dio 63.9, 1.
66 Suetonius *Life of Nero* 2–5.
67 Syme 1939, p. 421.
68 Suetonius *Life of Nero* 4.
69 Suetonius *Life of Nero* 5.
70 Tacitus *Annals* 6.47, 2; Bauman 1974, pp. 130ff.
71 Suetonius *Life of Nero* 5.
72 Suetonius *Life of Nero* 7, 1.
73 The Arval Brethren (*Fratres Arvales*) were a College of priests concerned with the fertility of the fields; they appear to have become defunct as a College in the latter years of the Republic, but were revived by Augustus (in *c*. 29 BC) largely for ceremonial purposes, and to enhance the traditionalist façade of his regime. Many of the priests were senators of importance, and they enacted vows and sacrifice in response to requests and events (Syme 1980, pp. 100ff). Their surviving records (*Acta*), albeit chronologically patchy, provide a brief commentary on contemporary events. Nero became their master (*magister*) in AD 66; on this, see below on p. 228 and note 148.
74 Tacitus *Annals* 13.10; Suetonius *Life of Nero* 9; *Acts of the Arval Brethren* for 11 December, AD 57 (Smallwood 1967, no. 19).
75 Tacitus *Annals* 15.23, 2.
76 Suetonius *Life of Nero* 41; see below on p. 157.
77 Suetonius *Life of Nero* 41, 1.
78 Pliny *Natural History* 2.92, 4.
79 E.g. Lucan *Pharsalia* 2.508–25.
80 Juvenal *Satire* 8.224–30.
81 Tacitus *Annals* 12.64, 4.
82 Barrett 1996, p. 45.
83 Tacitus *Annals* 12.64, 5; Suetonius *Life of Nero* 5, 2.
84 Barrett 1996, p. 233.
85 Suetonius *Life of Nero* 5, 2; Quintilian 6.1, 50.
86 Tacitus *Annals* 13.21, 6; Dio 61.17, 2.
87 Tacitus *Annals* 13.21, 4; Dio 61.17, 1.
88 Tacitus *Annals* 12.7, 5.

89 Tacitus *Annals* 12.7, 6–7.
90 *RIC* 1² (Gaius), no. 33; note Suetonius' observation (*Life of Gaius* 15, 4) that the names of Gaius' sisters were included in oaths.
91 *RIC* 1² (Gaius), no. 58; this appears to contradict Suetonius (*Life of Gaius* 23, 1), who claims that Caligula flew into a rage at any mention of his descent from the plebeian, Marcus Agrippa. It may be conjectured that Caligula's anger derived not from mentions of Marcus Agrippa (*sic*) but from the inclusion of his rare but unimpressive family-name, Vipsanius; most inscriptions appear to omit this family-name.
92 Suetonius *Life of Gaius* 24, 2.
93 *Acts of the Arval Brethren* for 27 October, AD 39 (Smallwood 1967, no. 9), where a sacrifice is recorded 'on account of the detection of the wicked plans of Gn. Lentulus Gaetulicus against C. Germanicus'; for details of this conspiracy against Caligula, see Barrett 1989, pp. 91ff.
94 Suetonius *Life of Gaius* 24, 3.
95 Suetonius *Life of Nero* 6, 3.
96 Suetonius *Life of Nero* 6, 3.
97 Tacitus *Annals* 12.65, 1; Suetonius *Life of Nero* 7, 1.
98 Suetonius *Life of Nero* 6, 3.
99 Suetonius *Life of the Deified Claudius* 27.
100 Tacitus *Annals* 13.15–17; Suetonius *Life of Nero* 33, 2; Dio 61.1, 2 and 7, 4; Barrett 1996, pp. 170–3; Woods 2004, p. 112.
101 Tacitus *Life of Agricola* 3, 1; von Fritz 1957; Shotter 1978.

Chapter 3 The Path to Power

1 Suetonius *Life of Nero* 6, 1.
2 See Shotter 1968 (Germanicus); Barrett 1996, pp. 13ff and Shotter 2000 (Agrippina).
3 Suetonius *Life of Nero* 6–7.
4 Balsdon 1934, pp. 58ff; Barrett 1989, pp. 91ff; *Acts of the Arval Brethren* (Smallwood 1967, no. 9) for 27 October, AD 39.
5 On this, see above in chapter 2, p. 39.
6 Wilkinson 2005, pp. 10ff.
7 Suetonius *Life of Nero* 6, 2.
8 Josephus *Jewish Antiquities* 20.183; Suetonius *Life of Nero* 35, 2; Tacitus *Annals* 14.3–8; Warmington 1969, p. 26.
9 Josephus *Jewish Antiquities* 20.8.
10 Tacitus *Annals* 14.7–8; Suetonius *Life of Nero* 35, 2; for a discussion of the question of whether there may have been two different men with the name, Anicetus, see Woods 2006.
11 Griffin 1984, p. 31.
12 Tacitus *Annals* 12.64, 6.

13 Tacitus *Annals* 11.37, 4.

14 Tacitus *Annals* 6.20, 2; Seneca *On Benefits* 1.15, 5; Griffin 1984, p. 28; Barrett 1996, pp. 84–6.

15 For the problems of distinguishing between references to Ahenobarbus' two sisters, Domitia and Domitia Lepida, see Barrett 1996, pp. 84ff and p. 233; also above in chapter 2 (p. 39).

16 Barrett 1996, pp. 84ff.

17 Barrett 1996, p. 86 and p. 222.

18 He was dead by AD 48; Syme 1958, Vol. I, p. 328.

19 Tacitus *Annals* 12.7, 5–7.

20 Suetonius *Life of Nero* 22.

21 Suetonius *Life of Nero* 20, 1.

22 Suetonius *Life of Nero* 20, 1.

23 See *RIC* 1² (Nero), no. 73 etc; the coin-type received a specific mention by Suetonius (*Life of Nero* 25, 3).

24 Suetonius *Life of Nero* 52, 1.

25 Tacitus *Life of Agricola* 4, 2–3.

26 On the 'political application' of the 'virtue' of *clementia*, see Earl 1967, p. 60.

27 Suetonius *Life of Nero* 52, 1.

28 Suetonius *Life of Nero* 52, 1.

29 Suetonius *Life of Nero* 7, 1.

30 Tacitus *Annals* 12.7, 5–7.

31 Her father was Marcus Valerius Messala Barbatus (Levick 1990, p. 54).

32 For the problems surrounding the date of Britannicus' birth, see Henderson 1903, p. 453.

33 Suetonius *Life of Nero* 6, 4; Dio 61.2, 4.

34 Tacitus *Annals* 4.39–40.

35 Tacitus *Annals* 4.52; Shotter 2000.

36 Tacitus *Annals* 11.26–38; Suetonius *Life of the Deified Claudius* 26, 2; Levick 1990, pp. 64ff.

37 Tacitus *Annals* 11.12, 2; she was probably the daughter of Marcus Junius Silanus, consul in AD 15 (Tacitus *Annals* 3.24, 5), and sister of Junia Claudilla, wife of Caligula (Tacitus *Annals* 6.20, 1).

38 Tacitus *Annals* 4.17, 4; Rogers 1931; for Silius' family and connections, see Shotter 1967b.

39 See above in chapter 2 (pp. 40ff).

40 Publius Vitellius, who was with Germanicus in Germany and the East (Tacitus *Annals* 1.70; 3.17, 4), and his brother, Lucius, who was a 'courtier' of both Caligula and Claudius, sharing the censorship with the latter in AD 47–8.

41 Tacitus *Annals* 12.7, 5–6.

42 Tacitus *Annals* 1.69; Shotter 2000.

43 Tacitus *Annals* 12.4.

44 Tacitus *Annals* 12.3–4.

45 Nero was eleven years of age at the time of his engagement to Octavia, and fifteen when they were married.

46 *Res Gestae Divi Augusti* 14; Suetonius *Life of Tiberius* 23.

47 Shotter 1974c.

48 Claudius had Octavia adopted into another family to obviate the appearance of incest in a marriage between brother and sister (Dio 60.33, 2a).

49 Tacitus *Annals* 12.26, 1; *ILS* 224.

50 Barrett 1996, pp. 108–9; Tacitus *Annals* 12.26, 1.

51 As can be seen in early representations in sculpture and on coins (Suetonius *Life of Nero* 51; coin-illustrations 1 and 3–5).

52 Tacitus *Annals* 12.41; Suetonius *Life of Nero* 7; Griffin 1984, p. 29.

53 Smallwood 1967, no. 105; Grant 1950, p. 78; 1954, p. 109; 1970, p. 26.

54 Suetonius *Life of Nero* 7, 2.

55 Tacitus *Annals* 12.41, 8.

56 Tacitus *Annals* 12.42, 1.

57 Tacitus *Annals* 4.2, 1–3.

58 Tacitus *Annals* 12.64, 5.

59 E.g. Dio 60.33, 9.

60 See Smallwood 1967, no. 105b.

61 Suetonius *Life of the Deified Claudius* 43.

62 Dio 60.34, 1–2; in general on this, see Champlin 2003, pp. 44–6.

63 Tacitus *Annals* 12.66–7; Suetonius *Life of the Deified Claudius* 44–6; Dio 60.34, 1–6; Pliny *Natural History* 22.92; Martial *De Spectaculis* 1.21, 4; Juvenal *Satires* 5, 146–8 and 6.620–3; Seneca *Apocolocyntosis*; 'Pseudo-Seneca' *Octavia* 31; Philostratus *Life of Apollonius of Tyana* 5.32. For the extensive modern bibliography, see Barrett 1996, p. 287.

64 Josephus *Jewish Antiquities* 20. 148–51.

65 Suetonius *Life of Nero* 33, 1.

66 The Younger Seneca *Apocolocyntosis* 4; Levick 1990, p. 77.

67 Tacitus *Annals* 12.69, 2; Dio 60.33, 10.

68 Tacitus *Annals* 12.69, 3; Suetonius *Life of the Deified Claudius* 10.

69 Warmington 1969, p. 34.

70 Tacitus *Annals* 12.69; Suetonius *Life of the Deified Claudius* 44; Dio 61.1, 2; Barrett 1996, p. 144.

71 *Oxyrhynchus Papyrus* 1021; Smallwood 1967, no. 47.

Chapter 4 The Expectation and Hope of all the World

1 Seneca *On Benefits* 2.20, 2; Rudich 1997, p. 66.

2 *Oxyrhynchus Papyrus* 2435 (Turner 1959, p. 102); Shotter 1968, pp. 204ff.

3 *Cambridge Ancient History* 1966, Vol. X^1, p. 703.

4 *RIC* 1² (Claudius), no. 7.

5 *RIC* 1² (Nero), no. 6; coin-illustration 4.

6 See Bishop 1964, pp. 34ff. and Barrett 2002, pp. 103ff.

7 Tacitus *Annals* 13.1, 1.

8 Tacitus *Annals* 1.6, 1.

9 Aurelius Victor *On the Emperors* 5; the writer goes on to talk (in 5, 2–4) of the corruption of Nero. For the notion of the inception of a 'golden age', see Calpurnius Siculus *Eclogues* 1, 42; Lepper 1957; Murray 1965; Warmington 1969, pp. 34ff; Griffin 1984, p. 37; Malitz 2005, pp. 15ff.

10 Dio 61.3, 1 (except for the title of *Pater Patriae*, for which he said that he was too young; he did, however, accept it in AD 56).

11 Dio 60.33, 10.

12 *ILS* 244 (*Lex de Imperio Vespasiani*).

13 Tacitus *Annals* 13.4, 3.

14 Suetonius *Life of Nero* 9, 1.

15 Dio 61.3, 2.

16 Tacitus *Annals* 13.1, 1.

17 Tacitus *Annals* 13.1, 4.

18 Sutherland 1951, pp. 143ff.

19 *RIC* 1² (Nero), nos. 1–2; coin-illustrations 3–4.

20 E.g. Milne 1971, pp. 4ff; Burnett *et al.* 1992.

21 *RIC* 1² (Nero), nos. 6–7.

22 Tacitus *Annals* 13.14, 1.

23 Tacitus *Annals* 13.5, 1–3; 13.12, 2; 14.2, 2.

24 Griffin 1984, p. 39.

25 Shotter 1966a.

26 Tacitus *Annals* 13.2, 5–6; Suetonius *Life of Nero* 9; Dio 61.3, 2.

27 Tacitus *Annals* 13.5, 2.

28 *RIC* 1² (Gaius), p. 105; Sutherland 1951, pp. 107ff.

29 Tacitus *Annals* 13.5, 3.

30 Tacitus *Annals* 13.12–13; Suetonius *Life of Nero* 28, 1; Dio 61.3, 2. Her name is recorded as Claudia Acte.

31 Dio 61.7, 1.

32 Tacitus *Annals* 13.13, 1.

33 Tacitus *Annals* 13.2, 3–4; 13.14, 1.

34 Tacitus *Annals* 13.2, 5; Tacitus' wording appears to imply insincerity on Nero's part.

35 Juvenal *Satire* 10, 71–2; Dio 58.10.

36 Griffin 1984, p. 40.

37 Dio 60.35, 4.

38 Seneca *Apocolocyntosis* 4; see also Calpurnius Siculus *Eclogues* 1.44–5; 4.90–1; 7.84.

39 Champlin 2003, p. 113; Seager 2005, pp. 220ff.

40 Tacitus *Annals* 14.14, 1.

41 Tacitus *Annals* 6.46, 6; the remark was made to Macro, the Praetorian Prefect.

42 Shotter 2000, p. 352.

43 Tacitus *Annals* 12.41, 6; Suetonius *Life of Nero* 7, 1; it is worth noting that, whilst Tacitus tells us that the name used by Britannicus was 'Domitius', Suetonius says it was Nero's *cognomen*, 'Ahenobarbus'. One might wonder, however, how much of an insult this really was, as Nero certainly did not neglect his place amongst the Domitii. The real point of the story might be that Britannicus used Nero's *nomen* or *cognomen* in preference to what, in the context of the family, would have been more usual, the *praenomen*, Lucius.

44 Champlin 2003, p. 151.

45 Tacitus *Annals* 13.15, 3.

46 Suetonius *Life of Nero* 53.

47 Tacitus *Annals* 13.17, 3.

48 Tacitus *Annals* 15.62, 2.

49 Tacitus *Annals* 13.15–17; Suetonius *Life of Nero* 33, 3; Dio 61.7, 4.

50 Tacitus *Annals* 13.19, 3; both were great-great-grandsons of Augustus.

51 Tacitus *Annals* 13.19–22.

52 Tacitus *Annals* 14.12, 6–7.

53 Tacitus *Annals* 13.25 and 47, 2; Suetonius *Life of Nero* 26; Dio 61.8, 1–4; Eyben 1993; Marcus Antonius is said to have indulged in similar behaviour (Plutarch *Marcus Antonius* 29, 2–4; cf. Cicero *Philippic* 2.4; Lintott 1968, p. 110).

54 Champlin 2003, pp. 152–3.

55 Tacitus *Annals* 13.25, 4.

56 Champlin 2003, pp. 150ff.

57 Tacitus *Annals* 13.14–17.

58 The *Domus Aurea*, or Golden House, was the new palace which Nero built following the Fire of Rome in AD 64.

59 Suetonius *Life of Nero* 34, 1.

60 Tacitus *Annals* 13.20, 2.

61 Tacitus *Annals* 13.58.

62 Tacitus *Annals* 14.1, 1.

63 Tacitus *Annals* 14.13, 3.

64 Tacitus *Annals* 14.51, 1.

65 Dio 61.4, 1.

66 Seneca *Apocolocyntosis* 4; Tacitus *Annals* 14.14–15; Dio 61.19–20; Calpurnius Siculus *Eclogues* 1.44–5 (see Horsfall 1997, p. 166 for the dating of Calpurnius Siculus); Lucan *Pharsalia* 1.47–50; Champlin 2003, p. 114.

67 Lucan *Pharsalia* 1.33ff.

68 *Oxyrhynchus Papyrus* 1021; see above on p. 54.

69 Picard (1966, p. 125) argues that Nero's interest in the concerns of the masses was 'more or less pure'.

70 Seneca *Apocolocyntosis* 4; but compare, for example, Philostratus *Life of Apollonius of Tyana* 4.39 and 42.

71 *RIC* 1² (Nero), no. 73 etc; Sutherland 1951, p. 170.

72 Tacitus *Life of Agricola* 3, 1; Shotter 1978.

73 Tacitus *Histories* 1.15–16 (Oration of Galba); for the Senate under Claudius and Nero, see McAlindon 1956.

74 *RIC* 1² (Nero), nos. 1ff.

75 *RIC* 1² (Nero), nos. 1–43; for a discussion of the significance of this, see Griffin 1984, pp. 58ff and below on p. 195.

76 Earl 1967, p. 60.

77 Suetonius *Life of Nero* 10.

78 Calpurnius Siculus *Eclogues* 1.59f; Griffin 1984, p. 64.

79 Seneca *On Clemency* 2.1, 1.

80 Sutherland 1938.

81 See, for example, the observations made by Marcus Lepidus during the trial of Clutorius Priscus in AD 21 (Tacitus *Annals* 3.50, 3; Shotter 1969a).

82 Seneca *On Clemency* 1.1, 2–3.

83 Marcus Aurelius *Meditations* 1.16 and 6.30.

84 Suetonius *Life of Nero* 43, 1.

85 For example, Tacitus *Annals* 15.57 (conspiracy of Piso); Suetonius *Life of Nero* 36, 1 (conspiracies of Piso and Vinicianus) and 43, 1 (rebellion of Vindex).

86 Suetonius *Life of the Deified Vespasian* 9, 1; Martial *On Spectacles* 2.

87 See, for example, Smallwood 1967, p. 319 (= *ILS* 5640) of AD 57 and p. 321 (of AD 61–2).

88 Tacitus *Annals* 13.23, 1; Dio 60.30, 6a.

89 Tacitus *Annals* 15.53.

90 Tacitus *Annals* 14.1, 1.

91 Chilver 1957 and Gallivan 1974c.

92 Tiberius became excessively exasperated with what he saw as senatorial sycophancy (see Tacitus *Annals* 3.65, 3–4); see also Galba's observation on the evil of flattery (Tacitus *Histories* 1.15, 4).

93 Tacitus *Annals* 13.8, 1.

94 Tacitus *Annals* 13.10–11.

95 Tiberius had twinned *moderatio* with *clementia* as virtues to advertise on his coinage (*RIC* 1² (Tiberius), nos. 38–9); Sutherland 1938.

96 Griffin 1984, p. 60.

97 By contrast, Tiberius was in the habit of conducting searching and embarrassing examinations of the circumstances before offering such help (Tacitus *Annals* 2.37–8).

98 See Potter 1987, pp. 192ff.

99 In Britain, Colchester provides an example of a *colonia* founded in AD 49 (during Claudius' reign) for legionary veterans.

100 See Tacitus *Annals* 14.27; Stevenson 1939, p. 168.

101 Puteoli had been expanded and developed by Augustus, and had received *colonia*-status from Nero in AD 60 (D'Arms 1970, p. 98).

102 Tacitus *Annals* 14.17; Grant 1974, p. 73; see plate 13.

103 The effects of the earthquake are graphically depicted in reliefs on the shrine of the household gods in the House of Lucius Caecilius Iucundus at Pompeii (Grant 1974, p. 26; see plate 10).

104 Tacitus *Annals* 13.50–1.

105 Tacitus *Annals* 12.65, 1.

106 Tacitus *Annals* 14.61.

107 Tacitus *Annals* 15.46.

108 Tacitus *Annals* 13.24, 1 and 13.25, 4.

109 During discussion in the Senate when, during his censorship, Claudius had proposed the adlection to the Senate of leading Gauls, some senators had been dismayed enough to question a policy that they evidently saw as harmful to Italy's interests (Tacitus *Annals* 11.23, 2).

110 Suetonius *Life of Nero* 15, 1.

111 On this, see further below on pp. 92ff; see also Tacitus *Annals* 14.29–39 and Webster 1978.

112 See above on p. 59.

113 Tacitus *Annals* 13.50.

114 Tacitus *Life of Agricola* 19, 4.

115 Dio 56.18, 2–3.

116 Syme 1971, pp. 106–10.

117 Aurelius Victor *On the Emperors* 5; on Victor, see Bird 1994.

Chapter 5 The End of the Beginning

1 Tacitus *Annals* 13.58.

2 Horace *Odes* 3.6, 33ff.

3 Dio 63.22, 3; Warmington 1969, p. 46.

4 For Tacitus' account of the episode, see *Annals* 14.1–13.

5 Tacitus *Annals* 14.2; Suetonius *Life of Nero* 28; Champlin 2003, p. 42.

6 Bishop 1960.

7 Tacitus *Annals* 14.6–7.

8 Dio 61.12, 1.

9 Baldwin 1979, p. 380f.

10 Tacitus *Annals* 14.9, 1. Compare Suetonius *Life of Nero* 34 and Dio 61.14, 2; Griffin 1984, p. 236.

11 Tacitus *Annals* 14.1, 1 and 14.60; Dio 61.12 and 62.13, 1–4.

12 Tacitus *Histories* 1.13; Tacitus *Annals* 13.45–6; Suetonius *Life of Otho* 3; Plutarch *Life of Galba* 19–20; Dio 61.11, 2; Champlin 2003, pp. 46–8 and p. 281 (notes 23 and 24).

13 Titus Ollius perished with Sejanus in AD 31 (Tacitus *Annals* 13.45, 1) before he had entered on an official career. Although Poppaea preferred to take the name of her maternal grandfather, Gaius Poppaeus Sabinus (*Annals* 1.80, 1; 6.39, 3), a strong 'establishment-figure' in Tiberius' reign, some of the popular support in Rome shown to Sejanus (*ILS* 6044; Syme 1956) may have rubbed off onto the daughter of Ollius.

14 Griffin 1984, p. 102 and note 15; see Maiuri 1971, p. 95 and p. 102f. It may be significant that Poppaea is said to have had an interest in religions (Josephus *Jewish Antiquities* 20.189–95), and that the 'House of the Golden Cupids' is decorated with painted scenes from Egyptian religion (see plates 7–9).

15 Champlin 2003, p. 297 (note 48).

16 Sear 1982, p. 24 and p. 108; Potter 1987, p. 94; Giubelli 1991 (see plates 3–6).

17 Suetonius *Life of Nero* 35, 5.

18 Tacitus *Annals* 13.45–6.

19 Plutarch *Life of Galba* 19, 3.

20 Tacitus *Annals* 13.45, 3.

21 This province occupied parts of what is now Spain and Portugal.

22 Plutarch *Life of Galba* 20, 1.

23 John of Antioch (in a gloss on Dio 62.13, 1–2) notes Burrus' continued insistence upon the importance to the legality of Nero's position of the marriage to Octavia.

24 Tacitus *Annals* 14.51, 1.

25 Tacitus *Annals* 14.52ff.

26 Warmington 1969, p. 47.

27 Suetonius *Life of Nero* 28, 2.

28 Tacitus *Annals* 14.13, 2.

29 See, for example, the range of reasons for quitting life in Rome, given by the central character in Juvenal *Satire* 3.

30 Tacitus *Annals* 14.10.

31 Tacitus *Annals* 14.10, 2–3; Manning 1975.

32 Tacitus *Annals* 14.11, 3.

33 Tacitus *Annals* 14.11, 1 (cf. 13.5, 1–2).

34 It seems likely that, in AD 68, Gaius Julius Vindex chose the same period for the inauguration of his rebellion against Nero (Shotter 1975, 61ff; see also below on pp. 157).

35 Tacitus *Annals* 14.12–13; Suetonius *Life of Nero* 11–12; Dio 61.15–16; Champlin 2003, p. 70.

36 Dio 61.16–18.

37 Tacitus *Annals* 16.21–35; for the rôle of Stoics in the opposition to Nero, see Warmington 1969, pp. 142ff; Sandbach 1975, pp. 140ff; Griffin 1984, pp. 171ff; Rudich 1992.

38 Tacitus *Annals* 14.12, 1.

39 Tacitus *Life of Agricola* 42, 4, where he compares the moderate conduct of his father-in-law under Domitian with those who, like Thrasea Paetus under Nero,

courted a melodramatic death that may have brought them personal fame, but that was of no value to the Republic.

40 Champlin 2003, p. 69.

41 Tacitus *Annals* 14.13, 2; Dio (61.16) says that, although people paid Nero reverence in public, 'in private they tore his character to shreds'.

42 Barrett 1996, p. 233.

43 Tacitus *Annals* 14.22; Rogers 1955.

44 D'Arms 1970, pp. 94–99; the mineral waters of Baiae were regarded as the 'richest on earth' (The Elder Pliny *Natural History* 31.4–5; D'Arms 1970, pp. 139ff).

45 Champlin 2003, p. 157.

46 See *RIC* 1² (Nero), no. 73 etc; Mac Dowell 1979, p. 82 and plates IX and X; Suetonius *Life of Nero* 25, 2 (coin-illustation 15).

47 Boethius and Ward-Perkins 1970, p. 211.

48 Tacitus *Annals* 14.14, 3; Hind 1970.

49 Juvenal *Satire* 1.59–62.

50 Boethius and Ward-Perkins 1970, p. 211.

51 Tacitus *Annals* 12.56, 1; 14.15; for the location, see *Res Gestae Divi Augusti* 23.

52 Suetonius *Life of Nero* 20, 3.

53 Tacitus *Annals* 14.20; Mac Dowall 1958.

54 *RIC* 1² (Nero), nos. 91–2.

55 See below on pp. 92ff.

56 Shotter 2004c, 31–36.

57 Tacitus *Annals* 14.48.

58 Tacitus *Annals* 3.50, 2.

59 Tacitus *Annals* 14.51, 1.

60 Tacitus *Annals* 14.51, 2–3.

61 Tacitus *Annals* 14.52ff.

62 Tacitus *Annals* 14.57–59.

63 For Corbulo's position in the East, see below on pp. 96ff.

64 Dio 62.13, 1–2; Warmington 1969, p. 50 and Gallivan 1974b.

65 Tacitus *Annals* 14.61.

66 Tacitus *Annals* 14.62.

67 Tacitus *Annals* 14.63, 2.

68 *Octavia* 125; Dio 62.13, 1 (who uses the same terminology for Poppaea); Champlin 2003, p. 103 and p. 305.

69 Tacitus *Annals* 14.65, 2.

Chapter 6 Nero and the Empire

1 Chilver 1957; Fabius Valens, when encouraging Vitellius to make a bid for power at the end of AD 68, pointed out that Verginius Rufus had been right to hesitate, when offered the throne by his soldiers earlier in the year, because

he came from an equestrian family and because his father was a social 'nobody' (Tacitus *Histories* 1.52, 4).

2 Shotter 1969b; for implied criticism of the practice under Tiberius, see Tacitus *Annals* 2.36, 1–2. It would seem that Caecina Alienus provides another example under Galba, when he was given a legionary command in Germany as a reward for supporting Galba in the *bellum Neronis*. In general, see Birley E. B. 1953.

3 Birley E. B. 1953.

4 See below in Appendix 2.

5 Tacitus *Annals* 2.59, 3; Shotter 1966a.

6 The temple was rescued in 1963 from the area to be flooded by the new Aswan Dam, and in 1965 was presented by the Egyptian government to the United States of America; it can now be seen, reconstructed, in the Metropolitan Museum of Art in New York.

7 Livy 5.34ff.

8 See Carney 1970, pp. 31ff.

9 See Clunn 1999 for a review of recent field-study at the site of this event.

10 Suetonius *Life of the Deified Augustus* 23; Campbell 1984.

11 These military districts lacked some aspects of civilian administration that were handled from the neighbouring province of Belgica; for the Roman Frontiers see Whittaker 1994.

12 For Germanicus on the Rhine, see Wells 1972 and Shotter 1968.

13 Tacitus *Annals* 2.26.

14 Tacitus *Annals* 1.55–71.

15 Seneca the Elder *Suasoriae* 1.15; see also Tacitus *Annals* 2.23–4.

16 For a recent edition of the *Germania*, see Benario 1999.

17 See Wellesley 1989, pp. 168–83.

18 Tacitus *Annals* 13.53, 4; see also Tacitus *Histories* 5.19, 3; Griffin 1984, p. 61.

19 Tacitus *Annals* 13.53–57.

20 Seneca *On Anger* 1.11, 3 and 2.15, 4; Tacitus *Germania* 28, 4. See Tacitus *Annals* 13.53, 2 for Pompeius Paulinus.

21 Schönberger 1969, pp. 151–5.

22 Dio 63.17–18.

23 *ILS* 986.

24 See, for example, the likely honour done to Claudius' memory on the Richborough monument (Shotter 2004a), and Vespasian's resumption of building-work on the Temple of *Divus Claudius* in Rome, that had been started by Agrippina, but interrupted by Nero who wanted the site on the Caelian Hill for part of his *Domus Aurea* project (Suetonius *Life of the Deified Vespasian* 9, 1; also below on pp. 118ff).

25 Tacitus *Annals* 14.29–39.

26 See the inscription that was placed on the Arch of Claudius in Rome (*ILS* 216), recording the submission to Claudius of eleven British leaders; for the invasion of AD 43 and its aftermath, see now Manley 2002.

27 Tacitus *Annals* 12.36–7.

28 Tacitus *Annals* 12.40; 14.29, 1; *Life of Agricola* 14, 2; Shotter 1994.

29 Shotter 2004b, p. 17.

30 Birley A. R. 2005, pp. 302–3.

31 For the course of events, see Tacitus *Annals* 14.29–39; Dio 62.1–12; also Webster 1978 and Benario 2007.

32 Tacitus *Annals* 14.31, 4.

33 Suetonius *Life of Nero* 18.

34 Dio 62.2, 1; Curchin 1991, p. 80.

35 Tacitus *Annals* 14.33, 5.

36 Tacitus *Annals* 14.32–3; although Tacitus says that it was the Temple of *Divus Claudius* that was sacked, it remains uncertain whether the Imperial Cult-centre at Colchester existed in the form of a temple prior to the Flavian period, or whether the cult-centre may initially have taken the simpler form of an altar to *Roma et Augustus*, as at Lyon (*Lugdunum*); see Fishwick 1972 and 1991 and Shotter 2004a, p. 4. It would have been in keeping with Vespasian's regard for Claudius (Suetonius *Life of the Deified Vespasian* 9, 1) that he should have instituted what he regarded as a fitting 'reparation' to the deified Emperor.

37 It was subsequently found in the river, and is now in the British Museum.

38 Birley A. R. 2005, p. 303.

39 Tacitus *Annals* 14.31, 4.

40 See Birley A. R. 1973, pp. 179ff.

41 Tacitus *Annals* 14.39.

42 See Birley A. R. 2005, pp. 50–2.

43 Shotter 2002; Birley A. R. 2005, pp. 52–6. Tacitus (*Annals* 14.39, 4–5) is scathing in his criticism of the lack of action shown by Petronius Turpilianus.

44 Birley A. R. 2005, p. 237f; it appears that the legion acquired its titles ('valiant' and 'victorious') as a result of its service during Boudica's rebellion (McPake 1981, pp. 293ff; Keppie 1984, p. 138f).

45 It is possible that the poor relationship that seems to have existed between Agricola and Tacitus on the one hand and Petillius Cerialis on the other may have originated in part in the events of the rebellion, particularly if Polyclitus' report placed the bulk of the blame for the problems on Suetonius Paullinus, to whom Agricola, as *tribunus militum* may have been attached as an aide (Birley A. R. 1973, p. 186; Shotter 2000, p. 189).

46 As, for example, in his threat in AD 68, when he heard of Galba's rebellion, to initiate dire reprisals, including setting fire to Rome again and releasing wild beasts into the streets of the city to hamper the fire-fighting; needless to say, he actually did none of these things (Suetonius *Life of Nero* 43, 1).

47 Excavation at Gresham Street in London has suggested the possibility there of monumental building in the Neronian period (Burnham, Keppie and Fitzpatrick 2001, p. 365; Burnham, Hunter and Fitzpatrick 2002, p. 327); this may represent renewed investment following Boudica's rebellion. It has been

suggested by Professor Michael Fulford that traces of a substantial building at Silchester, which are evidently of Neronian date, could be interpreted as representing an expression of the Emperor's gratitude to Cogidubnus for his support during Boudica's uprising (Fulford 2008; also *Britanuia* 12 (1981), p. 290f). Such a gesture would have been entirely characteristic of Nero; I am very grateful to Professor Fulford for allowing me access to this interpretation prior to its full publication.

48 Seager 1979, pp. 44–55; King Mithridates of Pontus, a long-standing 'thorn in the flesh' to the Romans in the East, despairing of defeating the Roman army, committed suicide in 63 BC.

49 The occasion was duly celebrated on the coinage (*RIC* 1² (Augustus), no. 287).

50 See Tacitus *Annals* 2.1–4.

51 Tacitus *Annals* 6.31–37.

52 His brother, Publius Vitellius, had been a companion (*comes*) of Germanicus in the East (Tacitus *Annals* 3.10ff).

53 See Tacitus *Annals* 11.8–10; 12.10–21 and 44–51.

54 Syme 1970; Goldsworthy 2003, pp. 297ff.

55 Tacitus *Annals* 13.8, 1.

56 Chilver 1957.

57 Tacitus *Annals* 15.1–17.

58 Caesennius Paetus is memorably described by J. G. C. Anderson (*Cambridge Ancient History* 1966, Vol. X, p. 768) as 'an incompetent soldier, an insufferable braggart, and an absolute poltroon'.

59 For Tacitus' estimate of Corbulo, see Syme 1958, Vol. II, pp. 492ff; despite the fact that Corbulo, in Tacitus' eyes, was not without flaws, reminders are constantly present of Republican predecessors in the East, such as Lucius Licinius Lucullus and Gnaeus Pompeius Magnus.

60 Tacitus *Annals* 15.16, 3; evidently Tacitus did not regard Corbulo's memoirs as a totally reliable source for these events.

61 Tacitus *Annals* 15.17, 2.

62 Levick 1999, pp. 134ff.

63 Tacitus *Annals* 13.41 and 15.18, 1; *RIC* 1² (Nero), no. 393 and plate 21; Suetonius *Life of Nero* 13, 2.

64 See below in chapter 8.

65 *RIC* 1² (Nero), no. 458; Tameanko 1999, p. 219.

66 Champlin 2003, p. 221; for an account, see Dio 63.1–7.

67 Dio 63.1–3; the amphitheatre now has an inscription of the Flavian period, reflecting Flavian favour to the town in return for its support of Vespasian during the civil war of AD 69.

68 Dio 63.5, 2.

69 See below on p. 151.

70 Tacitus *Annals* 15.74, 1.

71 Dio 63.6, 3–4.

72 See the Elder Pliny *Natural History* 33.54; as Champlin notes (2003, p. 126), Pliny must have seen this spectacle for himself.

73 See Tacitus *Annals* 16.23–4; Suetonius *Life of Nero* 13; Dio 63.1–6.

74 Seneca *Moral Epistles* 115.12–13; compare Petronius *Satyricon* 120 for an attack on the current obsession with gold (Hemsoll 1990).

75 See Barrett 1989, pp. 182–91.

76 For the full text of Claudius' letter, see Smallwood 1967, no. 370; for a translation, see Miller 1971, no. 27.

77 Josephus *The Jewish War* 2.120–61.

78 Josephus *The Jewish War* 2.651.

79 Furneaux 1973, p. 26; see also Watt 1989.

80 Josephus *The Jewish War* 2.184–203.

81 Tacitus *Annals* 12.54.

82 Josephus *The Jewish War* 2.277–9 and 293ff.

83 Josephus *Jewish Antiquities* 20.252; Griffin 1984, p. 101.

84 Yadin 1966.

85 Tacitus *Annals* 15.25, 3; Josephus *The Jewish War* 2.499ff; for Nero's outwardly low-key reaction, see *The Jewish War* 3.1.

86 Dio 63.17, 2–6; Suetonius *Life of Nero* 33, 2; see above on p. 91.

87 Tacitus *Histories* 2.5, 2; 2.76.

88 Suetonius *Life of the Deified Vespasian* 2, 3; Dio 59.12, 3.

89 Suetonius *Life of the Deified Vespasian* 4.

90 Tacitus *Histories* 4.7–8; Shotter 2004a.

91 Griffin 1984, p. 265.

92 Levick 1999, p. 119.

93 Although the name, Colosseum, derives from the Colossus, that had stood in the entrance to Nero's *Domus Aurea*, there is no evidence that it was applied to the amphitheatre until the eleventh century (Claridge 1998, p. 271).

94 Tacitus *Histories* 1.9, 3.

95 Tacitus *Histories* 2.11, 1.

96 Suetonius *Life of Nero* 19, 2; Dio 63.8, 1–2; Keppie 1984, p. 213.

97 Suetonius *Life of Nero* 19, 2; Webster 1985, p. 45 (and note 3).

98 Sanford 1937.

99 *Oxyrhynchus Papyrus* 2435 (Turner 1959, pp. 102ff).

100 *ILS* 985 and 986, and above on p. 91. See also Josephus *The Jewish War* 7.94 for later repetition of the symptoms of trouble.

101 Tacitus *Annals* 6.33; Josephus *Jewish Antiquities* 18.97.

102 Lucan *Pharsalia* 8.223; 10.454.

103 Tacitus *Histories* 1.6, 2.

104 Henderson 1903, pp. 224ff and p. 480.

105 The Elder Pliny *Natural History* 6.40; Dio 63.8, 2; Warmington 1977, p. 77; Griffin 1984, p. 228.

106 Suetonius *Life of Nero* 18.

107 Josephus *The Jewish War* 2.345ff.
108 Josephus *The Jewish War* 2.494 and 3.8; Tacitus *Annals* 15.33–36 (especially 36, 1); Suetonius *Life of Nero* 19, 1 and 35, 5; Woods 2004.
109 Seneca *Quaestiones Naturales* 6.8, 3–4; the Elder Pliny (*Natural History* 6.181ff) appears to have been unimpressed by this 'project'.
110 Tacitus *Annals* 13.4, 3; Millar 1966.
111 Warmington 1969, p. 71.
112 Suetonius *Life of Nero* 32, 1.
113 See below on p. 108; Millar 1966.
114 See, for example, his treatment of the Alpine tribes of the *Anauni*, the *Tulliasses* and the *Sinduni* (*ILS* 206; Smallwood 1967, no. 368), whom he permitted to retain the citizenship which technically they had usurped, but which they had used responsibly.
115 Suetonius *Life of the Deified Claudius* 16.
116 *ILS* 212; Tacitus *Annals* 11.24.
117 Tacitus *Annals* 11.23.
118 Birley A. R. 2002.
119 Dio 56.18, 2–3; see above on p. 72. See further, Woolf 1998.
120 Tacitus *Life of Agricola* 19, 4.
121 For Capito's expulsion from the Senate, see Tacitus *Annals* 13.33, 3 and 16.21, 3; for his restoration, see *Annals* 14.48, 2.
122 See Juvenal's comment (*Satire* 1.49–50) on the case of Marius Priscus in the province of Africa; Marius Priscus was convicted in AD 100 but, wrote Juvenal, 'the province still weeps'; see also the Younger Pliny *Letters* 2.11.
123 Tacitus *Annals* 13.31, 4; Suetonius *Life of Nero* 12, 1.
124 Tacitus *Annals* 13.50–1.
125 Tacitus *Annals* 15.22, 1–2; Griffin 1984, p. 80.
126 Josephus *The Jewish War* 2.372; Warmington 1969, p. 54; see plate 18.
127 Tacitus *Histories* 1.73; see below on p. 160.
128 Tacitus *Histories* 1.89, 2.

Chapter 7 The Imperial Builder

1 Suetonius *Life of Nero* 49, 2; Champlin 2003, pp. 49–51; see further below on p. 153.
2 Horace *The Art of Poetry* 268–9; Wardman 1976, p. 62.
3 Horace *Epistles* 2.1, 156.
4 Suetonius *Life of the Deified Augustus* 28.
5 See, in particular, *Res Gestae Divi Augusti* 19–21.
6 Tacitus *Annals* 3.72, 1. The building is recorded on a *denarius* of 61 BC (Crawford 1974, no. 419, 3a).
7 As Juvenal put it (*Satire* 10.81), it was essential for an Emperor to keep his people fed and entertained.

8 Suetonius *Life of the Deified Vespasian* 18.

9 Horace *Odes* 3.6, 1–4.

10 *Res Gestae Divi Augusti* 20.4.

11 Zanker 1968; Thornton and Thornton 1989.

12 Simon 1967.

13 *RIC* 1^2 (Nero), no. 418.

14 Champlin 2003, pp. 149ff and pp. 168ff.

15 Crescenzi, Gizzi and Vigilante 1992.

16 Suetonius *Life of Nero* 6, 1; Blake 1959, pp. 40–1; Ling 1979.

17 The Elder Pliny *Natural History* 36.74; Toynbee and Ward-Perkins 1956, pp. 7ff; Boethius and Ward-Perkins 1970, p. 211; Townend 1958; Humphrey 1986.

18 Toynbee and Ward-Perkins 1956, p. 10.

19 Tacitus *Annals* 13.13, 1; Champlin 2003, p. 68; Balsdon 1974, p. 256f.

20 Suetonius *Life of Nero* 12; the Elder Pliny *Natural History* 16.200 and 19.24.

21 Calpurnius Siculus *Eclogue* 7.

22 Suetonius *Life of Nero* 21, 1; Dio 61.9, 5.

23 Blake 1959, p. 34.

24 Tacitus *Annals* 13.41, 5; Blake 1959, p. 33; Kleiner 1985.

25 Tacitus *Annals* 15.18, 1.

26 *RIC* 1^2 (Nero), nos. 148ff; Tameanko 1999, pp. 197–9; see coin-illustration 11.

27 Frontinus *On the Aqueducts of the City of Rome* 1.20; 2.70 and 87; Platner and Ashby 1926, p. 40; Evans 1983; Claridge 1998, p. 308.

28 *RIC* 1^2 (Nero), nos. 184ff; Sutherland 1951, p. 169; Tameanko 1999, pp. 200–2; Platner and Ashby 1926, p. 323; Rainbird and Sear 1971; see coin-illustration 13.

29 Sear 1982, p. 36.

30 *RIC* 1^2 (Nero), nos. 178ff; Tameanko 1999, pp. 83–7; see coin-illustration 12.

31 Suetonius *Life of the Deified Vespasian* 9, 1; Shotter 2004a.

32 Martial *Epigrams* 7.34: 'Who was worse than Nero? Whose baths were better than Nero's?'

33 Holland 2000, p. 129.

34 Philostratus *Life of Apollonius of Tyana* 4.42; Tamm 1970.

35 Dio 61.21, 1.

36 Tacitus *Annals* 14.47, 2.

37 Tacitus *Annals* 15.22, 3.

38 Blake 1959, p. 36; Platner and Ashby 1926, pp. 178–9.

39 Suetonius *Life of Nero* 31.

40 Boethius and Ward-Perkins 1970, p. 212; Sear 1982, p. 96.

41 The Elder Pliny *Natural History* 35.120; Blake 1959, p. 50. The painter's precise name is uncertain, and may have been Fabullus or Amulius.

42 Griffin 1984, p. 126.

43 *RIC* 1^2 (Nero), no. 61f; Tacitus *Annals* 15.41, 1; Sutherland 1951, p. 167; Lugli 1960; see coin-illustration 9 and plate 24.

44 Tacitus *Annals* 15.36, 3.

45 Suetonius *Life of Nero* 55.

46 Tacitus *Annals* 15.42, 1; Tacitus' account of the fire is given in *Annals* 15.38–44.

47 Suetonius *Life of Nero* 16.

48 Tacitus *Annals* 15.44.

49 Tacitus *Annals* 15.38, 1; Suetonius *Life of Nero* 38; Dio 62.16, 1.

50 Tacitus *Annals* 15.67, 2; Statius *Silvae* 2.7, 60–1.

51 Suetonius *Life of Nero* 38, 2; see also *Octavia* 831–3; Dio 62.18, 1. Tacitus (*Annals* 15.39, 3) gives this story, but as a rumour.

52 Tacitus *Annals* 15.40, 1.

53 Blake 1959, pp. 46–54; Boethius and Ward-Perkins 1970, pp. 214–6 and pp. 248–51; Hemsoll 1989 and 1990; Iacopi 2001.

54 Suetonius *Life of Nero* 39, 2.

55 Blake 1959, p. 48; see plate 26.

56 Tacitus *Annals* 15.42, 1.

57 Tacitus *Annals* 15.42, 1, translated by Michael Grant in *Tacitus: The Annals of Imperial Rome* (Harmondsworth, 1996).

58 Tacitus *Annals* 15.46, 2–3; Warmington 1969, pp. 131–2.

59 The Elder Pliny *Natural History* 14.68; Statius *Silvae* 4.3, 7–8; Tacitus *Annals* 15.42, 2–4; Suetonius *Life of Nero* 31, 3; D'Arms 1970, p. 97.

60 Suetonius *Life of Nero* 31 (the translation is from Robert Graves' *Suetonius: The Twelve Caesars* (Harmondsworth, 1957)). For the house, see Boethius 1960, pp. 94–128; MacDonald 1965, pp. 31–46; Boethius and Ward-Perkins 1970, pp. 214–6; McKay 1998, pp. 128–31; Sear 1982, pp. 97–102.

61 Martial *On Spectacles* 2.5–6.

62 Champlin 2003, p. 132.

63 Champlin 2003, pp. 156ff.

64 Champlin 2003, pp. 207ff.

65 As can be seen in wall-paintings at Pompeii, amongst them the House of Venus in a Sea-Shell (Plate 22).

66 Sallust *The Catilinarian Conspiracy* 20.11; Horace *Odes* 2.18, 17–22; 3.1, 33–46; 3.24, 4; D'Arms 1970, p. 42.

67 Boethius and Ward-Perkins 1970, p. 248; see plate 21.

68 Boethius and Ward-Perkins 1970, pp. 248ff; see also Ball 2003.

69 See Champlin 2003, pp. 129ff for a discussion of where the statue stood, when it was placed there, and whom it represented.

70 The Elder Pliny *Natural History* 34.45.

71 Suetonius *Life of the Deified Vespasian* 18; Martial *On Spectacles* 2.1; Dio 65.15.

72 Writers of the Augustan History, *Life of Hadrian* 19.

73 Dio 72.22; Writers of the Augustan History, *Life of Commodus* 17.

74 Cf. A similar representation on the coinage in *RIC* 3 (Commodus), nos. 637ff.

75 Herodian 1.15, 9.

76 Claridge 1998, p. 271.

77 Tacitus *Histories* 1.78, 2; Plutarch *Life of Otho* 3.1–2.

78 Suetonius *Life of Otho* 7.

79 Dio 64.4.

80 The Elder Pliny *Natural History* 33.54; 36.111; Martial *On Spectacles* 2; see plate 17.

81 The Elder Pliny *Natural History* 34.84.

82 The mythological son of the Trojan king and queen, Priam and Hecuba; see Virgil *Aeneid* 2.41.

83 The Elder Pliny *Natural History* 36.37; for the 'Laocoon group', see Della Portella 2000, pp. 234–5.

84 Orosius 7.12.

85 Juvenal comments on the frequency of fires in Rome and the poor quality of domestic building (*Satire* 3.7ff; 194ff; 214).

86 Tacitus *Annals* 15.43, where the historian gives a favourable reaction to the new regulations.

87 Strabo *Geographia* 5.3, 7.

88 Victor *Epitome de Caesaribus* 13.13.

89 Suetonius *Life of Nero* 16, 1; Blake 1959, p. 42.

90 Boethius and Ward-Perkins 1970, p. 216.

91 D'Arms 1970, pp. 94–9.

92 Suetonius *Life of Nero* 40, 4; see below on p. 160f.

93 See above on p. 99.

94 Tacitus *Annals* 16.10, 4; Dio 62.2–3.

95 The poet, Horace, regarded Baiae highly for its beauty (*Epistles* 1.1, 83); for Seneca's view, see his *Moral Epistles* 51.1–4; in general, see D'Arms 1970, pp. 73ff; Miniero 2000.

96 See below on pp. 146ff.

97 Tacitus *Annals* 15.42, 2–4; Meiggs 1960, p. 57; Rickman 1980, p. 59 and p. 76.

98 Tacitus *Annals* 14.27, 2.

99 Seneca *Moral Epistles* 77, 1; Josephus *The Jewish War* 2.383–5; see Rickman 1980, p. 68, p. 75 and pp. 231ff.

100 Suetonius *Life of Nero* 31, 2; D'Arms 1970, p. 98.

101 Tacitus *Annals* 15.42, 4.

102 Warmington 1969, p. 132.

103 See Yavetz 1968; also above on p. 121.

104 Tacitus *Annals* 15.36–7; Dio 62.15. Suetonius also (*Life of Nero* 29) appears to refer to this event, although he names the freedman involved in the 'wedding' as Doryphorus who, according to Tacitus (*Annals* 14.65, 1), had been put to death two years earlier for opposing Nero's marriage to Poppaea.

Chapter 8 The Beginning of the End

1 Tacitus *Annals* 14.65.

2 Tacitus *Annals* 14.61–4.

3 Tacitus *Annals* 3.65.

4 Tacitus *Histories* 1.15, 3–4; in the event, however, Galba showed himself unable to distinguish between genuine advice and banal flattery (Tacitus *Histories* 1.35).

5 Gwyn 1991; Holland 2000, p. 142.

6 Suetonius *Life of Nero* 12, 1.

7 Tacitus *Annals* 14.48–9.

8 Seneca *On Clemency* 1.2.

9 See Rogers (1953b), who compares it with the trial of Clutorius Priscus in the reign of Tiberius (see Shotter 1969a); see also Bauman 1974, pp. 143ff.

10 Tacitus *Annals* 2.27–32; Shotter 1972.

11 Tacitus *Annals* 14.65, 1.

12 Tacitus *Annals* 14.65, 2.

13 As Tacitus indicates in *Life of Agricola* 42, 5.

14 Roper 1979.

15 Dio 59.23, 9.

16 Seneca quotes the tag disapprovingly to Nero as a road with a very slippery slope (*On Clemency* 1.12, 4); the tag appears to have originated with Accius, a tragedian of the second century BC (Cicero *De Officiis* 1.28, 97); it is applied in a number of forms to Roman Emperors (Suetonius *Life of Tiberius* 59, 2 and *Life of Gaius Caligula* 30, 1).

17 Tacitus *Histories* 1.72; see also Juvenal *Satire* 1.155.

18 The translation is taken from K. Wellesley, *Tacitus: The Histories* (Harmondsworth, 1972).

19 Suetonius *Life of Nero* 10.

20 Tacitus *Annals* 4.1, 3.

21 Suetonius *Life of Nero* 53.

22 Barrett 1996, p. 49 and note 34.

23 Dio 61.9, 1–4.

24 See above on p. 112; Bowersock 1965.

25 *ILS* 18.

26 Tacitus *Annals* 2.55, 1.

27 *Oxyrhynchus Papyrus* 2435 (Turner 1959, pp. 102ff).

28 Juvenal *Satire* 3, 60ff.

29 Suetonius *Life of Nero* 12, 4; Dio 61.21, 2; Champlin 2003, p. 72.

30 Warmington 1969, p. 111.

31 Tacitus *Annals* 14.16; Suetonius *Life of Nero* 52; Martial *Epigrams* 8.70.

32 Townend 1967, p. 87.

33 Brisset 1964; Krautter 1992.

34 Tacitus *Annals* 12.2–3.

35 Dio 62.22, 2–6.

36 Suetonius *Life of Nero* 53.

37 Tacitus *Annals* 14.14.

38 Juvenal *Satire* 1.1ff.

39 Tacitus *Annals* 15.33.

40 Suetonius *Life of Nero* 21.

41 Suetonius *Life of Nero* 22; Bradley 1978b.

42 Woods 2004.

43 Dio 63.14, 3–4; 63, 21; Philostratus *Life of Apollonius of Tyana* 5.8–9. Nero was awarded one of his victor's prizes despite having fallen out of his chariot during the race! (Champlin 2003, p. 54).

44 Plutarch *Life of Flamininus* 12, 8; Suetonius *Life of Nero* 19, 2 and 24, 2; Gallivan 1973b; Griffin 1984, p. 162.

45 Warmington 1969, p. 117; *ILS* 8794 (for a translation of Nero's speech and the official local response, see Henderson 1903, pp. 389–92).

46 See above in footnote 26.

47 Pausanias *Description of Greece* 7.17, 3.

48 Philostratus *Life of Apollonius of Tyana* 5.41.

49 Warmington 1969, p. 133; Champlin 2003, p. 137.

50 Philostratus *Life of Apollonius of Tyana* 4.35; Sandbach 1975, p. 162.

51 See below on p. 155.

52 Suetonius *Life of the Deified Julius* 76.

53 Taylor 1931.

54 Tacitus *Annals* 4.37–8.

55 *SEG* 11.922–3 (Ehrenberg and Jones 1955, no. 102).

56 Suetonius *Life of the Deified Vespasian* 23, 4.

57 Tacitus *Annals* 4.15, 5.

58 Ehrenberg and Jones 1955, no. 320b.

59 Tacitus *Annals* 2.59, 2–3.

60 See above on p. 54.

61 Champlin 2003, pp. 106–7 and pp. 135–8.

62 Note Trajan's representation of his Column on the coinage as the club of Hercules (*RIC* 2 (Trajan), no. 581).

63 See Champlin 2003, p. 307 (and note 86), citing Wiseman, J. 1978.

64 Suetonius *Life of Nero* 21, 3; Dio 63.9, 4–5; 63.10, 2.

65 Tacitus *Annals* 13.8, 1.

66 The Elder Pliny *Natural History* 33.54; Tacitus *Annals* 16.23–4; Suetonius *Life of Nero* 13; Dio 63.1–6; Champlin 2003, p. 126.

67 *RIC* 1^2 (Nero), no. 52; coin-illustration 8.

68 *RIC* 1^2 (Nero), no. 77 etc; coin-illustration 15.

69 Suetonius *Life of Nero* 25, 3.

70 *RIC* 1^2 (Nero), no. 46; coin-illustration 7.

71 Suetonius *Life of Nero* 56.

72 Rudich 1992.

73 Tacitus *Annals* 15.23.

74 For example, Tacitus *Annals* 14.12, 1 and 14.48, 3–4.

75 Tacitus *Annals* 15.38–45; Suetonius *Life of Nero* 38; Dio 62.16–18.

76 Beaujeu 1960.
77 Lactantius *On the Deaths of the Persecutors* 2, 5–7.
78 The Younger Pliny *Letters* 10.96–7.
79 Eusebius *Ecclesiastical History* 2.25; Frend 1965, 160–71.
80 Tacitus *Annals* 15.44, 5.
81 Wiedemann 1992, pp. 68ff.
82 See above on pp. 118ff; for consequences of the Fire, see Newbold 1974.
83 Tacitus *Annals* 15.45, 1–4.
84 Tacitus *Histories* 1.20; Suetonius *Life of Galba* 15; Dio 63.14, 2.
85 Tacitus *Life of Agricola* 6, 5.
86 See above on pp. 71ff.
87 Tacitus *Annals* 13.28–31.
88 The Younger Seneca *On the Brevity of Life* 19, 1; Rickman 1980, p. 86.
89 Watson 1969, p. 108; Rickman 1980, p. 181.
90 Suetonius *Life of Nero* 10, 1.
91 Tacitus *Annals* 13.34.
92 Griffin 1984, p. 204.
93 Tacitus *Annals* 13.13, 2.
94 Tacitus *Annals* 15.18.
95 For example, Tacitus *Annals* 16.13, 5.
96 Suetonius *Life of Nero* 11; Rickman 1980, p. 244. Statius (*Silvae* 3.5) records that the distribution of grain was under the control of the Emperor's financial secretary (*a rationibus*), Claudius Etruscus, who kept an account of grain from the public provinces as well as from the imperial provinces.
97 See above on p. 123.
98 The Elder Pliny *Natural History* 37.45–6 and 50; Champlin 2003, pp. 134–5.
99 Tacitus *Annals* 16.1–2; Suetonius *Life of Nero* 31–2; Champlin 2003, p. 126.
100 Suetonius *Life of Nero* 32; Griffin 1984, pp. 186–7.
101 Dio 62.18, 5; Rickman 1980, p. 187.
102 Suetonius *Life of Nero* 32, 4.
103 Tacitus *Annals* 16.14, 3; 16.17; Dio 63.11, 3.
104 Mac Dowall 1979, pp. 9–15, pp. 31–5 and (especially) pp. 135–44; Griffin 1984, p. 198 and p. 238; for a note on the money-system, see below on pp. 193ff.
105 D. Walker (1976, p. 45) puts the reduction at almost fifteen percent.
106 The Elder Pliny *Natural History* 33.132.
107 The Elder Pliny *Natural History* 6.162 and 12.84.
108 Tacitus *Annals* 13.50.
109 Tacitus *Annals* 15.47.
110 Tacitus *Life of Agricola* 42, 5.
111 Tacitus *Annals* 1.72, 2.
112 Tacitus *Annals* 14.48–9.
113 Tacitus *Annals* 15.48ff.
114 Sandbach 1975, pp. 140–8.

115 Tacitus *Annals* 4.34–5.

116 Wirszubski 1950, pp. 143–50.

117 Toynbee 1944; Brunt 1975; Clarke 1981, pp. 13–14.

118 Dyson 1970; Griffin 1974 and 1976.

119 Sallust *The Catilinarian Conspiracy* 51–2.

120 Cicero *Letters to Atticus* 2.1, 8.

121 See Plutarch *Cicero* 39.

122 Tacitus *Annals* 14.12, 2 and 14.49, 5; *Histories* 4.8.

123 Suetonius *Life of the Deified Vespasian* 15; Dio 66.12, 1. This hardening of Stoic attitudes may have had much to do with rivalry between philosophical sects.

124 Rogers 1960; Jones 1992, p. 186.

125 Tacitus *Life of Agricola* 42, 5; cf. *Histories* 1.15–16.

126 Tacitus *Histories* 3.81, 1.

127 Tacitus *Annals* 16.22, 3.

128 The tribunes of the plebeians retained under the Principate the veto that had been the most powerful element of their office during the Old Republic; few, however, risked using it against the Emperors, particularly since their office lost so much of its significance, dwarfed as it was by the Emperors' tribunician power (*tribunicia potestas*). In fact, under the Principate, many senators omitted holding the office of tribune of the plebeians, regarding it as effectively a hindrance to their careers.

129 Tacitus *Annals* 16.21, 1.

130 Tacitus *Annals* 16.21–35, where the text breaks off abruptly in mid-sentence.

131 Tacitus *Annals* 16.22. (Translation from M. Grant, *The Annals of Imperial Rome* (Harmondsworth, 1996).

132 Tacitus *Annals* 15.49, 3.

133 Tacitus *Annals* 15.61–4; Dio 62.25.

134 Tacitus *Annals* 15.48.

135 Tacitus *Annals* 15.48, 4; the translation is taken from M. Grant, *Tacitus: The Annals of Imperial Rome* (Harmondsworth, 1996).

136 Tacitus *Histories* 1.16, 3.

137 Tacitus *Annals* 15.67, 2.

138 Tacitus *Annals* 16.30, 1.

139 Tacitus *Annals* 14.58.

140 Tacitus *Annals* 15.57, 1–3.

141 Tacitus *Annals* 15.58, 3; the translation is taken from M. Grant, *Tacitus: The Annals of Imperial Rome* (Harmondsworth, 1996).

142 The Younger Pliny *Letters* 3.7; Syme 1958, Vol. I, p. 89.

143 See below on p. 191. Petronius' *praenomen* is uncertain (see below on p. 233 and note 12).

144 Suetonius *Life of Nero* 36, 1; Syme 1958, Vol. II, p. 560.

145 Crawford 1974, no. 508, 3; *RIC* I² (Civil War: Spain), no. 24.

146 Lucan *Pharsalia* 1.33–45; it is difficult to determine from Lucan's excessive language whether this is serious flattery of the Emperor, or whether it is written ironically.

147 Dio 63.17–18; Willems 1902, p. 116.

148 Nero appears to have become the *magister* of the Arval Brethren in AD 66 (Syme 1980, p. 99), perhaps to enable him to keep a closer eye on men who might have been involved in conspiracy.

149 Neverov 1986; Champlin 2003, pp. 112ff.

150 Tacitus *Annals* 15.74, 1.

151 Tacitus *Annals* 16.17, 7; Willems 1902, p. 7. For ruler-apotheosis, see Toynbee 1947.

152 Tacitus *Annals* 15.74, 4.

153 Tacitus *Annals* 15.74, 2; this was subsequently interpreted as an omen of Nero's eventual fate in AD 68 at the hands of Gaius Julius Vindex.

154 *RIC* 1² (Nero), no. 52.

155 *RIC* 1² (Nero), nos. 46, 48, 50, 54.

156 *RIC* 1² (Nero), no. 44; coin-illustration 6.

157 Tacitus *Annals* 15.72, 2; Suetonius *Life of Nero* 15; *CIL* 11.5743, Grainger (2003, p. 29) suggests that this military honour was bestowed in return for the provision of information on the Pisonian conspirators.

158 Tacitus *Histories* 1.5–6.

159 Tacitus *Annals* 16.6, 1; Mayer 1982.

160 Tacitus *Annals* 15.68, 2–3.

161 Suetonius *Life of Nero* 28, 1; Champlin 2003, pp. 145–50. This appears to have been a very different matter from the 'marriage' that Nero is said to have entered into with his freedman, Pythagoras (Tacitus *Annals* 15.37, 7–9).

162 Suetonius *Life of Nero* 36.

Chapter 9 Rebellion and the Fall of Nero

1 Murison 1993, p. 6; see Morgan 2006 (especially chapter 1).

2 Suetonius *Life of Nero* 47–49; Dio 63. 27–28; Wallace-Hadrill 1983, p. 113; Reece 1969.

3 Suetonius *Life of Nero* 49, 2; see Sansone 1993.

4 Champlin 2003, pp. 49–51.

5 Townend 1964. For further discussions of the source material for these events, see Murison 1979, 1991, 1992 and 1993; Shotter 1993.

6 Champlin 2003, pp. 145–50.

7 Plutarch *Life of Galba* 7. For Plutarch's account see Little and Ehrhardt 1994.

8 Wellesley 1989.

9 Tacitus *Histories* 1.26, 1.

10 See above on p. 152.

11 Chilver 1957.

12 Shotter 1967a; Levick 1999, pp. 23ff.

13 For the date, see Griffin 1984, p. 162 and p. 280.

14 Plutarch *Life of Galba* 4, 2; Philostratus *Life of Apollonius of Tyana* 5.10; cf. Dio 63.19, 1.

15 For the reference, see Shotter 1975, p. 61 and note p. 18.

16 Suetonius *Life of Nero* 43, 1.

17 Suetonius *Life of Galba* 9, 2.

18 Dio 63.12 and 19, 1.

19 For a discussion of the numismatic evidence, see Kraay 1949 and Mattingly 1954. See also Raoss 1958 and 1960.

20 Suetonius *Life of Nero* 41; Dio 63.22, 2–6.

21 *RIC* 1² (The Civil Wars), pp. 206ff; *RIC* 1² (Galba), nos. 142ff.

22 Shotter 1975; Levick 1985; Murison 1993.

23 Tacitus *Histories* 2.27, 2; Bessone 1977 and 1978.

24 Dio 63.22, 3–4.

25 *RIC* 1² (The Civil Wars), p. 205, nos. 24–5; cf. Crawford 1974, no. 508, 3. It is said that, when news of Nero's death was received at Rome, people ran into the streets wearing the 'cap of freedom' (Suetonius *Life of Nero* 57, 1; Dio 63.29, 1).

26 Suetonius *Life of Galba* 3–4.

27 Suetonius *Life of Galba* 6–8.

28 Suetonius *Life of Galba* 5, 1.

29 Suetonius *Life of Galba* 5, 2.

30 Tacitus (*Histories* 2.86) refers to the legion by the name, *Galbiana*, although Keppie believes (1984, p. 213) that this may have been simply a nickname. Its official name may have been *Hispana*, which was later (in AD 70) changed to *Gemina*.

31 Plutarch *Life of Galba* 8–9, especially 8, 1–2.

32 Tacitus *Histories* 1.51, 4 and 4.17, 3; Brunt 1959, pp. 532–7 and Chilver 1957, p. 32; the Treveri and the Lingones, however, stood apart (Tacitus *Histories* 1.53, 3).

33 Tacitus *Histories* 1.37, 3.

34 Tacitus *Histories* 2.27, 2; Saddington 2005, p. 67.

35 Josephus *The Jewish War* 4.440; Tacitus *Histories* 2.94, 2; Suetonius *Life of Vitellius* 18.

36 *ILS* 982 from Mediolanum (Milan), that has been dated to AD 68.

37 Syme 1937 and 1958, Vol. II, p. 683f.

38 Dio 64.6, 5a.

39 Plutarch *Life of Galba* 5, 2.

40 Syme 1982; Murison 1993, p. 46. For Vinius' name, see Salomies 1987, p. 348f.

41 Tacitus *Histories* 1.52, 3.

42 Tacitus *Histories* 1.7, 1.

43 Tacitus *Histories* 1.73; 2.97, 2; 4.49, 4; Plutarch *Life of Galba* 6, 1–2; Bessone 1979.

44 Dio 63.12, 3–4; Champlin 2003, p. 146; Calvia Crispinilla was saved by Otho (Tacitus *Histories* 1.73) from those who demanded her punishment, and she evidently survived into old age.

45 Griffin 1984, p. 198.

46 *RIC* 1² (L. Clodius Macer), nos. 1ff.

47 Suetonius *Life of Nero* 45, 1; Morgan 2000.

48 Suetonius *Life of Nero* 41–42.

49 Suetonius *Life of Nero* 43, 1–2.

50 Keppie 1984, p. 213.

51 Tacitus *Histories* 1.9, 3; Murison 1993, pp. 13ff.

52 Tacitus *Histories* 2.11, 1; for its reputation, see Tacitus *Annals* 14.34 and *Histories* 5.16, 3, where the men of legion XIV are called 'conquerors of Britain' (*domitores Britanniae*).

53 Tacitus *Annals* 15.72, 2.

54 Suetonius *Life of Nero* 28, 1; Murison 1993, p. 24 (and note 82).

55 See Josephus *The Jewish War* 7.91; he is later found as an advisor (*amicus*) of Domitian (Juvenal *Satire* 4, 104–6).

56 Dio 63.27, 1a.

57 Tacitus *Histories* 1.6, 1 and 1.37, 3; Plutarch *Life of Galba* 15, 2–4; Dio 63.27, 1a.

58 Tacitus *Histories* 1.8, 1–2; Shotter 1967a and 1975; Murison 1993, pp. 15ff (and bibliography on p. 2).

59 Syme 1937, p. 12.

60 Brunt 1959, p. 540.

61 Dio 63.24, 1–2; Townend 1961a.

62 Shotter 1975, p. 69 and note 84.

63 Seneca *Moral Epistles* 91.14; Tacitus *Annals* 16.13, 5.

64 Suetonius *Life of Galba* 10, 5.

65 Dio 63.24, 1. For Verginius' persence at Vesontio, see Daly 1975.

66 Dio 63.24, 2.

67 Dio 63.24, 4; Plutarch *Life of Galba* 6, 3.

68 Dio 63.25; Plutarch *Life of Galba* 6, 3.

69 Pliny *Letters* 9.19; Shotter 2001; Verginius had composed his own epitaph that was to be inscribed on his tomb; it read 'Here lies Rufus who long ago after the defeat of Vindex laid claim to imperial power not for himself, but for his country'. This put a far more positive gloss on Verginius' part in these events than appears justified by the surviving evidence. For Tacitus' view of Verginius Rufus, see Hainsworth 1962 and 1964; Shotter 1967d; also Levick 1985.

70 Tacitus *Histories* 2.51; Shotter 1967a.

71 Dio 63.25.

72 Suetonius *Life of Galba* 11; Plutarch *Life of Galba* 6, 4.

73 Tacitus *Histories* 1.89, 2; Bessone 1980.

74 See above in footnote 36.

75 Tacitus *Histories* 1.72; see also Plutarch *Life of Galba* 8, 2 and 13, 2; Josephus *The Jewish War* 4.492. Tigellinus was evidently protected by Galba and Vinius (Suetonius *Life of Galba* 13; Plutarch *Life of Galba* 17, 2).

76 Dio 63.29, 6.

77 Tacitus *Histories* 1.7, 2; Suetonius *Life of Galba* 11; Plutarch *Life of Galba* 15, 2.
78 Tacitus *Histories* 1.30, 2.
79 Tacitus *Histories* 1.9, 1.
80 Tacitus *Histories* 1.4, 2.
81 Tacitus *Histories* 3.45.
82 Tacitus *Histories* 1.15–16; Syme 1958, Vol. I, pp. 148ff.
83 Tacitus *Histories* 1.16, 1.
84 Tacitus *Histories* 1.16, 2.
85 Tacitus *Histories* 1.16, 3.
86 Juvenal *Satire* 4.37–8: 'When the last of the Flavians was lashing a half-dead world and Rome was playing the slave to the bald Nero . . .'.

Epilogue

1 Tacitus *Histories* 4.73–4 (especially 74, 2).
2 Tacitus *Histories* 1.15–16.
3 Tacitus *Life of Agricola* 3, 1; the Younger Pliny *Panegyric of Trajan* 69–71.
4 Tacitus *Histories* 1.1, 4; see also Von Fritz 1957; Shotter 1978. Not everyone, however, was as happy with the situation as Tacitus seems to have been; Dio (68.1, 3) reports Fronto (consul in AD 96) as having said of Nerva that 'it was bad to have an Emperor under whom nobody was permitted to do anything, but worse to have one under whom everybody was permitted to do everything'.
5 The Younger Pliny *Panegyric of Trajan* 66, 4; compare Martial's famous comment (*Epigrams* 11.5, 14): 'If Cato were to return now, he would be a Caesarian'; Bruère 1954, pp. 161–79.
6 Tacitus *Histories* 1.78, 2; Suetonius *Life of Otho* 7, 1; Plutarch *Life of Otho* 3, 1.
7 Tacitus *Histories* 1.78, 2.
8 Suetonius *Life of Otho* 7, 1.
9 Plutarch *Life of Otho* 3, 1.
10 Plutarch *Life of Otho* 3, 2.
11 Tacitus *Histories* 2.50, 1.
12 Tacitus *Histories* 1.81; Plutarch (*Life of Otho* 3, 4–8) gives the number of senators present as eighty.
13 Tacitus *Histories* 2.95, 1; Suetonius *Life of Vitellius* 11; Dio 65.7, 3. See also Suetonius *Life of Vitellius* 4.
14 Herodian 1.3, 4.
15 Writers of the Augustan History, *Life of Antoninus Elagabalus* 23, 1; Champlin 2003, p. 277 and n. 52; see *Lives of the Later Caesars*, translated by A. R. Birley in the *Penguin Classics* series (Harmondsworth, 1976).
16 Writers of the Augustan History, *Life of Severus Alexander* 25, 3.
17 Grant 1958, plate 9, no. 6.
18 Dio Chrysostom *Orations* 21.9–10; Jones C. P. 1978, especially p. 13, p. 63, p. 127; Champlin 2003, p. 10.

19 Tacitus *Histories* 1.2, 1 and 2.8, 1; Gallivan 1973a; Tuplin 1989, pp. 364–71; Champlin 2003, pp. 10–12.

20 See above on pp. 96ff.

21 Tacitus *Histories* 2.8–9; Dio 64.9, 3; Champlin (2003, p. 11) prefers a date in the summer of AD 68.

22 Champlin 2003, p. 218; Tacitus *Annals* 15.72. He became consul in AD 72, and proconsul of the province of Africa in AD 83, where his career-inscription has survived (McCrum and Woodhead 1961, no. 303).

23 Dio 66.19, 3b; Tuplin 1989, pp. 372–7; Champlin 2003, p. 11.

24 Suetonius *Life of Nero* 57, 2; Tuplin 1989, pp. 377–81; Champlin 2003, p. 12; Grainger (2003, pp. 82–3) suggests that the 'false Nero' of AD 88/89 may have been a reappearance of Terentius Maximus.

25 Jones B. W. 1983, pp. 126ff.

26 Champlin 2003, p. 24 and detailed note on pp. 274ff.

27 Champlin 2003, pp. 12–17.

28 *Revelation of St John the Divine* 13.18.

29 Tertullian *Apologeticum* (quoted by Eusebius *Ecclesiastical History* 2.25, 4).

30 Christenson 1980.

31 Lactantius *On the Deaths of the Persecutors* 2.5–9 (translated and published privately by J. L. Creed, 1980).

32 Augustine *On the City of God* 20.19, 3; Augustine believed that the view that Nero was the Antichrist was wrong-headed.

33 Grant 1970, p. 208.

34 Tacitus *Histories* 1.15–16.

Appendix 4

1 See, in particular, Griffin 1974 and 1976 and Sandbach 1975, pp. 149ff.

2 Translated by J. W. Basore in *Seneca: Moral Essays* (vol. 1), *Loeb Classical Library* series (Cambridge, MA, 1928). See Fears 1975.

3 Translated by R. Campbell in the *Penguin Classics* series (Harmondsworth, 1969).

4 Toynbee 1942; Coffey 1976, pp. 165ff; translated by J. P. Sullivan in the *Penguin Classics* series (Harmondsworth, 1979).

5 See above on pp. 59ff.

6 Translated by F. J. Miller in *Seneca's Tragedies* (vol. 2), *Loeb Classical Library* series, London, 1917; see Herington 1961 and Garson 1975; Kragelund 1988.

7 Henderson 1903, p. 432f; Herington 1961; Garson 1975; Barnes 1982; Kragelund 1987 and 1988.

8 *Octavia* 629–31.

9 See above on p. 5f.

10 Translated by H. Rackham in the *Loeb Classical Library* series (Cambridge, MA, 1940–63).

11 Josephus *The Jewish War* 2–4; translated by G. A. Williamson in the *Penguin Classics* series (Harmondsworth, 1970).

12 Rudich 1997, pp. 186ff; Rose 1971; George 1974; Sullivan 1985; Syme (1958, Vol. I, p. 387) suggests that he may have been Titus Petronius Niger, consul in AD 62; Sullivan 1968; Coffey 1976, pp. 178ff; translated by J. P. Sullivan in the *Penguin Classics* series (Harmondsworth, 1979).

13 Tacitus *Annals* 16.18, 4.

14 Tacitus *Annals* 16.17–20; Syme 1958, Vol. II, p. 538.

15 Translated by C. P. Jones in the *Penguin Classics* series (Harmondsworth, 1970), (with an Introduction by G. W. Bowersock).

16 Dio 78.18, 4.

17 See above on p. 116.

18 Philostratus *Life of Apollonius of Tyana* 4.42 and 5.19.

19 Philostratus *Life of Apollonius of Tyana* 5.10 and 35; see above on p. 155.

20 Brisset 1964; Thompson 1964; Rudich 1997, pp. 107ff; translated by R. Graves in the *Penguin Classics* series (Harmondsworth, 1956).

21 Tacitus *Annals* 15.70, 1; Syme 1958, Vol. II, pp. 142–3.

22 Champlin 1978; Mayer 1980; Townend 1980a; Verdière 1985; Krautter 1992; Horsfall 1997; translated by A. M. Duff in *Minor Latin Poets* (vol. 1), *Loeb Classical Library* series (Cambridge, MA, 1934).

23 See especially *Eclogue* 4.

24 Comets are recorded in AD 60 and AD 64 (Tacitus *Annals* 14.22, 1; 15.47, 1; Rogers 1953a; Holland 2000, p. 129). Seneca (*Natural Questions* 7.17, 2) seems to have regarded the former of these as not having the usual dire significance; the Elder Pliny (*Natural History* 2.92) appears to have thought that the comet of AD 64 was a reappearance of the earlier one, and that its significance was sinister.

25 Tacitus *Annals* 12.58, 1; Suetonius *Life of Nero* 7.

26 Sandbach 1975, 16; Coffey 1976, pp. 98ff; translated by G. G. Ramsay in the *Loeb Classical Library* series (London, 1918).

27 Highet 1954; Coffey 1976, pp. 119ff; translated by P. Green in the *Penguin Classics* series (Harmondsworth, 1967).

28 See above on p. 10.

29 There is a considerable literature on this topic; see, for example, Sydenham 1920; Sutherland 1951, pp. 148–72; 1976; 1984; 1987; Mac Dowall 1978; 1979; Griffin 1984, p. 238f; Champlin 2003, p. 142f.

30 See above on pp. 141ff.

31 The Roman coinage in the first century AD consisted of the following:

    1 *aureus* (gold) = 25 *denarii*

    1 *denarius* (silver) = 4 *sestertii*

    1 *sestertius* (orichalcum) = 2 *dupondii*

    1 *dupondius* (orichalcum) = 2 *asses*

    1 *as* (copper) = 2 *semisses*

    1 *semis* (copper) = 2 *quadrantes* (copper)

Note: the *sestertius, dupondius, as, semis* and *quadrans* are collectively referred to as the *aes*-coinage, and represent the 'small change' of the Roman system.

32 Griffin 1984, p. 59.

33 Sydenham 1920, pp. 39ff; Burnett *et al.*, 1992.

34 Tacitus *Annals* 1.11–12.

35 Sutherland 1951, p. 160.

36 For the timing of these issues, see Mac Dowall 1979, pp. 32ff. For portraits of Nero see Hiesinger 1975.

37 Tacitus *Annals* 15.74, 4.

38 *RIC* 2 (Hadrian), pp. 358ff.

39 Grant 1950, p. 80f.

40 See above on p. 151. Note that Tacitus states that Nero's particular divine interest in the wake of the conspiracy was in Jupiter Vindex ('the Avenger') and Sol (Tacitus *Annals* 15.74, 1–2); for the temple of Janus, see Townend 1980b.

41 Tacitus *Annals* 15.41.

42 Tacitus *Annals* 15.36, 3; Woods 2004.

43 *RIC* 1² (Nero), nos. 178 and 138; Rickman 1980, pp. 76–7 and 260–1.

44 See above on p. 124.

45 E.g. *RIC* 1² (Nero), no. 427; these were issued from the mint at Lyon, a town favourably disposed towards the Emperor.

46 Suetonius *Life of Nero* 25, 3; Sutherland 1951, p. 170; Shiel 1976.

47 Sutherland 1984, pp. 196–200 and 203–12.

48 *RIC* 1² (Civil Wars), no. 24.

Abbreviations

AJA	*American Journal of Archaeology*
AJAH	*American Journal of Ancient History*
AJP	*American Journal of Philology*
Anc. Soc.	*Ancient Society*
BAR	*British Archaeological Reports*
BCAR	*Bullettino della Commissione Archeologica Comunale di Roma*
BMC	*Coins of the Roman Empire in the British Museum*
CIL	*Corpus Inscriptionum Latinarum*
Class. Phil.	*Classical Philology*
CQ	*Classical Quarterly*
CW	*Transactions of the Cumberland and Westmorland Antiquarian and Archaeological Society*
G & R	*Greece and Rome*
HSCP	*Harvard Studies in Classical Philology*
ICS	*Illinois Classical Studies*
ILS	*Inscriptiones Latinae Selectae*
JRS	*Journal of Roman Studies*
NAC	*Numismatica e Antichità Classiche*
Num. Chron.	*Numismatic Chronicle*
PBSR	*Papers of the British School at Rome*
Proc. Brit. Ac.	*Proceedings of the British Academy*
RFIC	*Rivista di Filologia e di Istruzione Classica*
Rh. M.	*Rheinisches Museum*
RIC	*Roman Imperial Coinage*

RSA	*Rivista Storica dell' Antichità*
SEG	*Supplementum Epigraphicum Graecum*
Tac. Ann.	Tacitus, *The Annals*
TAPA	*Transactions of the American Philological Association*

Bibliography

Anderson, J. G. C., 1966: 'The Eastern Frontier from Tiberius to Nero', pp. 743–80 in Cook, S. A., Adcock, F. E. and Charlesworth, M. P. (eds), *The Cambridge Ancient History X: The Augustan Empire, 44 BC–AD 70* (Cambridge).

Baldwin, B., 1979: 'Nero and his Mother's Corpse', *Mnemosyne* 32, 380–1.

Ball, L. F., 2003: *The Domus Aurea and the Roman Architectural Revolution* (Cambridge).

Balsdon, J. P., 1934: *The Emperor Gaius (Caligula)* (Oxford).

Balsdon, J. P., 1974: *Life and Leisure in Ancient Rome* (London).

Barnes, T. D., 1982: 'The Date of the *Octavia*', *Museum Helveticum* 39, 215–7.

Barrett, A. A., 1989: *Caligula: The Corruption of Power* (London).

Barrett, A. A., 1996: *Agrippina* (London).

Barrett, A. A., 2002: *Livia: First Lady of Imperial Rome* (New Haven, CT).

Bauman, R. A., 1974: *Impietas in Principem* (Munich).

Bauman, R. A., 1992: *Women and Politics in Ancient Rome* (London).

Beard, M. and Crawford, M. H., 1999: *Rome in the Late Republic*, second edition (London).

Beaujeu, J., 1960: *L'Incendie de Rome en 64 et les Chrétiens* (Brussels).

Benario, H. W., 1999: *Tacitus: Germany: Germania* (Warminster).

Benario, H. W., 2007: 'Boudica Warrior Queen', *Classical Outlook* 84, 70–3.

Bessone, L., 1977: 'Suet. *Nero* xl.7 e gli Inizi del *bellum Neronis*', *RSA* 6–7, 343–9.

Bessone, L., 1978: 'Cluvio Rufo sul *bellum Neronis*', *Aevum* 52, 100–14.

Bessone, L., 1979: 'Clodio Macro e la fine di Nerone', *RSA* 9, 39–59.

Bessone, L., 1980: '*Nero nuntiis magis et rumoribus quam armis depulsus*', *NAC* 9, 219–36.

Bird, H. W., 1994: *Aurelius Victor: De Caesaribus* (Liverpool).

Birley, A. R., 1973: 'Petillius Cerialis and the Conquest of Brigantia', *Britannia* 4, 173–90.

Birley, A. R., 2000: 'The Life and Death of Cornelius Tacitus', *Historia* 49, 230–47.

Birley, A. R., 2002: *Garrison Life at Vindolanda: A Band of Brothers* (Stroud).

Birley, A. R., 2005: *The Roman Government of Britain* (Oxford).

Birley, A. R., 2007: 'Sejanus: His Fall', pp. 121–50 in Sekunda N. (ed.), *Corolla Cosmo Rodewald* (Gdańsk).

Birley, E. B., 1953: 'Senators in the Emperors' Service', *Proc. Brit. Ac.* 39, 197–214.

Bishop, J. D., 1960: 'Dating in Tacitus by Moonless Nights', *Class. Phil.* 55, 164–70.

Bishop, J. H., 1964: *Nero: The Man and the Legend* (London).

Blake, M. E., 1959: *Roman Construction in Italy from Tiberius through the Flavians* (Washington, DC).

Boddington, A., 1963: 'Sejanus: Whose Conspiracy?', *AJP* 84, 1–16.

Boethius, A., 1960: *The Golden House of Nero* (Ann Arbor, MI).

Boethius, A. and Ward-Perkins, J. B., 1970: *Etruscan and Roman Architecture* (Harmondsworth).

Bowersock, G. W., 1965: *Augustus and the Greek World* (Oxford).

Bradley, K. R., 1978a: *Suetonius' Life of Nero: An Historical Commentary* (Brussels).

Bradley, K. R., 1978b: 'The Chronology of Nero's Visit to Greece, AD 66/67', *Latomus* 37, 61–72.

Brisset, J., 1964: *Les Idées Politiques de Lucain* (Paris).

Bruère, R. T., 1954: 'Tacitus and Pliny's *Panegyricus*', *Class. Phil.* 49, 161–79.

Brunt, P. A., 1959: 'The Revolt of Vindex and the Fall of Nero', *Latomus* 18, 531–59.

Brunt, P. A., 1975: 'Stoicism and the Principate', *PBSR* 43, 7–35.

Brunt, P. A. and Moore, J. M., 1967: *Res Gestae Divi Augusti* (Oxford).

Burnett, A. M., Amandry, M. and Ripolles, P. (eds), 1992: *Roman Provincial Coinage: I. From the Death of Caesar to the Death of Vitellius (44 BC – AD 69)* (London).

Burnham, B. C., Keppie, L. J. F. and Fitzpatrick, A. P., 2001: 'Roman Britain in 2000: I Sites Explored', *Britannia* 32, 311–85.

Burnham, B. C., Hunter, F. and Fitzpatrick, A. P., 2002: 'Roman Britain in 2001: I Sites Explored', *Britannia* 33, 276–354.

Campbell, J. B., 1984: *The Emperor and the Roman Army* (New York, NY).

Carney, T. F., 1970: *A Biography of Gaius Marius* (Chicago, IL).

Castrén, P. and Lilius, H., 1970: *Graffiti del Palatino: II Domus Tiberiana* (Helsinki).

Champlin, E., 1978: 'The Life and Times of Calpurnius Siculus', *JRS* 68, 95–110.

Champlin, E., 2003: *Nero* (Cambridge, MA).

Charlesworth, M. P., 1950: 'Nero: Some Aspects', *JRS* 40, 69–76.

Chilver, G. E. F., 1957: 'The Army in Politics, AD 68–70', *JRS* 47, 29–35.

Chilver, G. E. F., 1979: *A Historical Commentary on Tacitus' Histories I and II* (Oxford).

Christensen, A. S., 1980: *Lactantius the Historian* (Copenhagen).

Claridge, A., 1998: *Rome: An Archaeological Guide* (Oxford).

Clarke, M. L., 1981: *The Noblest Roman* (London).

Clunn, A., 1999: *In Quest of the Lost Legions* (London).

Coffey, M., 1976: *Roman Satire* (London).

Collingwood, R. G., 1946: *The Idea of History* (Oxford).

Correra, L., 1894: 'Graffiti di Roma', *BCAR* 22, 89–100.

Crawford, M. H., 1974: *Roman Republican Coinage* (Cambridge).

Crescenzi, L., Gizzi, S. and Vigilante, P., 1992: *Anzio: Villa di Nerone. Restauri 1989–1992* (Rome).

Crook, J., 1955: *Consilium Principis* (Cambridge).

Curchin, L. A., 1991: *Roman Spain: Conquest and Assimilation* (London).

Daly, L. J., 1975: 'Verginius at Vesontio: The Incongruity of the *Bellum Neronis*', *Historia* 24, 75–100.

D'Arms, J. H., 1970: *Romans on the Bay of Naples* (Cambridge, MA).

Della Portella, I., 2000: *Subterranean Rome* (Cologne).

Durry, M., 1968: *Les Cohortes Prétoriennes* (Paris).

Dyson, S. L., 1970: 'The Portrait of Seneca in Tacitus', *Arethusa* 3, 71–83.

Earl, D. C., 1967: *The Moral and Political Tradition of Rome* (London).

Eck, W., Caballos, A. and Fernandez, F., 1996: *Das Senatus Consultum de Cn. Pisone Patre* (Munich).

Ehrenberg, V. and Jones, A. H. M., 1955: *Documents Illustrating the Reigns of Augustus and Tiberius* (Oxford).

Elsner, J. and Masters, J. (eds), 1994: *Reflections on Nero: Culture, History and Representation* (London).

Evans, H. B., 1983: 'Nero's *Arcus Caelimontanus*', *AJA* 87, 392–9.

Everett, A., 2001: *Cicero: A Turbulent Life* (London).

Eyben, E., 1993: *Restless Youth in Ancient Rome* (London).

Fears, J. K., 1975: 'Nero as Vice-Gerent of the Gods in Seneca's *De Clementia*', *Hermes* 103, 486–96.

Ferguson, J., 1970: *The Religions of the Roman Empire* (London).

Fishwick, D., 1972: '*Templum Divo Claudio Constitutum*', *Britannia* 3, 164–81.

Fishwick, D., 1991: *The Imperial Cult in the Latin West: Studies in the Ruler Cult of the Western Provinces of the Roman Empire* (Leiden).

Frend, W. H. C., 1965: *Martyrdom and Persecution in the Early Church* (Oxford).

Fulford, M. G., 'Nero and Britain: The Palace of the Client King at *Calleva* and Imperial Policy towards the Province after Boudicca', *Britannia* 39 (forthcoming).

Furneaux, R., 1973: *The Roman Siege of Jerusalem* (London).

Gallivan, P. A., 1973a: 'The False Neros: A Reconsideration', *Historia* 22, 364–5.

Gallivan, P. A., 1973b: 'Nero's Liberation of Greece', *Hermes* 101, 230–4.

Gallivan, P. A., 1974a: 'Suetonius and Chronology in the *De Vita Neronis*', *Historia* 23, 297–318.

Gallivan, P. A., 1974b: 'Confusion concerning the Age of Octavia', *Latomus* 33, 116–7.

Gallivan, P. A., 1974c: 'Some Comments on the Fasti for the Reign of Nero', *CQ* 24, 290–311.

Garson, R. W., 1975: 'The Pseudo-Senecan *Octavia*: A Plea for Nero?', *Latomus* 34, 754–6.

Gelzer, M., 1968: *Caesar: Politician and Statesman* (Oxford).

Gelzer, M., 1969: *The Roman Nobility* (Oxford).

George, P., 1974: 'Petronius and Lucan *De Bello Civile*', *CQ* 24, 119–33.

Giubelli, G., 1991: *Oplontis: Poppaea's Villa* (Naples).

Goldsworthy, A., 2003: *In the Name of Rome* (London).

Grainger, J. D., 2003: *Nerva and the Roman Succession Crisis of AD 96–99* (London).

Grant, M., 1950: *Roman Anniversary Issues* (Cambridge).

Grant, M., 1954: *Roman Imperial Money* (London).

Grant, M., 1958: *Roman History from Coins* (Cambridge).

Grant, M., 1970: *Nero* (New York, NY).

Grant, M., 1974: *Cities of Vesuvius: Pompeii and Herculaneum* (London).

Griffin, M. T., 1974: '*Imago Vitae Suae*', pp. 1–38 in Costa, C. D. N. (ed.), *Seneca* (London).

Griffin, M. T., 1976: *Seneca: A Philosopher in Politics* (Oxford).

Griffin, M. T., 1984: *Nero: The End of a Dynasty* (New Haven, CT).

Griffin, M. T., 1997: 'The Senate's Story', *JRS* 87, 249–63.

Gwyn, W. B., 1991: 'Cruel Nero: The Concept of the Tyrant and the Image of Nero in Western Political Thought', *History of Political Thought* 12, 421–55.

Hainsworth, J. B., 1962: 'Verginius and Vindex', *Historia* 11, 86–96.

Hainsworth, J. B., 1964: 'The Starting-Point of Tacitus' *Historiae*: Fear or Favour by Omission', *G & R* 11, 128–36.

Hemsoll, D., 1989: 'Reconstructing the Octagonal Dining Room of Nero's Golden House', *Architectural History* 32, 1–17.

Hemsoll, D., 1990: 'The Architecture of Nero's Golden House', pp. 10–38 in Henig M. (ed.), *Architecture and Architectural Sculpture in the Roman Empire* (Oxford).

Henderson, B. W., 1903: *The Life and Principate of the Emperor Nero* (London).

Herington, C. J., 1961: '*Octavia Praetexta*: A Survey', *CQ* 11, 18–30.

Hiesinger, U. W., 1975: 'The Portraits of Nero', *AJA* 79, 113–24.

Highet, G., 1954: *Juvenal The Satirist* (Oxford).

Hind, J. G. F., 1970: 'The Middle Years of Nero's Reign', *Historia* 20, 488–505.

Holland, R., 2000: *Nero: The Man behind the Myth* (London).

Horsfall, N. M., 1997: 'Criteria for the Dating of Calpurnius Siculus', *RFIC* 125, 166–96.

Humphrey, J. H., 1986: *Roman Circuses: Arenas for Chariot Racing* (Berkeley, CA).

Hurley, D. W., 2003: 'The Politics of Agrippina the Younger's Birthplace', *AJAH*[2] 2, 95–117.

Huzar, E. G., 1978: *Mark Antony: A Biography* (Minneapolis, MN).

Iacopi, I., 2001: *Domus Aurea* (Milan).

Jones, B. W., 1983: 'C. Vettulenus Civica Cerialis and the False Nero of AD 88', *Athenaeum* 61, 516–21.

Jones, B. W., 1992: *The Emperor Domitian* (London).

Jones, C. P., 1978: *The Roman World of Dio Chrysostom* (Cambridge, MA).

Keaveney, A., 1982: *Sulla: The Last Republican* (London).

Keppie, L. J. F., 1984: *The Making of the Roman Army* (London).

Kleiner, F. S., 1985: *The Arch of Nero in Rome: A Study of Roman Honorary Arches Before and Under Nero* (Rome).

Kraay, C. M., 1949: 'The Coinage of Vindex and Galba, AD 68, and the Continuity of the Augustan Principate', *Num. Chron.*[6] 9, 129–49.

Kragelund, P., 1988: 'The Prefect's Dilemma and the Date of the *Octavia*', *CQ* 38, 492–508.

Krautter, K., 1992: 'Lucan, Calpurnius Siculus und Nero', *Philologus* 136, 188–201.

Lepper, F. A., 1957: 'Some Reflections on the *Quinquennium Neronis*', *JRS* 47, 95–103.

Levick, B., 1975: 'Julians and Claudians', *G & R* 22, 29–38.

Levick, B., 1985: 'L. Verginius Rufus and the Four Emperors', *Rh. M.* 128, 318–46.

Levick, B., 1990: *Claudius* (London).

Levick, B., 1999: *Vespasian* (London).

Ling, R., 1979: 'The Stanze di Venere at Baia', *Archaeologia* 106, 33–60.

Lintott, A. W., 1968: *Violence in Republican Rome* (Oxford).

Lintott, A. W., 2000: *The Roman Republic* (Stroud).

Little, D. and Ehrhardt, C., 1994: *Plutarch's Lives of Galba and Otho* (Bristol).

Lugli, G., 1960: *Regio Urbis Decima: Mons Palatinus: Testi e Documenti* (Rome).

MacDonald, W. L., 1965: *The Architecture of the Roman Empire* (New Haven, CT).

Mac Dowall, D. W., 1958: 'The Numismatic Evidence for the *Neronia*', *CQ* 8, 192–4.

Mac Dowall, D. W., 1978: 'The Organisation of the Julio-Claudian Mint at Rome', pp. 32–46 in Carson, R. A. G. and Kraay, C. M. (eds), *Scripta Nummaria Romana: Essays Presented to Humphrey Sutherland* (London).

Mac Dowall, D. W., 1979: *The Western Coinages of Nero* (New York, NY).

Macé, A., 1900: *Essai sur Suétone* (Paris).

Maiuri, A., 1971: *Pompeii* (Novara).

Malitz, J., 2005: *Nero*, translated into English by Allison Brown (Oxford).

Manley, J., 2002: *AD 43: The Roman Invasion of Britain: A Reassessment* (Stroud).

Manning, C. F., 1975: 'Acting and Nero's Conception of the Principate', *G & R* 22, 164–75.

Martin, R. H., 1981: *Tacitus* (London).

Mattingly, H., 1954: 'Verginius at Lugdunum', *Num. Chron.*[6] 14, 32–9.

Mayer, R., 1980: 'Calpurnius Siculus: Technique and Date', *JRS* 70, 175–6.

Mayer, R., 1982: 'What caused Poppaea's Death?', *Historia* 31, 248–9.

McAlindon, D., 1956: 'Senatorial Opposition to Claudius and Nero', *AJP* 77, 113–32.

McCrum, M. and Woodhead, A. G., 1961: *Select Documents of the Principates of the Flavian Emperors, AD 68–96* (Cambridge).

McKay, A. G., 1998: *Houses, Villas and Palaces in the Roman World* (Baltimore, MD).

McPake, R., 1981: 'A Note on the *cognomina* of Legio XX', *Britannia* 12, 293–5.

Meiggs, R., 1960: *Roman Ostia* (Oxford).

Mellor, R., 1993: *Tacitus* (London).

Millar, F. G. B., 1964: *A Study of Cassius Dio* (Oxford).

Millar, F. G. B., 1966: 'The Emperor, the Senate and the Provinces', *JRS* 56, 156–66.

Millar, F. G. B., 1977: *The Emperor in the Roman World* (London).

Millar, F. G. B., 2002: *The Roman Republic in Political Thought* (Hanover, NH).

Miller, S. J., 1971: *Inscriptions of the Roman Empire, AD 14–117* (London).

Milne, J. G., 1971: *A Catalogue of Alexandrian Coins* (Oxford).

Miniero, P., 2000: *Baia* (Naples).

Morgan, G., 2000: 'The *Publica Fames* of AD 68 (Suetonius *Nero* 45, 1)', *CQ* 50, 210–22.

Morgan, G., 2006: *AD 69: The Year of the Four Emperors* (Oxford).

Murison, C. L., 1979: 'Some Vitellian dates: An Exercise in Methodology', *TAPA* 109, 187–97.

Murison, C. L., 1991: 'The Historical Value of Tacitus' *Histories*', pp. 1686–1713 in Haase, W. and Temporini, H. (eds), *Aufstieg und Niedergang der Römischen Welt*, II. (Principat) 33, 3 (Berlin).

Murison, C. L., 1992: *Suetonius: Galba, Otho, Vitellius* (Bristol).

Murison, C. L., 1993: *Galba, Otho and Vitellius: Careers and Controversies* (Hildesheim).

Murison, C. L., 1999: *Rebellion and Reconstruction: Galba to Domitian* (Atlanta, GA).

Murray, O., 1965: 'The *Quinquennium Neronis* and the Stoics', *Historia* 14, 41–61.

Neverov, O., 1986: 'Nero-Helios', pp. 189–94 in Henig, M. and King, A. (eds), *Pagan Gods and Shrines of the Roman Empire* (Oxford).

Newbold, R. F., 1974: 'Some Social and Economic Consequences of the AD 64 Fire at Rome', *Latomus* 33, 858–69.

Ogilvie, R. M., 1969: *The Romans and Their Gods* (London).

Ogilvie, R. M. and Richmond, I. A., 1967: *Cornelii Taciti De Vita Agricolae* (Oxford).

Parker, H. M. D., 1928: *The Roman Legions* (Oxford).

Picard, G-C., 1966: *Augustus and Nero*, translated into English by Len Ortzen (London).

Platner, S. B. and Ashby, T., 1926: *A Topographical Dictionary of Rome* (Oxford).

Potter, T. W., 1987: *Roman Italy* (London).

Rainbird, J. S. and Sear, F. B., 1971: 'A Possible Description of the *Macellum Magnum* of Nero', *PBSR* 39, 40–6.

Raoss, M., 1958: 'La Rivolta di Vindice ed il Successo di Galba', *Epigraphica* 20, 46–120.

Raoss, M., 1960: 'La Rivolta di Vindice ed il Successo di Galba', *Epigraphica* 22, 37–151.

Reece, B. R., 1969: 'The Date of Nero's Death', *AJP* 90, 72–4.

Rickman, G. E., 1980: *The Corn Supply of Ancient Rome* (Oxford).

Rogers, R. S., 1931: 'The Conspiracy of Agrippina', *TAPA* 62, 141–68.

Rogers, R. S., 1953a: 'The Neronian Comets', *TAPA* 84, 237–49.

Rogers, R. S., 1953b: 'The Tacitean Account of a Neronian Trial', pp. 711–8 in Mylonas, G. E. and Raymond, D. (eds), *Studies presented to David Moore Robinson* (Saint Louis, MO).

Rogers, R. S., 1955: 'Heirs and Rivals to Nero', *TAPA* 86, 190–212.

Rogers, R. S., 1960: 'A Group of Domitianic Treason-Trials', *Class. Phil.* 55, 19–23.

Roper, T. K., 1979: 'Nero, Seneca and Tigellinus', *Historia* 28, 346–57.

Rose, K. F. C., 1971: *The Date and Author of the Satyricon* (Leiden).

Rowell, H. T., 1962: *Rome in the Augustan Age* (Norman, OK).

Rudich, V., 1992: *Political Dissidence under Nero: The Price of Dissimulation* (London).

Rudich, V., 1997: *Dissidence and Literature under Nero* (London).

Saddington, D. B., 2005: 'The Roman Government and the Roman *Auxilia*', pp. 63–9 in Visy, Z. (ed.), *Limes XIX: Proceedings of the XIXth International Congress of Roman Frontier Studies* (Pécs).

Saller, R. P., 1982: *Personal Patronage under the Early Caesars* (Cambridge).

Salomies, O., 1987: *Die Römischen Vornamen*, Helsinki.

Sandbach, F. H., 1975: *The Stoics* (London).

Sanford, E. M., 1937: 'Nero and the East', *HSCP* 48, 75–103.

Sansone, D., 1993: 'Nero's Final Hours', *ICS* 18, 179–89.

Schönberger, H., 1969: 'The Roman Frontier in Germany: An Archaeological Survey', *JRS* 59, 144–97.

Seager, R., 1979: *Pompey: A Political Biography* (Oxford).

Seager, R., 2005: *Tiberius*, second edition (Oxford).

Sear, F. B., 1982: *Roman Architecture* (London).

Shiel, N., 1976: 'Nero Citharoedus', *Euphrosyne* 7, 175–9.

Shotter, D. C. A., 1966a: 'Tiberius and the Spirit of Augustus', *G & R* 13, 359–65.

Shotter, D. C. A., 1966b: 'Elections under Tiberius', *CQ* 16, 321–32.

Shotter, D. C. A., 1967a: 'Tacitus and Verginius Rufus', *CQ* 17, 370–81.

Shotter, D. C. A., 1967b: 'The Trial of Gaius Silius', *Latomus* 26, 712–6.

Shotter, D. C. A., 1967c: 'The Debate on Augustus (Tac. *Ann.* 1.9–10)', *Mnemosyne* 20, 171–5.

Shotter, D. C. A., 1967d: 'The Starting-Dates of Tacitus' Historical Works', *CQ* 17, 158–63.

Shotter, D. C. A., 1968: 'Tacitus, Tiberius and Germanicus', *Historia* 17, 194–214.

Shotter, D. C. A., 1969a: 'The Trial of Clutorius Priscus', *G & R* 16, 14–18.

Shotter, D. C. A., 1969b: 'Irregular Legionary Commands', *CQ* 19, 371–3.

Shotter, D. C. A., 1971a: 'Julians, Claudians and the Accession of Tiberius', *Latomus* 30, 1117–23.

Shotter, D. C. A., 1971b: 'Tiberius and Asinius Gallus', *Historia* 20, 443–59.

Shotter, D. C. A., 1972: 'The Trial of M. Scribonius Libo Drusus', *Historia* 21, 88–98.

Shotter, D. C. A., 1974a: 'Gnaeus Calpurnius Piso, Legate of Syria', *Historia* 23, 229–45.

Shotter, D. C. A., 1974b: 'The Fall of Sejanus: Two Problems', *Class. Phil.* 69, 42–6.

Shotter, D. C. A., 1974c: 'Gnaeus Cornelius Cinna Magnus and the Adoption of Tiberius', *Latomus* 33, 306–13.

Shotter, D. C. A., 1975: 'A Timetable for the *Bellum Neronis*', *Historia* 24, 59–74.

Shotter, D. C. A., 1978: '*Principatus ac Libertas*', *Anc. Soc.* 9, 235–55.

Shotter, D. C. A., 1988: 'Tacitus and Tiberius', *Anc. Soc.* 19, 225–36.

Shotter, D. C. A., 1991: 'Tacitus' View of Emperors and the Principate', pp. 3263–3331 in Haase, W. and Temporini, H. (eds), *Aufstieg und Niedergang der Römischen Welt*, II (Principat) 33.5 (Berlin).

Shotter, D. C. A., 1993: *A Historical Commentary on Suetonius' Lives of Galba, Otho and Vitellius* (Warminster).

Shotter, D. C. A., 1994: 'Rome and the Brigantes: Early Hostilities', *CW²*, 21–34.

Shotter, D. C. A., 2000a: 'Agrippina the Elder: A Woman in a Man's World', *Historia* 49, 341–57.

Shotter, D. C. A., 2000b: 'Petillius Cerialis in Northern Britain', *Northern History* 36, 189–98.

Shotter, D. C. A., 2001: 'A Considered Epitaph', *Historia* 50, 253–5.

Shotter, D. C. A., 2002: 'Roman Britain and the Year of the Four Emperors', *CW³* 2, 79–86.

Shotter, D. C. A., 2004a: 'Vespasian, *Auctoritas* and Britain', *Britannia* 35, 1–8.

Shotter, D. C. A., 2004b: *Romans and Britons in North-West England* (Lancaster).

Shotter, D. C. A., 2004c: *Tiberius Caesar*, second edition (London).

Shotter, D. C. A., 2005a: *Augustus Caesar*, second edition (London).

Shotter, D. C. A., 2005b: *The Fall of the Roman Republic*, second edition (London).

Simon, E., 1967: *Ara Pacis Augustae* (Tübingen).

Smallwood, E. M., 1967: *Documents Illustrating the Principates of Gaius, Claudius and Nero* (Cambridge).

Staveley, E. S., 1972: *Greek and Roman Voting and Elections* (London).

Stevenson, G. H., 1939: *Roman Provincial Administration* (Oxford).

Stockton, D. L., 1971: *Cicero: A Political Biography* (Oxford).

Stolte, B., 1973: 'Tacitus on Nero and Otho', *Anc. Soc.* 4, 177–90.

Sullivan, J. P., 1968: *The Satyricon of Petronius* (London).

Sullivan, J. P., 1985: *Literature and Politics in the Age of Nero* (Ithaca, NY).

Sutherland, C. H. V., 1938: 'Two Virtues of Tiberius: A Numismatic Contribution to The History of his Reign', *JRS* 28, 129–40.

Sutherland, C. H. V., 1951: *Coinage in Roman Imperial Policy, 31 BC – AD 68* (London).

Sutherland, C. H. V., 1976: *The Emperor and the Coinage* (London).

Sutherland, C. H. V., 1984: *The Roman Imperial Coinage: Volume 1*, second edition (London).

Sutherland, C. H. V., 1987: *Roman History and Coinage, 44 BC – AD 69* (Oxford).

Sydenham, E. A., 1920: *The Coinage of Nero* (London).

Syme, R., 1937: 'The Colony of Cornelius Fuscus: An Episode in the *Bellum Neronis*', *AJP* 58, 7–18.

Syme, R., 1939: *The Roman Revolution* (Oxford).

Syme, R., 1956: 'Sejanus on the Aventine', *Hermes* 84, 257–66.

Syme, R., 1958: *Tacitus* (Oxford).

Syme, R., 1970: 'Domitius Corbulo', *JRS* 60, 27–39.

Syme, R., 1971: *Emperors and Biography* (Oxford).

Syme, R., 1980: *Some Arval Brethren* (Oxford).

Syme, R., 1982: 'Partisans of Galba', *Historia* 31, 346–57.

Syme, R., 1986: *The Augustan Aristocracy* (Oxford).

Talbot, R. J. A., 1984: *The Senate of Imperial Rome* (Princeton, NJ).

Tameanko, M., 1999: *Monumental Coins* (Iola, WI).

Tamm, B., 1970: *Nero's Gymnasium in Rome* (Stockholm).

Taylor, L. R., 1931: *The Divinity of the Roman Emperor* (Middletown, CT).

Taylor, L. R., 1966: *Roman Voting Assemblies* (Ann Arbor, MI).

Thompson, L., 1964: 'Lucan's Apotheosis of Nero', *Class. Phil.* 59, 147–53.

Thornton, M. K. and R. L., 1989: *Julio-Claudian Building Programs*, (Wauconda, IL).

Townend, G. B., 1958: 'The Circus of Nero and the Vatican Excavations', *AJA* 62, 216–8.

Townend, G. B., 1959: 'The Date of Composition of Suetonius' *Caesares*', *CQ* 9, 285–93.

Townend, G. B., 1961a: 'The Reputation of Verginius Rufus', *Latomus* 20, 337–41.

Townend, G. B., 1961b: 'The Hippo Inscription and the Career of Suetonius', *Historia* 10, 99–109.

Townend, G. B., 1964: 'Cluvius Rufus in the *Histories* of Tacitus', *AJP* 85, 337–77.

Townend, G. B., 1967: 'Suetonius and his Influence', pp. 79–111 in Dorey, T. A. (ed.), *Latin Biography* (London).

Townend, G. B., 1980a: 'Calpurnius Siculus and the *Munus Neronis*', *JRS* 70, 166–74.

Townend, G. B., 1980b: 'Tacitus, Suetonius and the Temple of Janus', *Hermes* 108, 233–42.

Toynbee, J. M. C., 1942: 'Nero Artifex: The *Apocolocyntosis* Reconsidered', *CQ* 36, 83–93.

Toynbee, J. M. C., 1944: 'Dictators and Philosophers in the First Century AD', *G & R* 38, 43–58.

Toynbee, J. M. C., 1947: 'Ruler-Apotheosis in Ancient Rome', *Num. Chron.*[6] 7, 126–49.

Toynbee, J. M. C. and Ward-Perkins, J. B., 1956: *The Shrine of St Peter* (London).

Tuplin, C., 1989: 'The False Neros of the First Century', pp. 364–404 in Deroux, C. (ed.), *Studies in Latin Literature and History 5* (Brussels).

Turner, E. G., 1959: '*Acta Alexandrinorum*', *Oxyrhynchus Papyri* 25, 102–12.

Van Ooteghem, J., 1968: 'Verginius et Vindex', *Les Etudes Classiques* 36, 18–27.

Verdière, R., 1985: 'Le Genre Bucolique à l'époque de Néron', pp. 1846–76 and 1902–4 in Temporini, H. and Haase, W. (eds), *Aufstieg und Niedergang der Römischen Welt*, II (Principat) 32, 3 (Berlin).

Veyne, P., 1992: *Bread and Circuses* (London).

Von Fritz, K., 1954: *The Theory of the Mixed Constitution in Antiquity* (New York, NY).

Von Fritz, K., 1957: 'Tacitus, Agricola, Domitian and the Problem of the Principate', *Class. Phil.* 52, 73–97.

Walker, B., 1960: *The Annals of Tacitus*, second edition (Manchester).

Walker, D., 1976: *The Metrology of the Roman Silver Coinage: Volume I* (Oxford), *BAR* S5.

Wallace-Hadrill, A., 1981: 'Galba's *Aequitas*', *Num. Chron.* 141, 20–39.

Wallace-Hadrill, A., 1982: '*Civilis Princeps.* Between Citizen and King', *JRS* 72, 32–48.

Wallace-Hadrill, A., 1983: *Suetonius: The Scholar and his Caesars* (London).

Wardle, D., 1992: 'Cluvius Rufus and Suetonius', *Hermes* 120, 466–82.

Wardman, A. E., 1976: *Rome's Debt to Greece* (London).

Warmington, B. H., 1969: *Nero: Reality and Legend* (London).

Warmington, B. H., 1977: *Suetonius: Nero* (Bristol).

Watson, G. R., 1969: *The Roman Soldier* (London).

Watt, W. C., 1989: '666', *Semiotica* 77, 369–92.

Weaver, P. C., 1972: *Familia Caesaris: A Social Study of the Emperor's Freedmen and Slaves* (Cambridge).

Webster, G., 1978: *Boudica* (London).

Webster, G., 1985: *The Roman Imperial Army*, third edition (London).

Wellesley, K., 1954: 'Can You Trust Tacitus?', *G & R* 1, 13–33.

Wellesley, K., 1989: *The Long Year: AD 69*, second edition (Bristol).

Wells, C. M., 1972: *The German Policy of Augustus* (Oxford).

Wheeler, R. E. M., 1964: *Roman Art and Architecture* (London).

Whittaker, C. R., 1994: *The Frontiers of the Roman Empire* (London).

Wiedemann, T. E. G., 1989: *The Julio-Claudian Emperors* (Bristol).

Wiedemann, T. E. G., 1992: *Emperors and Gladiators* (London).

Wilkinson, S., 2005: *Caligula* (London).

Willems, J., 1902: *Le Sénat Romain en l'An 65 Après Jésus-Christ* (Louvain).

Wirszubski, Ch., 1950: *Libertas as a Political Idea at Rome* (Cambridge).

Wiseman, J., 1978: *The Land of the Ancient Corinthians* (Goteborg).

Wiseman, T. P., 1965: 'The Mother of Livia Augusta', *Historia* 14, 333–4.

Woodman, A. J., 1977: *Velleius Paterculus: The Tiberian Narrative* (Cambridge).

Woods, D., 2004: 'The Consequences of Nero's Ill-Health in AD 64', *Eranos* 102, 109–16.

Woods, D., 2006: 'Tacitus, Nero, and the "Pirate" Anicetus', *Latomus* 65, 641–9.

Woolf, G., 1998: *Becoming Roman* (Cambridge).

Yadin, Y., 1966: *Masada* (London).

Yavetz, Z., 1969: *Plebs and Princeps* (Oxford).

Zanker, P., 1968: *Forum Augustum* (Tübingen).

General Index

❧❧❧

Achaea 87, 134
Acraephia 134
Actium, Battle of 11, 15, 18, 27, 29, 43, 140, 154
Aedui 1, 107, 158
Aegae 45
Aegean Sea 171
Aerarium 71, 72, 140
Africa 87, 109, 125, 141, 159, 160, 221n
Alani 105
Albani 105
Alde, river 93
Alexandria 22, 23, 45, 55, 101, 107, 131, 132, 136, 203n
Anauni 204n, 221n
Antichrist 172, 173
Antium (Anzio) 114, 117, 118, 138, 145
Aquileia 159
Aquitania (s.v. Gaul)
Argentoratum (Strasbourg) 89
Armenia 10, 59, 95ff, 104, 137, 171
Arval Brethren 38, 207n, 208n, 228n
Arverni 158
Asia 18, 46, 57, 80, 84, 87, 96, 98, 136, 148, 149, 171
Athens 3, 125, 131, 132
Auctoritas 15, 16, 17, 19, 181
Augustiani 82
Auxilia 26, 90, 104, 158, 161, 181

Baetica (s.v. Spain)
Baiae (Baia) 39, 75, 81, 114, 121, 124, 147, 172, 224n
Baltic Sea 115
Batavi 104, 157, 158, 161
Belgica (s.v. Gaul)

Beneventum (Benevento) 149, 152
Bithynia 2, 87, 139
Black Sea 104, 105, 106
Boeotia 134
Bonna (Bonn) 89
Bosporus 105
Brigantes 92
Britain 2, 6, 10, 23, 26, 42, 71, 72, 82, 86, 87, 91ff, 107, 109, 116, 141, 161, 166, 205n, 217n
Byzantium (Constantinople) 7

Caesarea 45
Calabria 39, 70
Calleva Atrebatum (Silchester) 218n
Campania (Campagna) 53, 85
Camulodunum (Colchester) 93, 213n
Cappadocia 96, 97, 191
Capreae (Capri) 10, 20, 21, 35, 36
Carrhae 98
Carthage 141
Caspian Gates 104, 105, 161
Catuvellauni 92
Caucasus 105
Cherusci 89
China 142
Christians 139, 172ff
Cilicia 109, 172
Cimbri 87
Clementia 8, 47, 66, 67, 68, 100, 142, 181, 189f
Client-Kingdom 71, 92, 96, 101
Clunia 164, 165
Coinage Reform 141, 142, 193ff, 234n
Colonia 76, 107, 124, 182
Colonia Claudia Ara Agrippinensium (Cologne) 89

· 248 ·

Index of Persons and Divinities

≋≋≋≋≋

(The names of Emperors will follow normal usage and feature in bold letters; the forms of the names of Classical authors will follow normal usage)

Accius 225n
Acte 59, 60, 77, 153, 211n
Aelius Sejanus, Lucius 16, 20, 34, 35, 36, 49, 52, 59, 60, 76, 129, 202n
Aemilius Lepidus, Marcus (*cos.* 46 BC) 11
Aemilius Lepidus, Marcus (*cos.* AD 6) 112, 213n
Aemilius Lepidus, Marcus (h. of Drusilla) 41, 44
Aeneas 18, 28, 113
Afranius Burrus, Sextus 25, 52, 54, 58, 59, 60, 61, 62, 63, 64, 66, 75, 77, 78, 81, 82, 83, 84, 85, 107, 110, 128, 129, 130, 142, 146, 194
Agricola (s.v. Julius)
Agrippa (s.v. Vipsanius)
Agrippa Postumus 30, 32, 33
Agrippina (the Elder) 21, 22, 25, 30, 32, 34, 35, 36, 40, 41, 43, 44, 45, 47, 48, 49, 50, 60, 85
Agrippina (the Younger) 6, 25, 28, 30, 35, 36, 39, 40, 41, 42, 44, 45, 46, 47, 48, 49, 50, 51, 53, 55, 56, 57, 58, 59, 60, 61, 62, 63, 66, 68, 71, 73, 74, 75, 76, 77, 78, 79, 80, 82, 84, 85, 96, 116, 127, 129, 130, 133, 140, 148, 149, 158, 190, 194
Albinovanus Pedo 90
Alexander (k. of Macedon) 104
Alexander of Aegae 45
Alexandria 153
Anicetus 45, 75, 85, 208n
Anicius Cerealis, Gaius 149, 151

Annaeus Lucanus, Marcus 39, 64, 132, 146, 149, 192
Annaeus Mela 149
Annaeus Seneca, Lucius 6, 8, 25, 46, 47, 54, 58, 59, 60, 61, 62, 63, 64, 66, 67, 68, 75, 77, 79, 81, 84, 85, 90, 93, 100, 107, 110, 128, 129, 130, 132, 142, 143, 146, 150, 181, 189, 190, 194
Annius Pollio 149
Annius Vinicianus 99, 103, 149, 152, 154
Anteia 149
Anteius Rufus, Publius 149
Antistius Sosianus 128, 142
Antistius Vetus, Lucius (*cos.* AD 55) 69, 149
Antonia 30, 36, 43
Antoninus Pius 67
Antonius Felix, Marcus 102
Antonius Pallas, Marcus 49, 50, 57, 59, 72, 102, 128, 194
Antonius Primus, Marcus 158
Antonius, Marcus 11, 15, 30, 50, 87
Apollo 46, 60, 64, 81, 99, 100, 122, 134, 135, 137, 141, 151, 192, 195, 196, 197
Apollonius of Tyana 134, 191
Aristotle 12
Arminius 89
Arruntius, Lucius 204n
Artabanus (Parthian Pretender) 172
Artabanus III (k. of Parthia) 96
Asinius Gallus, Gaius 30, 35
Atia 29, 205n
Atius Balbus, Marcus 205n